# Missing Pieces

*52 Vital Lessons Our Kids Should Be Learning at School (But Aren't)*

Jaime Richards

ISBN 978-0-9970112-2-7

Also by Jaime Richards

*What It Takes*
*A Teacher's Thoughts on Living an Extraordinary Life*

*Living the Decision*
*A Pocket Guide to Cramming 72 Years of Living into 27*

*Kids Can't Write!*
*and Neither Can Adults*

jaimerichards.org

For Mom
Your support and optimism are unwavering.

For Mandie
Your work ethic and design expertise are world class.

For Mr. Klum
You're still coaching me.

For Norma and Kylene
You teach your way, and it works. You're both magical.

And especially for Kyrra
Your encouragement, positive criticism and
relentless attention to detail enables me to believe,
*This is my best work.*

# Contents

# Prologue

*Non scholae sed vitae discumus*
(We learn, not for school, but for life.)

No we don't. We learn for school. At least most kids do. They cram to get the grade, to pass the class and earn the units with the vague hope that it will lead to something better. Even though motivated students will pretend to learn whatever we tell them to learn, they're not really learning. Discontented and unfulfilled, they play the school game (often exceptionally well) while wondering why education is supposed to be so great.

Less motivated kids have stopped wondering. They hate school. They hate it so much they quit. In the United States, 7,000 kids drop out of school each *day*. That's one every 26 seconds.[1]

American school retention rates are so lame that when *80%* of the class of 2012 received a high school diploma, Secretary of Education Arne Duncan called it "a profound milestone."[2] Around the world, unless you live in one of the top 20 ranked countries, students are more likely to quit than graduate from secondary school. Mexico (ranked 27 out of 100) graduates 45% of its students.[3]

Education should be magical, and for some it is. Visit a first grade classroom. Ask the six-year-olds a question. Any question. Every hand in the room will shoot up. Most will have no clue what the answer is, but so what? They're excited about school. They're enthused about learning because it's fascinating. It's relevant. They're learning to read, write, add and subtract. They're singing, reciting poems and learning how magnificent it is to make friends. School is fun!

Then it changes. It stops being fascinating. It stops being relevant. It stops being fun.

Why?

It's not just because learning gets harder. It's rarely easy, nor should it be. Education demands discipline and lots of long, intense hours of study and practice. But so does basketball. So does dance. So does acting, painting and playing the guitar.

Yet, kids consider sports, art and music fun. More kids go out for the basketball team than make the basketball team. More kids don't get the part than get the part. Few children are forced to try out or audition. They just do. You know why? Because work and fun are not mutually exclusive. They're symbiotic. Fun *requires* work.

One of the all-time best movie scenes is in *A League of Their Own*. Baseball manager Jimmy Dugan (Tom Hanks) scolds star catcher Dottie Hinson (Geena Davis), "It's supposed to be hard. If it wasn't hard, everyone would do it. The hard is what makes it great." Dugan was talking about baseball, but he could have been talking about almost anything, including education. "It's the hard that makes it great."

No, it's not the rigor that turns students off. It's the irrelevance. Isn't it ironic that kids believe sports – games – are more relevant than most of their school curriculum? As students are promoted up through the grades, they become increasingly adept at recognizing what classroom lessons are significant and useful and what are insignificant and useless.

The older students get, the more they recognize and detest what they perceive as useless curriculum.

Kids want and deserve to know...

"Why should I learn this?"

"Will learning it help me get ahead, be happier, make money?"

"How will knowing this make me better?"

"How will mastering it enable me to improve the world?"

The word *education* is thrown around loosely, usually as a panacea. All our lives, we're taught that education is omnipotent:

"Get an education!"

"You're not going anywhere without a good education!"

"Stay in school!"

"Go to college. Get your degree!"

Horace Mann, the founder of American public education, wrote, "Education is the gateway to equality." Nelson Mandela wrote, "Education is the most powerful weapon which you can use to change the world."

Agreed. But not all education. This unconditional love affair we're having with education isn't healthy. It's like the 15-year-old girl who's so infatuated with her 16-year-old boyfriend that she refuses to believe he's anything less than perfect. Because practically everybody is for education, almost nobody questions it. Not enough of us are asking, "What should an education include?" How can intangible skills (leadership, for instance) be assessed? And, most importantly, what really is a "good" education?

It's not like aspirin. All education isn't the same. All education isn't "good."

In many of Pakistan's madrassas, students are taught to hate America and murder Americans. That's education, but it sure isn't good. What is? What do students most need to learn that they're not being taught?

Let's start with social skills. Not just teaching them. But convincing kids (and their parents) that learning them is at least as important as learning algebra. The story of multi-billionaire Dhirubhai Ambani is an example of why.

At the time of his passing in 2002, Ambani was the fourth richest man in the world. Yet, his childhood was not extraordinary. He grew up in a two bedroom house in Chorvad, Gujarat, India that had a dirt floor. How did he go from such a humble start to living in a palace with a six story *parking garage*?

I found one answer in two mind-blowing, life-altering sentences. They were embedded in a story in the *Australian Financial Review*: "Indians complain that social connections trump hard work. But no one has worked harder than Dhirubhai at forging connections."

Yes! That's the answer! Most people wouldn't put "forging connections" on a list of things kids need to work hard at. But most people are wrong. "Forging connections" is a skill we need to teach kids to work on *every day*. Building relationships is not frivolous fun. It's essential work.

So is something else that most parents and teachers wish for their children and students – happiness. It's not something that magically appears when the stars align. Happiness must be sought. It has to be strived for, worked for. Gretchen Rubin writes about this in *The Happiness Project*.

"Acting happy and, even more, being happy is challenging... Zest and enthusiasm take energy, humility, and engagement... It's more selfless to act happy (than unhappy). It takes energy, generosity and discipline to be unfailingly lighthearted... Happiness takes energy and discipline."[4]

Happiness research, Rubin points out (yes, there is such a thing), shows that there are specific things we can do to be happier. But, just as it is with building meaningful relationships, happiness demands education, study, effort and work. Yet, how many curriculums include lessons on what it takes to live a happy (or happier) life?

It's startling how many incredibly successful people either quit high school, didn't attend college or left college early. Like the Scarecrow who was brilliant long before the Wizard of Oz awarded him a diploma, what they needed to know they learned without the help of traditional schooling. Quentin Tarantino didn't finish his sophomore year – of *high school*. What he didn't learn about making movies there (or in college) he learned while working at a video rental store where he paid close attention to the kinds of movies customers liked to rent. Everyone knows Bill Gates and Steve Jobs didn't need a college degree, but neither did Will Rogers, Alicia Keys, J.K. Rowling, John D. Rockefeller, Teddy Roosevelt, Tom Hanks, William Randolph Hearst, Robert Frost, P!nk, R. Buckminster Fuller, Will Smith, Dana White, Tony Hawk, Tony Robbins, William Saroyan, George Bernard Shaw, Simon Cowell, George Gershwin, Jimmy

Fallon, Walt Disney, Ellen DeGeneres or Mark Zuckerberg. (For a long list of "successful dropouts" see "The College Drop-out Hall of Fame.")[5]

I'm not suggesting that students follow their example and drop out. I'm advocating that schools formally teach the lessons that many of the greatest achievers *ever* somehow learned somewhere outside formal education's claustrophobic walls. Why aren't we teaching what they know?

"The most critical lesson in economics," I stress to my econ students, "is opportunity cost." Opportunity cost is about making choices. Whenever we choose to spend our money on something – say $100 dollars – it means we can't spend that $100 dollars on anything else. When we say yes to one thing, it means we're saying no to every other thing. When we say yes to one college, career or romantic partner, we're saying no to every other college, career or romantic partner (ideally, anyway). Our choices define our lives. We must choose wisely! Too often we don't, especially with how we spend our time and talent.

On a particularly congested day on the most clogged freeway in the United States – California's 405 – I had plenty of time to examine the graffiti on the highway overpasses. One conspicuous piece of freeway art had been painted on five overpasses in row. In huge block lettering was the word *SLUT*.

You've got to admit, painting anything, even SLUT, on a *single* freeway overpass is an impressive feat. But five in row? How did he (or she) do it? I couldn't have done it! It had to have been done by someone, somehow, suspended over multiple lanes of traffic. It must have taken meticulous planning, extraordinary determination and great courage. To succeed, the artist (or vandal) must have had powerful motivation and an urgent goal. He or she must have thought creatively and, perhaps, worked as part of a team.

But for what? What did it accomplish? What did it contribute? All that focused planning, determination, courage, motivation, goal setting, creativity and teamwork wasted on a pointless, destructive "mission." Imagine what could have been accomplished if that overpass painter's choice had been to spend that same kind of time and effort on something meaningful and constructive.

Something like what college dropout Jann Wenner constructed. When he was 20, (20!) he left the University of California, Berkeley and founded *Rolling Stone* magazine. But that was in the 60's. It couldn't happen today, right? What about Maggie Doyne? She didn't even go to college. Yet, after graduating from high school in 2005, she took a gap year "to see the world." She ended up in Nepal where she built an orphanage, founded a school and adopted over 30 children!

What did Wenner, Doyne and the rest of the successful *formal* education (not education) dropouts learn that everyone should know?

What they all have in common is a passion and a relentless desire to pursue it. It ought to be an outrage when our students graduate from high school – and even college – without a passion. When schools are being evaluated, they aren't judged by how many of their students have found and are actively pursuing a passion. Why not?

My favorite passion story is about a guy who *did* end up graduating from college – Jeff Van Gundy. Growing up, Van Gundy was a stellar student. He got into Yale. But his passion was basketball. After he was cut from the Yale basketball team, he finished out his freshman year, then transferred to Menlo College.

Unless you're from California's Bay Area (and maybe even if you are), you've probably never heard of Menlo. Van Gundy's girlfriend, Kim (now his wife), thought he was nuts. Who leaves Yale for Menlo? Who leaves Yale?

But the decision made perfect sense to Van Gundy. He couldn't play ball at Yale. He could at Menlo. It was a no-brainer. An important part of the story is how Van Gundy's parents reacted. They weren't thrilled, but they understood and supported him. (Probably because Jeff's father, college coach Bill Van Gundy, could relate to his son's infatuation.) And they continued to support him when, chasing his dream, he left Menlo for SUNY – Brockport so he could play for his father. Unfortunately, Bill Van Gundy was fired, so Jeff transferred again, this time to Nazareth College in Rochester, New York.

Finally, at Nazareth, he thrived. The not-so-athletically-gifted, 5' 9", 150 pound point guard led the Golden Flyers to the 1984 NCAA Division III Eastern Regional Championship.

Yale, Menlo, Nazareth, it didn't matter. Whatever Van Gundy needed to succeed, he already had. For the next 11 years, he worked his way up the coaching ranks, culminating with the New York Knicks improbably hiring him to be their head coach. The Yale dropout has since made millions coaching and broadcasting professional basketball games.

How does something like this happen? What can we learn from Van Gundy's story that will inspire us to help our kids live great lives?

In a perfect world, all courses would include only interesting, relevant and useful lessons that would inspire students to learn and seek more education. But, alas, we live on Earth where perfect exists only in our imagination. As anyone who has ever been to school knows, a lot of what's "taught" is boring, irrelevant and useless. In *What I Talk About When I Talk About Running*, the renowned Japanese novelist, Haruki Murakami, wrote, "The most important thing we learn at school is the fact that the most important things can't be learned at school."

Sure, some of education is about overcoming obstacles. That's why the type of degree earned isn't nearly as important as just getting one. Finding a way to get over the crazy hurdles is part of the game. Battling their way through our imperfect school system prepares kids to battle their way around our imperfect world.

I get that.

Nevertheless, I despise it. Life is hard enough as it is. We don't need to make it *artificially* harder. Group initiations are archaic. Jumping jacks suck.

To test if potential players want to make my basketball team badly enough, I could demand that they do 1,000 jumping jacks. Players who did it would be demonstrating that they're willing to do whatever it takes to make it. But why not let them demonstrate their resolve by requiring them to do something worthwhile? The problem is not so much *what* we're teaching. The tragedy is what we're *not* teaching.

Doing jumping jacks isn't much different than studying the Ordinances of 1785 and 1787. They're better than nothing, but there are a zillion healthier alternatives. Instead of jumping jacks, players could be doing plyometric push-ups or box jumps – challenging exercises that are useful, too.

Teachers have a one-time chance to teach students critically important lessons that can turn them on to education – and life. But when we teach obscure material of questionable value, that opportunity is lost. Because there is an infinite amount of material to teach, those making the decisions about what students should learn have a gigantic responsibility to be super selective. Whenever a book is assigned, every other book is *not* assigned. So it better be one heck of a great book! Whenever a lesson is taught, every other lesson is *not* taught. So it better be one heck of a great lesson.

You could spend a lifetime reading great book after great book and never come close to reading all the great books. So why waste time reading anything mediocre? Likewise, you could spend every minute of every class teaching interesting, relevant and useful lessons and never come close to teaching everything that's interesting, relevant and useful. So why waste time teaching mediocre, relatively irrelevant lessons? Why misuse even a minute of it doing jumping jacks?

What lessons are not included in *The Missing Pieces*? Lots! Personal finance, for example, is not in the curriculum. How can we send kids out into the world without teaching them about investing, checking accounts, life, health and auto insurance, how credit cards work and why mortgage interest is so important at tax time? We don't require kids to learn how to perform CPR, jump start a car, plan a party or prepare a meal. Why not?

These skills are important, but they didn't make the cut. I didn't include them because they are just that - *skills.* They're needed, but relatively easy to teach and master. They can be learned in a day or at a weekend seminar.

In America, despite high unemployment, there are millions of jobs - from accountants to machinists to diagnostic medical sonographers - that remain unfilled. The pool of applicants with the proper training in these specializations is pitifully small. [3] Although providing the specific training required to be hired in these fields is obviously necessary and important, it's not the focus of *Missing Pieces.* Here, we take a broader view of what it takes to succeed in *any* job, career or enterprise.

# Introduction

After my daughters, Kyrra and Kylene, had grown and moved away from our San Francisco Bay Area home, I was visiting them in Los Angeles. I awoke early on a Sunday morning and was on my way to the beach for a workout run. While waiting for a light to turn green, I watched as a haggard-looking, 30-something man made his way across a Santa Monica Boulevard intersection.

I'd seen him before. Well, not *him*. People like him.

It was a little before 7:00 AM. There aren't many times in LA when the streets are empty, but that morning they were.

Except for the man.

He had pressed the button so he could cross the street. I was irritated. Those crosswalk lights allow way too much time. A three-legged turtle could make it to the other side before the light changes, so I had plenty of time to watch him.

He may have been homeless, but I don't think he was. It seemed like he was on his way somewhere. Probably to a job that required him to work for someone else for a low wage. A job that demanded him to be up early on a Sunday morning. I felt sad for him.

The year I began teaching, Kyrra was three. Kylene was born that October. My first class was a combination class - 18 third graders and 12 fourth graders. Some of them stood out. They did well academically. They were vibrant and fun. The other kids liked them and wanted to be around them. I hoped my kids would grow up to be like them.

Others stood out, too. But for the opposite reasons. They struggled academically. They were disruptive. The other kids didn't like them and avoided them. I hoped my kids *wouldn't* grow up to be like them.

Harsh? Perhaps. But honest. I wanted my kids to be happy and successful. I wanted them to live meaningful, extraordinary lives. So, initially informally, later formally - my Master's thesis at San Jose State was *A Study of the Factors Contributing to Student Success* - I became obsessed with learning what it takes to live well. Originally, it was for my daughters but later for my students, especially the ones headed for heartache. I didn't want them living a life where they'd have to be up before seven on Sundays, heading off to a job they hate, looking hopeless and miserable.

As I drove onto the westbound Interstate 10 on-ramp, I thought about Kyrra and Kylene. They've grown up and are living good lives. They aren't completely satisfied yet (Is anyone? Ever?), but they're pursuing their passions and working toward their dreams. Maybe the guy crossing the street was, too. But I doubt it. I got the feeling he was just trying to survive.

What was he like when he was ten? Did he have dreams back then? If so, what were they? More importantly, when did they die, and what was the cause of death? Tragedy? Injury? Illness? Addiction? Settling? Financial misfortune? A love affair gone bad?

What murders dreams? And what must I teach to prevent my students from ending up like the man crossing the street?

52 Lessons.

## The New Report Card

*If gross miscalculations of a person's value could occur on a baseball field, before a live audience of thirty thousand, and a television audience of millions more, what did that say about the measurement of performance in other lines of work? If professional baseball players could be over or under valued, who couldn't?*

- Michael Lewis

*Moneyball: The Art of Winning an Unfair Game*

Yeah, who couldn't? I encounter overvalued and undervalued students each year. I see overvalued high school seniors who, because they have impressive grades and test scores, get into top tier universities. (Top tier according to tradition, bias and the controversial *U.S. News & World Report*'s ranking system.) They shouldn't have been accepted. They're better on paper than in real life. They may have cheated their way through high school, spent hours in SAT prep classes, had their college entrance essay ghostwritten and/or just played the high school game exceptionally well.

I also see undervalued seniors with less stellar grades and test scores not get into top tier colleges because they aren't as good on paper as they are in real life. Like the valuable baseball player the scouts didn't notice because they were measuring the wrong attributes, colleges miss out on some of the best kids because they're obsessed with numbers - the wrong numbers.

Let's initiate the education revolution with a renovation of report cards. The ones we have now – at least at the secondary school level - are archaic. Even though they don't tell us nearly enough, they *are* taken seriously. Getting a report card is still a big deal. Grades matter. They matter to parents, and they matter to kids. Management consultant/author Tom Peters says, "What gets measured gets done." Trouble is, because we don't measure a lot of what's important, a lot of what's important doesn't get done. It's not taught. Yet, perhaps the greatest and most iconic theoretical physicist of our era, Albert Einstein, ironically stated, “Not everything that can be counted counts, and not everything that counts can be counted.” It’s ironic because physics is such a precise, measurable, “countable” science.

What do parents get from today’s report cards? Other than whether or not their child is mastering a specific subject, not much. Obviously, how well a student learns the course curriculum is critical. But isn’t there more – a lot more? As important as intellect and discipline are, they aren’t adequate indicators of the *whole* child. *In addition to* (not instead of) the traditional report card grades, don’t you think it’s crucial that we measure how students are doing in the areas most relevant to their overall success?

*Overall* success. Wise parents know that their children are much, much more than what’s reflected in a math, science, English or social studies grade. And what about the students? Don’t they need to know how they’re doing at what it takes to be happy, successful and fulfilled in the out-of-school world? In kid logic, “If it’s not on the report card, it can’t be that important.”

Let’s make it important. Let’s demand more than we’re currently demanding from our kids. They’re capable of learning, developing and delivering more, but not unless we put it in writing.

In the 1960’s, at St. Barnabas School, we’d get an A,B,C grade for *effort* (how hard we tried) and *conduct* (how well we behaved). I’m all for bringing those grades back. My mom used to insist that they were the most important marks on my report card. I didn’t get it then, but I do now.

Let’s reinstate effort and conduct onto today’s report cards. Let’s also find a way to measure these other vital but difficult-to-count characteristics:

- **Integrity:** Can the student be trusted? During a test, if the teacher left the room, would the student cheat? How does he/she act when no one is watching?

- **Initiative:** Has the student ever started anything? A club? A protest?

A movement? Or does he or she just sit back, waiting to be told what to do? World changers don't join stuff. They *start* stuff.

- **Special Interest:** Does the student have one? How into it is he or she? Kids who aren't interested in anything are headed for trouble.

- **Passion:** Has the student found an activity that provides both joy and heartache? Finding a passion should be required. Without one, life is hollow, meaningless and boring.

- **Goal Setting:** Goals motivate. Is the student working toward both short and long-term goals? Goal setting has to be encouraged – and taught.

- **Motivation:** How motivated is the student? Is the motivation extrinsic or intrinsic? Intrinsic is the goal.

- **Determination and Perseverance:** How quickly does the student give up or give in? Is he or she a fighter (in the best sense)? Remember Thomas Edison? *Ten thousand* tries until he got the light bulb right.

- **Mentorship:** How many mentors does the student have, especially in his or her special interest and passion? They won't magically pop into students' lives. Cinderella is fiction. There are no magical fairy godmothers or godfathers. But there are real ones.

- **Critical Thinking / Resourcefulness / Problem Solving:** While maintaining morals, does the student find a way to get it done? Sometimes, especially when they're blazing a trail, there won't be any mentors. It will be up to them to figure it out.

- **Social Skills:** Is the student someone others want to be around? If not, he or she will be miserable and could become dangerous.

- **Manners:** Does the student have them? Some do. Some don't. Either way, manners matter, and they're not that hard to teach.

- **Ability to Meet People:** Can the student make connections and build relationships? Overall happiness and career success rely heavily on both – skills that can be mastered.

- **Empathy:** Can the student put him/herself in the place of others? Or, does the world revolve around him or her? Selfishness or selflessness?

- **Use of Time:** Does the student use it prudently? Is the bulk of it spent on life-augmenting activities?

- **Balance:** Where is the student "too much" or "too little"? Kids won't learn balance unless we teach them how necessary it is and how harmful not having it can be.

- **Design:** Does the student's work show effort? Pride of ownership? Creativity? Form *and* function matter.

- **Leadership:** Can the student rally others? Does he or she make life better for others? Does he or she walk the walk? (It takes leaders to train leaders.)

- **Autonomous Learning:** Is the student able to "self-teach"? Students who don't require constant coaxing become self-motivated, lifelong learners. Online resources make learning almost anything possible. Roy Chin, a revolutionary medical device entrepreneur, taught himself how to perform heart surgery!

- **Self-control (Willingness to sacrifice immediate gratification for a long-term reward):** Can the student control his or her urges? The difference between immaturity and maturity, childhood and man/womanhood is self-control. Has the student demonstrated the ability to ignore those powerful "I-need-it-now" urges and focus on large-picture, future goals?

- **Presentation Skills:** How well does the student speak and present? Kids who can talk are respected and ultimately hired, promoted, worked with and invested in.

- **Writing:** Can the student produce clearly-communicated, error-free, emotion-generating prose? An A in English doesn't mean the student can write. Good writers are scarce - and valuable.

- **Human Capital:** Is the student developing positive talents, skills and behaviors that separate him/her from the masses? Kids who are good at stuff – especially in-demand stuff - have confidence and an identity. Human capital leads to social capital which can lead to financial capital.

  Human capital ➔ Social Capital ➔ Financial Capital

- **Patience:** Can he or she wait? The "patience muscle" must be developed.

- **Creativity/Originality:** How distinct (in a good way) is the student's work? Conformity has its place, but individuality improves the world.

- **Humility:** Does the student handle success with class? Isn't it refreshing when successful people don't act like successful people?

- **Health and Fitness:** Does the student value and work at his or her physicality? If adults don't take it seriously, kids won't either. Keeping fit will help their mental as well as their physical health.

- **Compassion/Inclination to help others and contribute to the world:** Is the student a good person? Isn't this one of the purposes of education? Shouldn't we be teaching kids to be kind? Shouldn't we be showing them how to contribute?

- **Attention Span/Listening Skills/Audience Skills:** Can the student focus, remain attentive and "get it"? Is his or her in-class body language animated or lifeless?

- **Sales:** Can the student market and promote? Knowing how to sell, whether it be a product, service or themselves, may be the most important skill for a student to master.

- **Curiosity:** Does the student ask questions? How good, interesting, creative and perceptive are they? Intelligence can be assessed by the quality of a question.

- **Humor:** Does the student "get funny"? It takes background knowledge and intelligence to understand humor. Actress/ comedian Tina Fey says she can tell how smart people are by what they laugh at.

- **Energy/Fire/Ambition/Enthusiasm:** Does the student show a zest for life? If not, why not? (Kids should be excited about living! When they aren't, it's a red flag.)

Are teachers qualified to evaluate these qualities?

Who better?

Often (especially at the elementary level), teachers spend more time with their students than parents do with their kids. Further, we have the opportunity to observe how our students are when they're out in the world, away from the familiar confines of their homes and families - something most parents seldom get to do.

Give us teachers some credit. Please, listen to our input. If you want to blow it off, fine. But how can such an extensive evaluation do anything but help? At the very least, it will get parents and students thinking, not just about grades, but about strengths and weaknesses and what's important and what's not.

Excelling in any (all?) of these capacities is at least as important as excelling in math, science, reading, writing and social studies. But you've got to take them seriously. If you do, and if you want to learn how to master them, read, study and teach this book.

# Empty Your Cup

*What we know is to what we do not know, as a grain of sand is to the beach.*

- Ivan Panin
Nobel Prize winner - Mathematics (1941)

Three-time Pulitzer Prize-winning *New York Times* columnist Thomas Friedman wrote, "The standard answer is that we need better leaders. The real answer is that we need better citizens."

Just as true is: The standard answer is we need better teachers (or better schools). The real answer is we need better students. In *Zen in the Martial Arts,* Joe Hyams writes about the time Bruce Lee told him a story about an arrogant student who is more concerned with impressing his master than learning from him.

When he enters the dojo, his attitude is more "Look at me" than "Teach me." He spends his once-in-a-lifetime opportunity talking about and showing off his *own* martial arts philosophies and techniques. He's so busy blabbing and boasting that he hasn't taken a single sip of his tea. When the master pours more boiling hot tea into his already full cup, the stunned student jumps up and yelps, "Master, can't you see? My cup is full!"

"Exactly," the master gently scolds, "and until you empty it, I won't be able to teach you anything."

Sometimes, because of their arrogance, students don't know when, why or how they're being taught. At the beginning of each school year, I show my students the scene from the original *The Karate Kid* (a great, timeless movie!) when the frustrated karate student, Daniel, learns *why* he was instructed to paint the house, sand the floor and wax the car. Before the light bulb came on, he had no idea that his sensei, Mr. Miyagi, was teaching him the muscle memory he'd need to deflect punches and kicks. Until that magnificent moment of understanding, Daniel hadn't trusted his teacher. He hadn't emptied his cup.

I don't care how great a teacher is. Socrates couldn't teach an American teenager who has no interest in learning. Sure, teachers need to be clear and empathetic and caring and understanding and inspiring. When I asked my Facebook friends for adjectives that describe an ideal teacher, I got almost 50 different answers, including *nurturing, driven, fun, inspiring, organized, imaginative* and *smart*. It takes a lot, a heck of a lot, to be a successful teacher.

But students have to do their part, too. They have to give us a chance. They have to be teachable. They have to empty their cups.

## Assignment

Before passing judgment, before deciding if a teacher is good or bad, empty your cup. Before deciding whether or not a lesson is effective, empty your cup. Before sharing what *you* know, empty your cup. And, while you're reading this book, I humbly ask you to, please, empty your cup.

## Balance

Don't be surprised at how often the solution is balance. Too much or too little of virtually anything is bad. It's true with the obvious - eating, sleeping, exercising, studying, working...

- Too much food and you're fat. Too little and you're skinny (and maybe you have an eating disorder).

- Sleep all day and you're lazy, nonproductive (or sick). Sleep too little and you're exhausted, ornery (and you end up becoming sick).

- Exercise too much and you're over-trained and obsessed. Exercise too little and you're out of shape and weak.

- Study all the time and you hate your life. Never study and you'll end up hating your life.

- Work too much and your relationships suffer - and you're boring. Work too little and you're ineffective, unsuccessful – and you're boring.

But balance is also the solution to the less obvious, more subtle life situations:

- When you're around others too much, you'll grate on them, and they'll take you for granted. If you're never around, you'll become insignificant, and they'll learn to live without you.

- Talking too much may make you someone others avoid. Talking too little may make you invisible.

- Shakespeare's *Macbeth* was a tragedy because Macbeth (and even more so, Lady Macbeth) was too ambitious. The overly-ambitious are more apt to try to achieve their goals illicitly. Too little ambition assures failure and leads to an unrewarding and unfulfilling life.

- Too much power can be dangerous. The United States began because of this belief. But too little power is maddening. When no one has any power, it's like America under the Articles of Confederation - nothing gets done.

- When you're beginning a romantic relationship, if you're too clingy, it's a turn-off (and kind of creepy). On the other hand, if you're not attentive enough, you'll end up alone and miserable.

- Being proud of your race, religion, school, city, state or country is good. Being *too* proud of any of those can lead to hate, violence and war.

- Sometimes, cool detachment is the right call. Other times, passionate involvement is necessary.

- Too much parental discipline is harmful to children. Radical "Tiger Moms" (and Dads) can make their children crazy. But too little discipline may be worse. Kids who haven't been disciplined enough become society's menaces. Too much or too little of just about any kind of discipline – teacher disciplining student, coach disciplining player, boss disciplining employee – won't work.

- Trust is good. Too much trust is bad. Having a healthy

> dose of skepticism is necessary for self-preservation. The world is full of kindhearted, trustworthy people. But it's also full of hardhearted, deceitful scumbags.

It's hard to find anything in which balance isn't important. Our bodies are incessantly seeking homeostasis. Too hot is uncomfortable. Too cold isn't any better. It's not healthy when our blood pressure or blood sugar is too high or too low.

The United States Constitution has worked because it balances power between the states and the federal government and among the three branches.

A basic teaching tenant when writing curriculum and planning lessons is to balance the difficulty. Too hard is overwhelming and discouraging. Too easy is unchallenging and boring.

Finding the center isn't easy. Kids are taught about the importance of balance the first time they read *Goldilocks and the Three Bears*. We don't want our porridge to be too hot or too cold. Chairs can be too hard or too soft. Finding "just right" is a challenge. It demands constant adjustment and endless fine-tuning. The search for balance is a lifetime quest.

## Assignment

1. Take inventory. What do you need to do more? Less? More exercise? Less work? More study? Less play? More volunteering? Less "me time"? After taking inventory, make the necessary adjustments. Sounds simple, but it's not. Balance takes time and effort. But it's worth it.

2. Be aware of how often you'll have to make a "balance decision." Having this awareness will enable you to make a better choice as to whether to do more or less. For example, walking our French bulldog, Kihei, can be frustrating! She's continually distracted. She hunts for lizards, sniffs almost everything and has no interest in arriving

anywhere before she's ready.

What should I do?

I could constantly tug at her leash, hurrying her along. But that would ruin the best part of her day. Or, I could ease up and let *her* set the pace. But that could keep me from doing something important *I* need to do. So, each time we walk, I make a balance decision. Sometimes, I stop, relax and let her do her thing. At other times, I tug the leash (not too much and not too little) to keep her moving.

Not exactly a life-altering choice, but indicative of how pervasive balance decisions are and will be throughout our lives.

## The Three Questions

*It is not the critic who counts; not the man who points how the strong man stumbles, or where the doer of deeds could have done them better. The credit belongs to the man who is actually in the arena, whose face is marred by dust and sweat and blood; who strives valiantly; who errs, who comes up short again and again, because there is no effort without error and shortcoming; but who does actually strive to do the deeds; who knows great enthusiasms, the great devotions; who spends himself in a worthy cause; who at the best knows in the end the triumph of high achievement, and who at the worst, if he fails, at least fails while daring greatly, so that his place shall never be with those cold and timid souls who neither know victory nor defeat.*

- Theodore Roosevelt,
Excerpt from the speech "Citizenship In A Republic"
delivered at the Sorbonne, in Paris, France on
April 23rd, 1910

In the greatest movie of all time, *Rocky* (the original), there's a scene in which Rocky is giving advice to an adolescent girl named Maria. His advice is solid. Essentially, he tells her how important it is for a girl to protect her reputation - that if she speaks crudely and hangs out with the wrong crowd, her reputation will be soiled.

Maria appears to be getting it, but when Rocky is through lecturing, all she says is, "Screw you, Creepo," and then slams the door. Rocky is left alone on the street. "Yeah, Creepo," he mutters to himself, "who are you to be giving advice?"

The point is, unless you've done something, unless you've had success, unless you've lived *your* life well, most people aren't going to care what you have to say. So...

- *Who are you?*
- *What have you done?*
- *Why should I listen to you?*

These are the three questions people are wondering about you. Even if they don't ask them out loud, even if they're doing it subconsciously, they're thinking them. For example, from my days of teaching speech and drama, here's a tale of two demonstration speeches:

> Student #1 chose to teach us how to shoot a basketball free throw. So, we went to the gym. He had us sit on the baseline while he stood on the foul line. He talked for a moment about the proper grip, elbow position, knee bend and follow-through. He seemed to know what he was talking about. His classmates were listening.
>
> Then he shot the ball. He shot it ten times. He made two. Twenty percent. (Seventy is decent.) It was terribly embarrassing. His credibility gone, his classmates stopped listening. Worse, before I could stop them, they laughed. It was brutal.

- *Who are you?*
- *What have you done?*
- *Why should I listen to you?*

> Student #2 began her presentation by passing out cookies. They were fantastic - chocolate chip oatmeal cookies made with a special kind of oatmeal and other natural, "secret" ingredients. She claimed her cookies not only tasted yummy, they were

nutritious, too. We loved them.

She asked us if we wanted to learn how to make them. Of course we did! So we listened attentively to her speech. No one laughed.

- *Who are you?*
  "I'm Laura, an eighth grade girl who loves to bake."

- *What have you done?*
  (While students are enjoying samples) "I've invented these great-tasting and nutritious cookies."

- *Why should I listen to you?*
  "Because if you do, you can learn how to make these delicious cookies, too."

Our parents and grandparents were taught to respect the position. Teachers were respected because they were teachers. Coaches were respected because they were coaches. Parents were respected because they were parents.

I wonder, though. When they were young, did Grandma and Grandpa actually feel the respect they were ordered to show? Or did they only pretend to be the respectful student, player or child? Either way, it's not like that anymore. Today, right or wrong, positions aren't respected. People are. It's not what you are. It's who you are. It's what you've done, what you do and what you can do. If you've never done anything or can't do anything, you're not going to be respected. Liked? Maybe. Respected? No.

Students should ask the three questions because it's reasonable to be skeptical. Just because some teacher, some coach, some *adult* is telling them something, it doesn't mean that it's right, that it's good advice or that they should accept it. I want them thinking *Who are you? What have you done? Why should I listen to you?* Only after they are satisfied that their "teacher" has good answers to those questions should they seriously consider what he or she says.

And when they're not satisfied? I suggest that, outwardly (as our grandparents were taught), they should feign respect. Blatant disrespect rarely accomplishes much. So just play the role. Inside, though, think, *I'm not buying it. You haven't done enough to earn my respect or my trust.*

The three questions are also pertinent to thoughts and opinions. Students need to know that not all thoughts and opinions are equal. Sure, everyone gets to have an opinion and anyone can say what he or she thinks. But the thoughts on global warming from a scholar with a PhD in atmospheric science and meteorology count more than the two cents from the layman who barely made it out of high school. When the woman who has traveled abroad extensively talks about foreign policy, it means more than what the girl who has never left her hometown thinks. It's especially important to ask the three questions in a world where any idiot can have a blog and rant on about whatever, pretending to be important.

I also want kids to reverse the roles. I want them to look at *themselves* as the teachers. I want them to work to develop their *own* excellent answers to the three questions. If they want to matter, if they want respect, they need to start by asking the three questions to *themselves.* Who am *I*? What have *I* done? Why should anyone listen to *me*? If they're not satisfied with their answers, they need to get to work. "Practice," I tell them. "Train. Study. Get skills. Improve. Get good. If you're exceptionally good at just about anything, people will want to be your friend. You'll be popular. You can get away with stuff that people without skills can't. If you're good, there are countless fringe benefits." (More on this in lesson 29 – Specialize and Get Good.)

Is this fair? Probably not. But it's the way it is. So work hard. Pay your dues. Be able to make those free throws!

## Assignment

1. Get into the habit of asking the three questions about whomever is teaching, coaching or advising you. Maybe not literally, but at least think them. When they don't have good answers, be skeptical about what they're selling. Then, as soon as you can, find someone better.

2. Truthfully, ruthlessly answer the three questions about yourself. Who are you? What have you done? Why should anyone listen to you? Create a list of what you've done. If there's not much on it, don't worry. Resumes are built over time.

Here's my list:

- High school graduate
- B.A. degree, Liberal Studies, Cal-State, Northridge (Cum Laude)
- Commissioned as a United States Air Force officer, promoted to captain, awarded Commendation Medal
- M.A. Degree, Secondary Education, San Jose State (Thesis Title: "Successful Secondary School Students – A Study of the Factors Contributing to Their Success")
- Credentials and Authorizations: Multiple Subject, Single Subject: English and Social Science, English as a Second Language, Preliminary Administrative Credential, CLAD, GLAD, ESL, GATE
- Thirty years of teaching experience, including elementary, junior high, high school, adult school, college and special education
- Fremont Unified School District, Mentor Teacher
- Coca Cola Scholars: Educator of Distinction

- 2014 Yale Educator Award
- Professional writer: Twelve years writing a column "What It Takes" (Never missed a deadline); Published in the *Oakland Tribune*, *San Jose Mercury News*, *Hayward Daily Review*, the *Argus*, *yahoo.com*, *what-it-takes.com*
- Published author: *What it Takes*, *Kids Can't Write*, *Living the Decision*; (and working on this one!)
- Founder, The Kefi Foundation, a 501(c)(3) organization that provides sports, art and recreational equipment and instruction to disadvantaged children around the world (See Lesson 7 – How to Find *Kefi*)
- Basketball player: Ann Arbor Huron High School – starter, Eastern Michigan University – (scored in double figures three times, scored 6 points in victory over Michigan State), Ellsworth AFB – base champions, Fremont City League – city champions
- Basketball coach: elementary, junior high, high school and military coaching experience; *junior high* team scored over 100 points six times in one season
- Martial Arts student: Belts include 2nd Degree black in Taekwondo, blue in Gracie Jiu-Jitsu, blue in Krav Maga, level three in Eskrima
- Martial Arts teacher: Five years experience teaching children and adults
- Martial Arts competitor: Placed in every tournament entered. Experience in point fighting, ground fighting and full-contact (Been "In the ring")
- Tour Coordinator: Led student travel trips to San Francisco, Washington D.C., Boston, New York, Mexico

and Nicaragua

- D.J. at KOHL (college radio station)

- TV Host *Homework Helpline* (education-themed cable television program)

- Surfer: Learned to surf (albeit far from expertly) after age 40 (Hey, it's tough learning *anything* after 40!)

- Personal Trainer: certification – National Academy of Sports Medicine (NASM)

- Scuba Diver: certification – Scuba Diving International (SDI)

- Triathlete: Completed a triathlon!

- Alcohol, cigarette and drug free; physically fit, work out daily

- Husband: happily married to Norma Richards for 35 years. No affairs.

- Father: two amazing daughters, both successful UCLA graduates, who love each other.

Should we *need* to make such a list? Gandhi said, "My life is my message," and that's how it should be. We should be judged by how we live, not by what we write. Further, constructing a bullet list of accomplishments seems arrogant, and I despise arrogance. So I debated with myself as to whether or not I should publish my list. On the other hand, I'm not Gandhi. Upon meeting me, most people won't know who I am, what I've done or why they should listen to me. So, how will they get the message, especially when it has to be delivered quickly? Only by building, producing and promoting a snapshot of my life.

Am I proud of my list? Yes. I know I've been "in the arena." Am

I satisfied with it? No. Not even close. It's not good enough. When I compare what I've accomplished with what others have done, I'm disheartened. (Barack Obama is younger than me.) When I compare what I've accomplished with what I had hoped to have accomplished, I'm disappointed with myself.

Still, my body of work includes enough successes that I believe I've earned respect. It also inspires me. As long as I'm breathing, I want to keep adding to it. I'm not done.

Are you?

## The Pleasures

Earth isn't heaven. It's a septic tank filled with war and violence, poverty and pain, sadness and stress, disappointment and frustration, unrequited love and unfulfilled expectations.

Depressed yet? Sorry, but I don't believe in that "ignorance is bliss" garbage. Sure, as much as we can, we need to expose kids to the best. (Lesson 11 - Immerse). But let's not sugarcoat life. Besides, the more we say, "Don't look," they're going to look. We can't hide reality, nor should we. Kids have to learn to recognize it, understand it, cope with it and, hopefully, do something about it.

That said, it's not all bad. Despite the surplus of pain, there's an abundance of pleasure. Life is loaded with good stuff that helps us cope with the bad stuff. Sometimes we forget this. And sometimes kids are not taught this.

So let this be a reminder to "see the blue" (Lesson 18) and become cognizant of those pleasures. Some are expensive and available to only a tiny portion of people. There's no doubt that living in a gorgeous home, driving a luxurious car, eating at five-star restaurants or traveling to fabulous vacation resorts is pleasurable. But since that stuff is out of reach for the majority, let's focus on the low-cost/no-cost pleasures available to almost all of us.

You can group the pleasures according to the senses:

- What *sights* make you happy?

- What *smells* wonderful?

- What *tastes* delicious?
- What *feels* pleasant? (Get past the obvious sexual jokes. Yes, sex belongs in this category, but it doesn't have to dominate.)
- What *sounds* make you happy and content?

Even though many of them are available to anyone, anytime, at no cost, pleasures are a lot like money. By themselves, they won't make us happy. If we have them too often or overdose on them, their effect wears off, and we take them for granted. Still, when they're managed well, pleasures can make a bad day better and a good day great.

Learning about or even pursuing pleasures isn't necessarily selfish. Not only can we teach others about them, we can help people experience them. Buying someone a favorite food or flower, especially when he or she is feeling sad, lonely, frustrated or angry, will help. It will help a lot. In J.D. Salinger's *The Catcher in the Rye*, Holden Caufield's mother gives him the wrong kind of skates. "I wanted racing skates and she bought hockey, but it made me sad anyway. Almost every time somebody gives me a present, it ends up making me sad."

Pathetic, right?

Maybe.

Before you dismiss Holden as a spoiled, ungrateful brat, consider *why* he was sad. It's not that his mother bought him the wrong kind of skates. Whether or not he got racing skates wasn't the point.

What upset him was that his mother didn't know him well enough to know what he really wanted. His own mother - the person who should have known him best – hadn't known that he wanted racing not hockey skates. That's why he was unhappy. His mom not knowing or taking the time to find out that there is a difference between speed and hockey skates seems like a little thing, but it really is a big thing. So, if you listen to people, if you take the time to learn about their specific, personal pleasures, you can surprise them with a gift that matters.

**Note:** University of Pennsylvania positive psychologist Martin Seligman teaches us that, with discipline, we can *enhance* our pleasures.[6] When we don't eat all the time, food tastes better. When we don't sleep all the time, sleep feels better. When we don't listen to it all the time, a favorite song sounds better… And we can further enhance pleasures by *combining* them. Try it! Eat your favorite burrito while sitting in a comfortable chair, gazing at the sea, listening to the waves crash while inhaling the fresh, salty air.

## Assignment

List at least five low-cost/no-cost pleasures for each of the five senses–25 in all. For example:

**Sight**

1. Little kids having fun on a playground
2. Hawaiian sunsets
3. My daughters, especially when they're laughing
4. Animals in the wild – deer, hawks, dolphins…
5. Awesome human-engineered structures e.g. the Golden Gate Bridge (Makes me think about what's possible)

**Smell**

1. The pine forests of Lake Tahoe
2. My puppy's distinctive scent
3. Ivory soap
4. Autumn
5. My wife's spaghetti

**Taste**

1. Gatorade (the original, lemon-lime kind) when I'm super thirsty after a good workout
2. Cold fruit – apples, oranges, grapes - when I'm really hot
3. Freshly baked, soft chocolate chip cookies
4. Peanut butter and jelly sandwiches!
5. Chipotle chicken or vegetarian burritos (extra cheese and guac)

**Touch**

1. Warm, dry socks
2. A cool pool (or lake) when it's hot outside. A hot shower (or hot tub) when it's cold outside.
3. A basketball with good grip
4. My bed when I'm exhausted
5. A hug from someone I love

**Sound**

1. The ocean, no matter its mood
2. The right song at the right time e.g. Stevie Wonder's "Love's in Need of Love Today" when the world is making me sad
3. Rain on the window panes and rooftop, especially when I'm dry, warm, comfortable and safe
4. Wind rustling tree leaves
5. A basketball swishing through the net – but only when it's one of my players (or me) shooting!

Put your "Pleasures List" in a conspicuous place. When you discover a new pleasure, add it. When you're feeling down, enjoy something on your list.

## Understanding Passion

*Streetlights, people*
*Livin' just to find emotion*
*Hidin', somewhere in the night*
- Jonathan Cain, Steve Perry and Neal Schon (Journey)
"Don't Stop Believin'"

To be happy, to be successful, to have a meaningful, fulfilling, extraordinary life, having a passion is mandatory. A passionless life is a C life. No highs. No lows. Every day just "OK." A life without a passion is a flat------line life. And, in hospitals, what does flatlining mean? Exactly. No heartbeat. No life.

*Passion* may be the most widely misunderstood and incorrectly used English word. It doesn't mean what most people think it means. And because of this misunderstanding, too many kids grow up without developing a passion. The quality of their lives suffers because they never learned what a passion is – and isn't.

One thing it often *isn't* is enjoyable. I enjoy eating and sleeping and reading on the beach. I enjoy watching football and basketball and going to the movies. But these aren't passions. They're pleasures, and pleasures don't require effort. Passions do.

The truth is, a lot of time we *hate* our passions. Even though they can provide massive joy, they are equally capable of causing searing pain. A passion causes an intense emotion but not always an enjoyable one. Rage, frustration and sorrow are generated by passion. Look it up. The word *passion* is derived from the Latin verb *patī* meaning "to suffer." One of its synonyms is "ache." *The Passion of Christ* was not about Jesus having a good time.

Passions fall into one of these categories:

- **Academics** – reading, writing, arithmetic – and beyond. Colleges offer dozens of majors and hundreds - sometimes thousands - of courses. Studying any one of them could be a passion.

- **Athletics** – team or individual sports

- **Performing Arts** – music, drama, dance

- **Visual Arts** – painting, drawing, ceramics, sculpture, animation, graphic design, fashion design, (any design!), photography, filmmaking

- **Work/Vocation/Career** – Obviously, one of the keys to happiness is being passionate about our work.

All are hard. All are frustrating. All are painful. If not physically, emotionally.

The aggravated artist who punches his imperfect painting and stuffs it into the trash is passionate about his work. So is the angry ballerina who determinedly rehearses a difficult turn sequence in front of the mirror, tears of passion trickling down her cheeks. And don't forget the dedicated accountant, working alone, late into the night, determined to make the balance sheet balance.

The lesson kids desperately need to learn is that sometimes – oftentimes - the thing they love the most they'll hate the most! That if what they think is a passion really is a passion, they *should* have a yin/yang, love/hate relationship with it.

I used to host a cable access educational television program called *Homework Helpline*. Each week I'd interview a student. On one show I asked a top-tier dancer if she ever *didn't* feel like going to dance class.

"Mr. Richards," she said, "I feel that way before *every* class."

That's passion. She hated it, but she loved it. She kept at it because dancing gave her her highest highs. It was her identity. It was who she was. By willing herself to go sweat when she would have rather stayed on the couch, she developed a priceless confidence that can never be stripped away from her. And when her dancing days are over, she'll transfer what she learned on the stage to some other platform.

If kids think that they should always love their passion, they're going to make a horrific mistake. When it gets hard (and it will), when it gets frustrating (and it will), when it gets physically or emotionally unbearable (and it will), they're going to quit. They're going to think, *This can't be my passion. I'm supposed to love my passion, and I'm definitely not loving this!* Then they'll try something else and stick with it – until it gets hard, frustrating and unbearable.

Whatever their passion is, kids won't love every moment of it. But that doesn't mean it isn't a passion. In fact, there's a good chance that means it is.

**Combining Pleasure and Passion:** For many, food tastes better after cooking it. The beach seems nicer after running on it. The view from the mountaintop appears grander after climbing it. By definition, you don't have to work for pleasures. A gourmet chef can cook for you. You can gaze at the beach from your hotel room. You can ride a tram to the top of the mountain. Yet, a lot of times, pleasures are sweeter when you've worked for them.

## Assignment

Read about your passion. Closely observe experts in your passion. Better, talk to them (Lesson 24 - Seek Sages). Learn everything you can about your passion. Orville Redenbacher, the king of popcorn, said, "Know one thing, but do it better than anyone else."

What are you trying to do better? What are you working on right now? What's your passion? If you don't have one, finding one should be your quest. Having one is critical because, as Tony Wagner writes in *Creating Innovators – The Making of Young People Who Will Change the World*, having a passion leads to having a purpose:

> *In the lives of young innovators whom I interviewed, I discovered a consistent link and a developmental arc in their progression from play to passion to purpose. These young people played a great deal - but their play was frequently less structured than most children's, and they had the opportunity to explore, experiment, and discover through trial and error – to take risks and fall down. Through this kind of more creative play as children, these young innovators discovered a passion – often as young adolescents. As they pursued their passions, though, their interests changed and took surprising turns. They developed new passions which, over time, evolved into a deeper and more mature sense of purpose...*[7]

So make life a buffet. Taste everything, choose something, then devour it ravenously.

What, besides the yin/yang, pleasure/pain aspect makes a passion a passion? Use this checklist:

**Can it be practiced alone?**
The runner, alone at sunrise, circling the track. The pianist, alone in a room, perfecting a challenging piece. The student, alone in the library, preparing for the exam... It's during those magical, solitary moments that we learn, create and dream.

**Note:** Even group members and team players need to develop their individual skills.

**Does it require repetition to perfect?**
I had a one-time opportunity to take a seminar from martial arts

legend Bill "Superfoot" Wallace. I was excited about the chance to learn the "secrets" that made Wallace an icon. Instead of revealing some mystical, hush-hush, never-fail technique, he had us put our hand on the wall and throw 50 side kicks. Then 50 hook kicks. Then 50 roundhouse kicks. Then he had us do it again. And again. Iteration is a marvelous teacher. Drenched in sweat, I understood. The "secret" was rigorous repetition. The "secret" was hard work.

**Does it take time to master?**

There are no shortcuts. In his book, *Mastery*, George Leonard writes that it takes a minimum of five years of persistent practice to master a skill.[8] In his book, *The Outliers*, Malcolm Gladwell concludes that it takes a minimum of 10,000 hours to get really good.[9] Putting this into perspective, say you take a typical three-unit college course. (That's 45 hours of class time.) And let's say you're a conscientious student, so for every hour you spend inside the classroom, you spend three hours outside the classroom studying and preparing for class. That's 180 hours per college course, which means you'd have to take *56* college courses on one subject before reaching the 10,000 hours of study necessary for mastery. Put another way, 10,000 hours is equivalent to practicing your passion two hours a day, seven days a week for *fourteen years.*

What it takes to master one passion is not much different from what it takes to master *any* passion. The important thing is learning what it takes to become successful at something meaningful and important (to you). Then, when your interests change, you can transfer what you know about mastery to your new pursuit. So it doesn't really matter what your passion is. There are people who are passionate about climbing trees and growing grass. (I'm serious. Check out treeclimbing.com. Search "Trey Rogers, Lawn Geek.") As long as it's at least relatively safe and entirely legal, if you love it, go for it – shamelessly.

## A Partial List of Potential *(and not always obvious)* Passions

Acting
Animals
Husbandry
Animation
Archaeology
Archery
Astronomy
Aviation
Baking
Baseball
Basketball
Biology
BMXing
Calculus
Carpentry
Ceramics
Cheerleading
Chemistry
Choreography
Comedy
Computer
Programming
Cosmetology
Crafts
Culinary Arts
Dancing
Directing
DJing
Drill Team
Drumming
Electronics
Entrepreneurship
Equestrian
Fashion Design
Fly Fishing
Football
Golf
Graphic Design
Guitar
Gymnastics
Hang Gliding
Hip-hop
Horticulture
Hurdling
Figure Skating
Speed Skating
Leadership
Martial Arts
Model Making
Motorcycling
Mountain Biking
Orienteering
Photography
Police/Fire
Cadets
Pool
Power Lifting
Rock Climbing
Rodeo
Running
Sailing
Scouting
Scuba Diving
Sculpture
Singing
Snowboarding
Soccer
Songwriting
Speech & Debate
Surfing
Swimming
Tennis
Tutoring
Violin
Water Polo
Writing
Working Out

## Flow

*I've got it all, but I feel so deprived*
*I go up, I come down and I'm emptier inside*
*Tell me what is this thing that I feel like I'm missing*
*And why can't I let it go*

*There's gotta be more to life...*
*Than chasing down every temporary high to satisfy me*
*Cause the more that I'm...*
*Tripping out thinking there must be more to life*
*Well there's life, but I'm sure... there's gotta be more*
*Than wanting more*

- Stacie Orrico
"(There's Gotta Be) More To Life"

Have you ever had an extremely hectic, demanding, yet productive day – one of those days where you barely had time to breathe, let alone relax or even eat? Then, as it finally wound down, as you were headed home and had a moment to regroup and think about all you accomplished, you felt a satisfying mixture of contentment and joy. That's good living.

That's flow.

Flow isn't new. Nearly a century ago, Helen Keller wrote, "Many persons have the wrong idea of what constitutes happiness. It is not attained through self-gratification but through fidelity of a worthy purpose."

But Mihaly Csikszentmihalyi – his name is Hungarian

(pronounced "Me-high Cheek-sent-me-high") - has studied and written about it in a series of published papers and bestselling books.[10]

Csikszentmihalyi grew up in a part of Italy (Fiume) that is now Rijeka, Croatia. After being on the losing side in World War II, he was intrigued by how differently people reacted to the devastation. Some were shattered. Others were able to put their lives back together and enjoy flickers of happiness.

Later, after immigrating to the United States and attending the University of Chicago, Csikszentmihalyi decided to spend his life studying and researching what makes humans happy. (If you're going to spend a lifetime researching anything, happiness is a pretty cool topic on which to focus.)

What Csikszentmihalyi discovered should be taught in every classroom in every school, everywhere. His work is that important. The absence of flow from school curriculums is especially confounding after you understand what Csikszentmihalyi and others (including UPenn's Seligman) say makes us happy and fulfilled. It's not what most people think. It's not taking a vacation, lying on the beach or sleeping in on Saturday morning. Those, Seligman would say, are pleasures. Pleasures, remember, are nice, but they shouldn't be the goal.

Flow should be the goal.

Flow, according to Csikszentmihalyi, "is being completely involved in an activity for its own sake. The ego falls away. Time flies. Every action, movement, and thought follows inevitably from the previous one, like playing jazz. Your whole being is involved, and you're using your skills to the utmost."

Flow isn't doing it for the grade. It's not memorizing and forgetting. It's not jumping through hoops. It's what education should be but usually isn't. Ideally, it's what we want kids to be doing with their time. It's what schools should be insisting their students find. Indeed, school should be the primary place where they look for it.

Flow happens when students find their passion and lose themselves in it. Csikszentmihalyi outlined what it involves:

- **Clear goals** - expectations and rules are discernible, and goals are attainable and align appropriately with one's skill set and abilities. Moreover, the challenge level and skill level should both be high.

- **Concentration** - a high degree of concentration on a limited field of attention (a person engaged in the activity will have the opportunity to focus and to delve deeply into it.

- **A loss of the feeling of self-consciousness** - the merging of action and awareness.

- **Distorted sense of time** - one's subjective experience of time is altered.

- **Direct and immediate feedback** - successes and failures in the course of the activity are apparent, so that behavior can be adjusted as needed.

- **Balance between ability level and challenge** - the activity is neither too easy nor too difficult.

- **A sense of personal control** - over the situation or activity.

- **The activity is intrinsically rewarding** - so there is an effortlessness of action.

- **A lack of awareness of bodily needs** - to the extent that one can reach a point of great hunger or fatigue without realizing it.

- **People become absorbed in their activity** - the focus of awareness is narrowed down to the activity itself, action and awareness merging.

**Note:** Csikszentmihalyi says you don't necessarily have to have *all* of these to experience flow.[11]

The point of flow is that happiness, enjoyment, satisfaction, gratification, fulfillment – whatever you want to call it - comes from *effort* and *action*. It's not passive. Flow is a product of passion. It's not *relaxing*, at least in the conventional definition of that word. Pleasures are passive. Eating a delicious dinner is a pleasure. Cooking one is a passion. Listening to music is a pleasure. Playing it is a passion. Looking at an amazing painting is a pleasure. Painting one is a passion. Watching a play is a pleasure. Directing one is a passion. Being a fan at a sporting event is a pleasure. Playing a sport is a passion. Reading a book is a pleasure. Writing one is a passion. This is crucial for students to grasp because passions (Seligman calls them gratifications), not pleasures, can lead to flow and, in turn, a happier, more fulfilling, more worthwhile life.

## Assignment

Think about a time you've experienced flow. What were you doing? Were you working on a project? Practicing a sport? Playing an instrument? Writing a story? Inventing a video game? When was the last time you lost yourself doing something you love (but sometimes hate)? What can you do to increase the number of these kinds of flow experiences?

## How to Find Kefi

*In daylights, in sunsets*
*In midnights, in cups of coffee*
*In inches, in miles, in laughter, in strife*
*In five hundred twenty-five thousand six hundred minutes*
*How do you measure a year in the life?*

- Jonathan Larson
Broadway musical *Rent*

I learned the word *kefi* while sitting in the Nederlander Theatre on 41st Street in Manhattan waiting to watch the Broadway musical, *Rent*. The playbill included *Rent*'s riveting yet heartbreaking background story, including the biography of its creator, Jonathan Larson.

*Rent* is the story of striving artists – singers, dancers, writers, poets, filmmakers and musicians – living in lower Manhattan in the early 1980's. Most had serious health, family and/or relationship problems. And because they hadn't yet "made it," all were struggling to pay their rent. Larson, a self-described drama geek from New York's White Plains High School and Adelphi University, moved to New York City with a mission – to modernize musical theater and make it relevant, especially for a new generation of theater patrons.

At Adelphi, Larson's theater instructor, Jacques Burdick, introduced him to the concept of *kefi* (pronounced keh-fee). It's about finding joy, especially in challenging times and difficult circumstances. "If you have *kefi*," Burdick taught Larson, "Wherever you live, whatever is going on in your life, it will feel wonderful."[12]

While Larson was waiting tables to support himself, he met many young artists who also had big but yet-to-be-fulfilled dreams. He took note that, regardless of their troubles, they still had moments of joy - *kefi*. Despite their difficulties, they were able to enjoy and appreciate life's undervalued treasures – hugs, smiles, jokes, steps toward success in their passions and, most of all, each other. When he wrote *Rent*, he incorporated his friends' *kefi* spirit into his musical.

The heartbreaking irony is that Larson's message – to live in the moment, value each day's blessings and have *kefi* experiences – became a thousand times more meaningful when, on the night before *Rent*'s opening, he suffered an aortic dissection. Shockingly, he passed away. He was only 35 years old.

After learning about Larson and *kefi*, I fell in love with its potential. Think about it. Almost anyone, practically anywhere, under nearly any condition can experience it. Most of us have felt it. Often, it comes from having a positive "flow" moment (Lesson 6) in one of our passions. These moments can be so joyous and satisfying that we never forget them. I can clearly recall a behind-the-back dribble and game-winning shot I made in a college basketball *practice*. You might remember the feeling of playing a demanding piano piece perfectly. Someone else may think back with *kefi* satisfaction about the time he or she masterfully performed a difficult dance move or solved an especially complicated algebraic equation.

*Kefi* is Greek. It's not easily interpreted. Google Translate simplistically calls it "fun," while listing *mirth*, *cheer*, *conviviality* and *joviality* as synonyms. But it's deeper, more important and more complex than that. *Kefi* is special because it's a satisfying moment of elation that we're capable of feeling, even when it wouldn't seem like elation is a reasonable emotion to feel. Once we understand *kefi*, joy will never be beyond our reach.

When my daughters were in high school, as part of a sister city service group called *Caravana Mexicana*, I spent several spring breaks with them in Puerto Peñasco, Mexico. Projects included building shelters, irrigating parks, maintaining playgrounds and painting schools.

One year, our *Caravana* group built a large play structure at a Mexican orphanage. While we worked, we were often (pleasantly) distracted watching the children play football (soccer) with a raggedy ball. *These kids seem happy,* I thought. *How can that be? Shouldn't they be more forlorn? Why aren't they feeling bad and acting sad?*

They were, after all, orphans. And poor. And living in relative squalor. Either their parents had died or were so bad at being parents - abusive, alcoholic or grossly negligent - that their children were taken from them. So how could these kids be laughing and having fun? From one perspective, it didn't make sense.

Yet, from another, it did. Playing football, even with a deflated ball and makeshift goals, made them happy. You may live in an orphanage but, as these kids proved, you can still have flashes of fun. It doesn't take much. A soccer match played on a dirt pitch with lousy equipment can still be gratifying and joyful. These kinds of enchanting moments are *kefi.*

While watching the kids play, I felt frustrated by my lack of forethought. *How great would it have been,* I thought, *if I had brought these kids a new, superior-quality soccer ball and real goals?* So, upon returning to California, I created the Kefi Foundation. Donations are used to fund the *kefi* spirit, specifically to purchase athletic gear, art supplies, musical instruments and – when possible - dance, drama and music instruction.

A primary way to create *kefi* is to actively participate in a passion. Soccer is emblematic. It can be practiced alone or with others. It requires repetition to perfect. It takes time to master. Obviously, it has that yin-yang, love-hate, magnificent highs-shattering lows aspect to it. And it doesn't cost anything. Well, barely anything. That's what makes *kefi* so glorious. It transcends place, circumstance and socioeconomic levels.

Although a wealthy person can have a *kefi* moment while sailing a million-dollar sailboat or playing a $100,000 Steinway piano, *kefi* can be equally experienced while surfing a $100 used surfboard or strumming a secondhand guitar. A ball, a glove, a bat, a hoop, canvas and paint, colored pencils and a sketchpad, a guitar, something on which to play recorded music… you don't have to be rich to pursue a passion and have a *kefi* moment.

Wiser after my Mexican orphanage mistake, I was better prepared when I traveled to Nicaragua as part of an award-winning organization called One Dollar for Life. ODFL invited me to Nicaragua to help build a school in rural Monte Grande. Deducing that the Nicaraguan children wouldn't have good quality baseball equipment, we brought them bats, balls and gloves. Turns out, they didn't have *any* baseball equipment. They were playing with a stick and some sort of large tropical rainforest nut. When I broke out a real baseball bat, they went crazy. "*El bate! El bate! El bate!*" they cried. Yet, even before they saw *mi bate*, they were able to practice their passion for baseball (even with limited means) and experience *kefi*.

The passion producing *kefi* theory explains Jonathan Larson's New York City friends. Despite their persistent money issues and ongoing troubles, why were they (Larson included) still able to experience *kefi*? Perhaps because, even though they hadn't yet made it big, they were able to practice and pursue their passions. Life wasn't perfect, but they were acting, composing, dancing, painting, singing and writing – all *kefi*-generating activities.

Although passions may be the most surefire way of feeling *kefi*, they aren't the only way. People – the right people - can bring us *kefi*. So often, joy stems from whom we're with (Lesson 32). Larson's friends in real life (and his characters in *Rent*) cared for and loved each other. There is nothing more joyous, more *kefi*, than spending good time with special people. They ignite our *kefi*.

Usually, *kefi* is planned and intentional, but it can also be captured in unintended, spontaneous moments. Even then, however, action is necessary. *Kefi* can't be experienced just by thinking about it. For example, when there's a rainstorm, large puddles form just outside my classroom door. "Take out a sheet of paper," I'll suggest to my students. "Use your origami skills, and fold your paper into a boat. Be creative. Figure out a way to make it float. Then go outside and race it across the puddles." Some will take advantage of the fleeting moment and experience *kefi*. Others will choose to remain in their seats and let the opportunity pass them by.

*Kefi* really isn't that hard to comprehend. Even Kihei seems to get it. If I find a sturdy, well-shaped twig, my doggy gets excited. She knows she's going to have a happy time chasing it, chewing it and playing tug-of-war. Kids should be taught to seek *kefi* like Kihei. They, too, should revel in the thrill of twig activities.

Well, maybe not. But what, exactly, should children be taught about *kefi*?

First, they need to know enough about it to recognize it. When others are engaged in *kefi*-augmenting behaviors, kids should not only think, *Hey, that's kefi*, they should be thinking, *I want to do that and feel that, too.*

Second, so they *can* feel it, they'll need to be nudged (or, if necessary, shoved) from their comfort zones. They'll need to be encouraged to aggressively pursue passions, seize opportunities, cultivate relationships and make memorable moments. Passivity doesn't lead to *kefi*. Boldness and action does. Kids have to be urged to take part in life.

Third, kids need to know that *kefi* is accessible. If it's available to starving artists in lower Manhattan, if it's available to orphaned children in northern Mexico and impoverished children in rural Nicaragua, it's available to them, too. Often, for free.

Finally, kids should be taught that they have the power to provide *kefi* experiences for others. They can start art, music, dance and athletic activities for those most in need of a *kefi* boost. They can introduce their passions to others by inviting them to the class, studio, gym, court or field. It's a win-win venture because they'll learn that when they give *kefi* to others, a lot of it will come right back to them.

## Assignment

Learn to spot *kefi*. Find or (even better) *take* and display pictures that depict it – street musicians, inner city kids playing ball, exuberant dancing...Make a *kefi* collage. And, to ensure participation, make sure that the collage includes photos of you.

# The Daffodil Principle

*The secret of getting ahead is getting started. The secret of getting started is breaking your complex overwhelming tasks into small manageable tasks, and then starting the first one.*

- Mark Twain

*Nothing is particularly hard if you divide it into small jobs.*

- Henry Ford

School teaches kids to cram. They learn that they can procrastinate and then, at the last second, pull an all-nighter and slip by. "I work best under pressure," some students allege.

Even though teachers and parents valiantly try to drum into their heads that they shouldn't put it off, kids put it off. It's human nature and human weakness. If we can get away with it, we'll defer until tomorrow.

No matter how much we preach against it, the truth is, for lots of stuff, especially school stuff (assignments and tests), cramming works. But it won't work for what's truly important.

When I was in eighth grade (back when schools had money), we had a full-contact football team. But there was a catch. You couldn't play if you weighed over 145 pounds. For most of us, this wasn't a problem. I weighed 115.

My friend, Dave, wasn't so unaffected by the weight limit. He started the season at 170. He may have been a little chunky, but mostly he was just a big strong guy who matured early.

Dave was determined to shed the 25 pounds he needed to lose to be eligible. So, while we practiced plays, he ran from goalpost to goalpost, futilely trying to melt away the excess weight.

Halfway through the season, still at 160 and desperate, Dave crammed weight loss. On the day before our fifth game, he put on a plastic sweat suit and sat in a sauna. In and out of the hot box he went - for several *hours.*

When he weighed in the next morning, we were startled when, not only did he make weight, he was seven pounds under the maximum. After losing 22 pounds in a day, he somehow played and played well. And he repeated the process before the final three games. We were in awe of his grit, but totally naïve about the danger.

Obviously, Dave's way was not a healthy way to lose weight. Successful, permanent weight loss can't be crammed. (A day or two after each game, he'd be back up to 160.)

To properly lose weight, use "The Daffodil Principle." Lose a pound every two weeks. In less than a year, 25 pounds will be gone - safely.

The Daffodil Principle is not a new concept. Its name comes from a lovely (and true) story by Jaroldeen Asplund Edwards. It's about a woman named Gene Bauer who, in 1958, began to plant daffodils "one bulb at a time" on a mountainside near Lake Arrowhead, California. After dozens of years of sustained effort, she created something spectacular.[13]

The beauty of the Daffodil Principle is that it doesn't take extraordinary effort. Just *consistent* effort over time. Time is powerful. By using it wisely, overwhelming, seemingly impossible tasks are made manageable. Achieving greatness becomes realistic.

Besides losing weight, what else can't be crammed? What else necessitates the Daffodil Principle?

- **Sleep** - Sleep experts agree that you can't sleep four hours a night Sunday through Thursday, then make up for it by crashing 14 hours on Friday and Saturday night. You can't store reserves of sleep.

- **Fitness** – If you're in lousy shape, you're not going to get fit over the weekend. To complete a triathlon, add 50 pounds to your bench press or six inches to your vertical leap, it's going to take many months of regular training.

- **Rehabilitation** – Baby steps over time is the only way.

- **Learning to play an instrument, speak a language or master a skill** – *Really* learning anything takes time. Not weeks. Not months. Years. *Decades.*

- **A valuable collection** – Whether it's furniture, art, coins, shoes, baseball cards, books or friends, real collecting takes time.

- **Truly *teaching* anything** - We teachers want our lessons to sink in immediately. Usually, they won't.

- **Saving/Investing money** - The surest road to wealth is dollar cost averaging. Invest money consistently, month after month, year after year and watch compound interest work its magic.

- **Building relationships** – Whether romantic or platonic, meaningful relationships are forged during shared experiences – both good and bad - over time.

- **Immersion** (Lesson 11) – Immersing for a day won't work. Neither will a week. Even a month may not be long enough. Immersing ourselves in the best will – in time - lift us.

- **Planning and completing a project** – Rushing won't work. Details will be forgotten.

- **Building a house** – Read *The Three Little Pigs.*

- **Earning trust** – It won't happen suddenly.

- **Change** – Lasting change is usually gradual. In the short term, it's barely perceptible. But, when you reflect back over time, it's obvious.

- **Getting out of debt** – Sadly, frustratingly, it takes a plan that may take years to complete.

- **Starting a business or non-profit organization** – Ask those who've successfully done it if it was an overnight success.

- **Parenting** – You can't ignore your kids for months, take them on a fun weekend outing, then ignore them for another month. Well, you can, but don't call it parenting.

- **Earning respect** – Sometimes it happens abruptly. But not usually.

- **Writing a book** – Write half a page a day and in two years you have 365 pages.

- **Achieving a goal** – Reaching worthwhile ones are like earning a blackbelt. You advance one color at a time.

- **Living a life** – Wasting 75 years living mediocrely, then trying to tack on a few years of spectacular living near the end won't work, will it?

Be careful. The Daffodil Principle has its dark side. Just as when you lose a half a pound a week, and it doesn't seem like much – until two years later when you weigh 50 pounds less – you can *gain* a half a pound a week and not notice until, yikes! Your favorite clothes no longer fit. As with every tool, every weapon, the Daffodil Principle can be helpful or harmful.

## Assignment

You can use The Daffodil Principle for unpleasant tasks like weeding a garden, but it's more fun and exciting when you apply it to something epic.

In the second century B.C.E., Indian philosopher and yoga master Patanjali wrote:

> *When you are inspired by some great purpose, some extraordinary project, all your thoughts break their bonds: Your mind transcends limitations, your consciousness expands in every direction, and you find yourself in a new, great and wonderful world. Dormant forces, faculties and talents become alive, and you discover yourself to be a greater person by far than you ever dreamed yourself to be.*

He wrote this over 2,200 years ago! Until I read it, I was prejudiced against the past. I used to believe that the people of today were so much smarter than people of yesterday. No more.

What extraordinary project do you want to begin (or continue)? Decide on a manageable amount of time you're willing and able to commit to your project. How many daffodils can you plant, and for how many days, weeks, months and years are you willing to plant them?

## The Reverse Daffodil Principle

The Daffodil Principle doesn't work for everything. Sometimes you don't have the luxury of time. Some things have to be done right now. What do you do then?

You get help. You substitute people for time. You use the Reverse Daffodil Principle. If the job is big – a fundraiser, beautifying a park or school, organizing an event – it doesn't make sense for you to plug away at it day after day, month after month, year after year. You may only have a day, a month or a year to get it done, and sometimes that's not enough time.

So instead of relying on time, you rely on people. Lots of people. Instead of you working an hour a day, every day, for 100 days, recruit 100 motivated people to work one hour for one day.

You'll need a whole different mindset. Instead of attacking it alone as a rugged individualist, you'll have to face the fact that you won't be able to reach your objective all by yourself.

Investment banker and former Coca-Cola president Donald Keough said, "What separates those who achieve from those who do not is in direct proportion to one's ability to ask for help."[14] The challenge, of course, is getting people to help you, and that's why mastering Lesson 19 - How to Build Social Capital - is vital if you plan to use the Reverse Daffodil Principle.

## Assignment

Try these:

1. Next Halloween, collect cash for UNICEF – the United Nations International Children's Emergency Fund. By yourself, you should be able to raise a few dollars. It doesn't take much to help a lot. Currently, according to UNICEF…

- 7¢ provides a packet of special powder that, when mixed with water, can save a child from dehydration.
- 50¢ will give an impoverished child a notebook and pencil.
- $1.00 pays for 24 protein biscuits for a starving child.
- $12.44 can buy a cold storage box to make sure medicines do not spoil in the heat.
- $18.57 can provide three bed nets to protect families from malaria-carrying mosquitoes.

All are doable – even by one person. But that's not how people with social capital think. Sure, do your part. Trick or treat for UNICEF. Or, find another way to raise a few dollars. The real challenge, however, is to see how many *other* people you can convince to join your cause. If you collect $12.44, great. Your effort will pay for one of those cold storage boxes.

But if you get nine others to collect $12.44, UNICEF can buy 10 cold storage boxes. And if you recruit 50 friends, relatives, classmates or co-workers, you'll make way more of a difference than you could have ever made on your own.

2. Initiate classroom cleanup. (Your teacher will love you!) Persuade every student in the room to clean for 10 minutes. You'll be amazed at how clean it will get in such a short time (*if* everyone works). What was done in 10 minutes by 30 people would have taken one person

several hours to do alone.

3. Organize a One Dollar for Life-type fundraiser. To fund the construction of schools in developing countries, the One Dollar for Life organization asks each student in an American school to donate just one dollar. By itself, a dollar won't buy much. But multiplied by hundreds or even thousands of students, it will buy a lot - especially in a third-world economy. One person may have to save for a year or more (probably more) to come up with a thousand dollars. Or, a thousand people could raise a thousand dollars – relatively painlessly – in an hour.

# The 10 Leading Life Indicators

One is not enough.

When economists are assessing the health of the economy, they don't look only at gross domestic product or the direction of the stock market. They also pour over the consumer price index, interest rates, initial jobless claims, factory managers' purchasing orders, housing permits and starts, retail sales – a whole list of economic indicators. Similarly, when someone asks us how we are, although they're expecting a curt answer based on one factor - our health, for instance - one (indicator) is not enough. Our lives are made up of many pieces. We may be doing well in some areas while others are in a slump. It's exceptionally uncommon for everything to be awesome or awful. The way we feel is based on the sum of all the different parts of our lives.

Ten leading life indicators need to be addressed and assessed:

**1. Physicality** – Remember how you felt the last time you had the stomach flu? All you cared about was getting better. Obviously, how you physically feel has a huge impact on your overall well-being. If you have no energy, if you're exhausted, if you're hurting or if you just feel yucky, every other part of your life is affected.

Physicality also includes how you feel when you look in the mirror. Be honest. You care what you look like. You feel better about yourself when you're looking good and less confident when you think you're not looking so hot. Very few of us are born gorgeous, but we can all do the best we can with what we have. Without being obsessive, we need to work at our physicality. That means exercising regularly, eating healthily, dressing nicely and grooming ourselves repeatedly.

**Relationships** * – The asterisk is added because relationships are the most important happiness indicators. Think about it. What's the best part of any day? What's the worst part? It's usually the same answer: our human contacts. Our interactions with others lift us up and bring us down. When our relationships – both our platonic (family and friends) and romantic - are going well, life is so sweet that we can cope with disappointments in other areas. On the other hand, when we're struggling with our relationships, it's hard to enjoy success in anything else. Face it. The health of our relationships influences our outlook on *everything*.

> **2. Family Relationships** - The family into which we are born or adopted is fate. Whether we like our parents, siblings, grandparents, aunts, uncles and cousins or not, they're ours for life. So, it makes sense that we naturally want our relationships with our family – adopted or blood – to be healthy and loving.
>
> **3. Friend Relationships** - Our adopted relationships – our chosen platonic family – are critical, especially during our formative years. The people we associate with shape us and help make us who we are. Meeting people and adding them to our support group is one of life's great delights. They love us because they want to, not because they have to or are supposed to. Having platonic friends affirms who we are and what we've become.
>
> **4. Romantic Relationships** – The vast majority of us crave a soulmate, that one special person meant for only us. When we have that person, life is complete. When we don't, it's not. When it's going well with that person, pleasures are amplified and disappointments are bearable. When it's not, it's the other way

around.

**5. Passion** – Without a passion it's hard to be truly happy and fully alive. There's no gratification quite like when you're succeeding at your passion – and no frustration quite like when you're failing at it.

**6. Education/Career** – When students are in school, education is their job. Whether they admit it or not, how they're doing in school matters. When it's interesting, when they have lots of friends, when they like their teachers and classes, when they're attending every day and getting good grades, life is good. When they're bored, when they don't have friends, when they're not getting along with their teachers, when they're absent a lot and not satisfied with their grades, life sucks.

How couldn't it? When adults don't like their job, co-workers or boss, when they're calling in sick whenever they can get away with it and generally not doing well at work, they hate life. How we're feeling about school and work (sometimes both) is, obviously, hugely important.

**7. Money** – *Money doesn't buy happiness. You can't take it with you. Money can't buy you love.* The clichés hint that money is overrated, and maybe it is. I think that when you *have* money, it's not a big deal. By itself, money doesn't guarantee anything, but it does make life less stressful. J.K. Rowling says money is *liberating*. When you *don't* have it, it's a big deal. A constant concern. Not knowing if or how you're going to pay the bills and live how you want to live induces middle-of-the-night terrors.

Even though they aren't the breadwinners, don't think that kids aren't affected by their parents' financial struggles. Yes, if the family is well off, the kids may take their good fortune for granted. But when mom and/or dad are stressed about finances, so are the kids.

Like it or not, money is essential.

**8. *la causa*** – That's what Cesar Chavez called it – "The Cause." His was to better the lives of migrant farm workers in the southwest

United States. Chavez's adult life was focused on *la causa.* He was so successful that every March 31st Americans are urged to remember him and celebrate his accomplishments on Cesar Chavez Day.

An eclectic collection of other icons also discerned that having a cause is a requirement for a happy, fulfilling, meaningful and complete life:

> Mark Twain: "The best way to cheer yourself up is to try to cheer somebody else up."
>
> The Dalai Lama: "If you want others to be happy, practice compassion. If you want to be happy, practice compassion."
>
> Muhammed Ali: "Service to others is the rent you pay for your room here on earth."
>
> Maya Angelou: "I've learned that you shouldn't go through life with a catcher's mitt on both hands. You need to be able to throw something back."
>
> Antoine de Saint-Exupéry in *The Wisdom of the Sands*: "In giving you are throwing a bridge across the chasm of your solitude."

My favorite quote on service is from public school activist Horace Mann:

> "Be ashamed to die until you have won some victory for humanity."

Whether you learn it from a parent, teacher, counselor, priest, minister, rabbi, psychologist or self-help book, the message is clear. To be happy, to live a meaningful and rewarding life, you need a cause. The opportunities are infinite:

- **Kids** - Tutor or coach local kids or help support a child in a third-world country.

- **Senior Citizens** - Volunteer at a senior center, assisted living facility or hospice.

- **Animals** - You can help your favorite animal! Work to save a threatened species (e.g. the International Elephant Foundation) or the abused and neglected dogs and cats at your local shelter or rescue center (e.g. Golden Gate Basset Rescue in the San Francisco Bay region).

- **The Environment** - Sadly, the whole planet has huge needs. Heal it by working with the Environmental Protection Agency, the Sierra Club, Earth First!, Greenpeace or the Third World Network.

- **The Sick** - Most hospitals need volunteers. Find a way to visit ill people in their homes.

- **The Disabled** - Ask special education teachers how you can befriend and help one or more of their students.

- **The Impoverished** - How can you help the poor help themselves? Consider learning about and supporting Heifer International, Kiva or the Grameen Bank.

Obviously, just having a cause isn't enough. Caring isn't enough. What counts is action. Get past the "I want to change the world!" cliché. First of all, changing the world is not necessarily a good thing. Hitler changed the world. What you want to do is *improve* the world.

Look around. There's so much need! Consequently, finding a cause should be relatively easy. (If you need ideas, check out *change.org*. It's loaded with worthwhile causes. There's bound to be at least one you'll want to get behind. If you already have a cause that needs mass support, consider using *change.org* to publicize it.) The work begins after you find your cause. Making a change – any change – is difficult.

In the 1880's, an Englishman named Walter Alcock perfected perforated toilet paper on a roll, then got it patented.[15] It was a huge improvement over anything previously used – sticks, sponges, leaves, grass, rocks, dry bones, corn cobs, pages torn from Sears catalogs... Still, because toilet paper was a change, it was resisted.

No matter how good the idea, no matter how *right* the idea, change is almost always resisted – at first. Alcock had to fervently *sell* his superior toilet paper. Galileo spent the last years of his life under house arrest for insisting that the earth revolves around the sun, not the other way around. (You'd think that if something is exceptionally good and clearly right, you wouldn't have to sell it. Unfortunately, this is definitely not the case.) Eventually, people embraced toilet paper, and nobody "believes" the earth is the center of the universe anymore. But it wasn't easy. Change requires vehement belief, a ton of time and effort and an army of people fighting for it.

There are tools that can help. *Change.org* will help you spread the word. The White House website, *whitehouse.gov*, allows you to create and sign petitions. But don't rely on only these. Think broader. Spread the word using social and traditional media. Launch a website. Create artsy t-shirts and well-designed posters. Get out there and talk to people face to face. Speak at city council and school board meetings. Meet people who can help you with your cause. Aggressively approach radio, TV and print journalists. Tell them your story so they will tell your story. Make friends with your elected representatives. How many CEO's and entrepreneurs do you know? Make calls. Visit offices.

Bottom line: To be happy, find your cause and get to work.

**9. Spirituality** – This is not a religious book. Although I was raised Catholic, I've spent my career teaching in public schools where I've met children who are deeply devoted to diverse religions. I'm convinced that there are great truths in all. For example, some form of the Golden Rule *(Do unto others as you would have them do unto you.)* can be found in all major religions. So, I'm certainly not advocating that anyone practice or convert to any specific organized religion. On the other hand, I've learned that research supports the belief that those who are spiritual tend to be happier and more satisfied with their lives than those who aren't. The point? Consider exploring this important aspect of life.

**10. Hope** – When most people are hurting, they sense that, somehow, someway, their lives will eventually get better. That's why it's imperative that, when we look ahead – whether it's later today, tomorrow, next week, next year or beyond – we have things we're excited about and looking forward to. Hope for a better future is our strongest and sometimes only buffer against life's torments.

All ten indicators can constantly be upgraded. There's a wonderful Japanese word, *kaizen* that means "continuous improvement." Toyota engineers will push a perfectly good assembly line until it breaks down. Then they'll find and fix the flaw and push the system again.[16] The idea is that we're never *there.* We should never stop growing, learning and improving. The A+ student still has a lot to learn. The world champion in anything is probably the best because he or she still strives.

It's not about being obsessed. It's about acknowledging that we can and should continue to grow. In his bestseller, *The Success Principles,* Jack Canfield writes about "The Most Valuable Question You May Ever Learn."[17] It's a question with two parts:

> **Part I:** "On a scale of 1 – 10, how would you rate the quality of our relationship (service/product) during the last week (two weeks/month/quarter/semester/season)?"
>
> Canfield asserts that the question or a form of the question can be used to improve just about anything we want to improve. For example, "On a scale of 1 – 10, how would

you rate the quality of my teaching?" Anytime the answer is less than 10, we should then follow up with...

**Part II:** "What would it take to make it a 10?"

It won't be easy to hear or admit to ourselves that we can be better, but it's important for our development to know where we need to put in more work.

## Assignment

On a scale from 1 to 10 (one is terrible, ten is terrific), rate how you're doing in each of the ten leading life indicators:

1. **Physicality**
*How are you feeling? How do you feel after you check yourself in the mirror?*

2. **Family Relationships**
*How are you getting along with your nuclear and extended family?*

3. **Friend Relationships**
*How's it going with your friends? Are they making your life better? They should be! How about you? Are you contributing to their lives?*

4. **Romantic Relationships**
*If you have a romantic love, are you making each other happy? If you don't have one, how is that affecting you?*

5. **Passion**
*Do you have one? If you do, how are you progressing with it?*

6. **Education/Career**
*How happy are you at school and/or on the job?*

**7. Money**
*Are you worried about it? How much? What's your financial status? Your family's?*

**8. *la causa***
*Are you contributing to the world? How so? Can you do more?*

**9. Spirituality**
*How spiritual are you? Do your beliefs comfort or scare you?*

**10. Hope**
*When you look to the future, does it excite or depress you?*

Add the scores, and treat the result like it's the score you earned on a tough test. A 100 is perfect - a perfect life. A 75 is a solid C. If you score below 60, your life – or at least parts of it – is in need of repair. If you're honest in your evaluation, you'll discover that living well is a never-ending study session. Not only is an A extremely difficult to earn, it's even harder to maintain.

Taking a truthful look at our leading life indicators enables us to pinpoint the areas that need more attention and work. It also allows us to see how fluid all ten indicators are. A high (or low) score today doesn't mean we'll have the same score tomorrow. Forces under and beyond our control can change each indicator in an instant.

## Immerse

When I was playing varsity basketball in high school, it was tradition, as a show of support, to watch the first half of the junior varsity game. During my senior year, our coach, Ed Klum, told us to stop. "I don't want you watching them," he said. "They're horrible."

So much for tradition. At the time, I thought it was funny. Today, I know it was brilliant. If we immerse ourselves in scum, we'll smell like it. It makes so much more sense to surround ourselves with success.

A myth about public schools is that there are good ones and bad ones. There really aren't. It's more like *rich* schools and *poor* schools. Most schools have a mixture of teachers, ranging from excellent to terrible. Many schools have wonderful, forward-thinking principals who love and support their students. Others have mediocre, follow-the-orders-from-above principals whom the students barely even know. Some schools have decent to good facilities. Others are architectural embarrassments.

Yet, when most people are describing a "good" school, they're not usually referring to the teachers, administration or buildings. They're referring to the school's students. "Good" schools are full of highly-motivated, hard-working, high-achieving students. "Bad" schools are full of – make that half full (due to absences) - of unmotivated, lethargic, low-achieving students. Yes, "good" schools have bad students and "bad" schools have good students, but we're talking generalities here.

Why are parents willing to pay extra – sometimes *a lot* extra - for a home in a neighborhood that, the real estate agent boasts, "has excellent schools"? The kind of schools UC Berkeley political economist Robert Reich calls "public-private" schools.

One word: *immersion*. Whether they're fully aware of it or not, parents are paying more so their kids can be immersed in an atmosphere of achievement. Nevermind that the "bad" school may have incredible teachers, the best principal or state-of-the-art facilities. If the students aren't on their way to a selective college, the school won't be perceived as "good."

Uninformed? Perhaps. Ridiculous? Probably. Unfair? Definitely.

Looking for a "good" school? Look in a wealthy neighborhood. A "bad" school? Try a poor neighborhood. The correlation between income and people's perceptions of "good" and "bad" schools is as strong as the correlation between exercise and obesity. Sure, there are slim people who don't exercise and heavy people who do, but they're exceptions.

That's the depressing reality, but all kids - even kids in the "worst" schools - can be taught how to succeed even if their peers *are* failing. The secret is to teach them to immerse. If they look for them, they can find friends who want to live well and have high aspirations.

Immersing themselves in good groups is the most critical aspect of immersion, but there's more. Kids should also be taught to seek and listen to high quality music, speakers and speeches. Google "The greatest albums, songs, classical music or speeches of all time." Listen to them. Study them. Figure out why they're considered great.

- View the best movies, plays, television programs and YouTube videos.

- Read excellent writing.

- Watch the most talented athletes.

- Examine outstanding art.

- Study interesting, uplifting subjects.

- Join worthwhile clubs and organizations.

- Visit intelligent websites.
- Spend time in beautiful places - natural or manmade.

I don't know why, but, left on their own, kids will gravitate toward scum. Don't let them. Steer them toward pure, refreshing water.

## **Assignment**

Research greatness. What's great? Who's claiming it's great? The American Film Institute, for example, lists the 100 greatest movies of all time (*Citizen Kane* was ranked #1). Watch those movies! They're legit. The American Film Institute is comprised of experienced and accomplished screenwriters, directors, actors, producers, editors, executives, film historians, cinematographers and critics. They ought to know what they're talking about! Immerse yourself in the great movies.

Or, find the best at whatever interests you. Search online for "The greatest doctors", "The greatest teachers" or "The greatest inventors." Visit the hall of fames of your interests. There's a hall of fame for practically everything:

- The Basketball Hall of Fame – Springfield, Massachusetts
- The Writers Hall of Fame - Springfield, Missouri
- The Insurance Hall of Fame - Tuscaloosa, Alabama
- The Rock and Roll Hall of Fame - Cleveland, Ohio
- The Astronaut Hall of Fame - Titusville, Florida
- The Toy Hall of Fame - Rochester, New York
- The Cowboy Hall of Fame - Oklahoma City, Oklahoma

- The Robot Hall of Fame - Pittsburgh, Pennsylvania (at Carnegie Mellon University)
- The National Museum of Dance and Hall of Fame – Saratoga Springs, New York
- The Mountain Bike Hall of Fame - Crested Butte, Colorado
- The National Inventors Hall of Fame – Alexandria, Virginia
- The California Social Work Hall of Distinction - Los Angeles, California (at University of Southern California)
- The Circus Hall of Fame - Peru, Indiana
- The U.S. Business Hall of Fame - Chicago, Illinois
- The Military Intelligence Hall of Fame - Fort Huachuca, Arizona
- The Songwriters Hall of Fame – Los Angeles, California
- The American Police Hall of Fame - Titusville, Florida
- The Mascot Hall of Fame – Whiting, Indiana
- The Hockey Hall of Fame – Toronto, Ontario, Canada
- The Aviation Hall of Fame – Dayton, Ohio
- The English Football Hall of Fame – Manchester, England

Learn about the greatest. Read about the greatest. Watch the greatest. Meet the greatest. Immerse yourself in the pool of their greatness. Let it wash over you. Allow it to motivate *you* to greatness.

# Mother Teresa

Early in my teaching career, I had an unpleasant conference with a parent who pretty much told me I was the worst teacher ever. I slunk into the faculty room, slumped onto a chair and thought, *I try hard to be a good teacher. How come I'm so underappreciated?* Feeling sorry for myself, I picked up a newspaper. I happened to see a short article about Mother Teresa (who, at the time, was still living). The small headline was "Mother Teresa forgives for negative view." The story was about a pair of documentary filmmakers who found Mother Teresa less than accommodating and condemned her in their film as "Hell's Angel."

Mother Teresa! Mother Teresa, the winner of the Nobel Peace Prize? Mother Teresa, who spent pretty much her entire life in the Calcutta, India slums helping the "poorest of the poor"? Mother Teresa, whom the Catholic Church is considering canonizing? How could anyone criticize Mother Teresa?

But people did. People still do. Not everyone liked Mother Teresa. After reading that article, I felt ashamed. *If Mother Teresa has critics,* I thought, *who am I to think I won't? If Mother Teresa has haters, we're all going to have haters.* Now, whenever I feel unfairly criticized, I think or even whisper to myself, "Mother Teresa."

We want to be liked. When people don't like us, it hurts. If you arrived a half-hour late to a party and the host said, "Hey, just before you rang the doorbell, we asked the 100 people here what they think of you, and guess what? Ninety-eight of them like you!"

If you're like most people, instead of feeling glad that such an overwhelming number of people like you, you'd be wondering, *Who are the two who don't?*

What kids need to know is that no matter who they are or what they do, there will be people who won't like them. If Mother Teresa couldn't get a 100% approval rating, who amongst us will? History's most beloved heroes were despised:

Abraham Lincoln: hated and assassinated

Gandhi: hated and assassinated

MLK Jr.: hated and assassinated

JFK, RFK: hated and assassinated

If you're not disliked by anyone, you're probably living such a meaningless life that you hardly matter, and who wants that? If nobody dislikes you, it's probably because nobody *knows* you. Which means nobody likes you either. People who matter inspire passion - on both sides. American essayist Elbert Hubbard wrote, "To avoid criticism, do nothing, say nothing, be nothing." And Eleanor Roosevelt said, "Do what you feel in your heart to be right – for you'll be criticized anyway. You'll be damned if you do, and damned if you don't."

And that's OK! Author and entrepreneur Seth Godin makes a life-altering point when he declares, "You don't need everyone!" All we need is a *tribe* – a small yet intense core of people who share our visions, passions and concerns. No matter how obscure our interest or cause, there's probably a group of like-minded people waiting for us to lead them.[18] (Hopefully, ideally, in a constructive direction)

Think about it. To be successful in politics, you only need 51% of the votes. In some elections, you don't even need that – you only need more votes than your opponent(s). In business, you don't have to sell to everyone. To make it huge, you only need to reach a tiny percentage of the market. Even the most popular and powerful companies don't appeal to everyone. Not everyone buys an iPhone. The bestselling authors aren't read by every reader. The highest grossing movies and the top-rated television programs aren't liked and watched by all.

Therefore, kids might as well be themselves. If they are, some people won't like them. But if they pretend to be someone they're not, other people won't like them. Either way there are haters, so they might as well be hated while showing their true colors.

## Assignment

Learn *both* parts of the Mother Teresa lesson:

**Part I:** Understand and accept the reality that no one is loved by everyone. Sometimes – often – it's out of our control. Some people won't like us because they're jealous. Some won't like us because we're White or Black or Asian or Latino. Some won't like us because we're male or female or because they have some misconception about us. Whatever the reason, if you're disliked, don't despair. Welcome to the world.

**Part II:** Pay attention and be responsive to the numbers. If a solid majority think you're pretty great while a few outliers don't, why worry? That's the Mother Teresa lesson. No one, not even Mother Teresa, will be loved by all. But if it's the other way around, if a solid majority thinks you're a fool, maybe you are! Maybe it's not the Mother Teresa lesson. Maybe it's *you*. Maybe *you* need to change. Maybe *you* need to improve.

**Extra Credit Thought:** The hardest people to like are the people who don't like us. The hardest people to dislike are the people who like us. Want more people to like you? Like them.

# Find a Way

My father died one month before his $70^{th}$ birthday. It was sudden and unexpected. He had checked into the hospital for a "routine" coronary artery bypass surgery, but it went tragically wrong. He lingered in a coma for three days – enough time for my brothers and sisters and me to join my mom at his bedside - but he never regained consciousness.

Moments after his passing, with the seven of us gathered around him, my big brother, J.T., shared a story I won't forget.

When he was seven (five years before I was born), J.T. was invited by his best friends to watch a movie at a movie theater (a huge deal back then). Naturally, he desperately "needed" to go. But my mom insisted that he had to attend church with her and my dad on that Sunday morning. The problem was, if he went to church, he probably wouldn't make it back in time, and his friends would leave without him.

That's exactly what happened. Understandably, J.T. was devastated. The movie was playing clear across town and, back then, my parents didn't own a car. It looked hopeless - until Dad saved his day. Swallowing his pride, Dad told J.T. to hop onto the handlebars. Then he pedaled his bike through the streets of Lansing, Michigan and got my brother to the theater in time to watch the opening credits of *War of the Worlds*.

My dad found a way. He always found a way to get us what we most wanted or thought we needed. Through actions more than words, he taught us that no matter the obstacle, a way can be found...

Which is why I have little patience for kids who claim they couldn't do their homework because of printer problems. It's not so much the missing piece of homework that burns me. The specific assignment isn't the issue. The lame excuse and the failure to find a way is. "The dog ate my homework" has morphed into "My printer ran out of ink." Yesterday's dog is today's printer is tomorrow's who knows what? It will be something, though. There will always be excuses.

Schools present students with plenty of opportunities to practice ways to meet all sorts of challenges. And what the teacher – later the boss or client - cares about most is whether or not the challenge was met. How it was met, when it was met, what obstacles had to be overcome... none of that matters. "Do or do not. There is no try," said Yoda.

The printer excuse is a contemporary "The Boy Who Cried Wolf." Because it's used so often, even if there really was a printer glitch, what teacher would believe it? But what if a student's printer truly didn't work? Could he or she find a way to print homework and turn it in on time?

Among the possibilities:

- Email it as an attachment to yourself. Then find a computer with a working printer on which you can open your mail and print it.

- Send it as an attachment to a friend. Ask him or her to print it for you. (If you have developed social capital - Lesson 19 - this may be your easiest and best option. If you haven't, it will be tougher. But you can still do it.)

- Send it as an attachment to your teacher asking him or her to print it for you (along with a note apologizing for the inconvenience). Include an offer to clean the classroom or show up the next day with chocolate chip cookies. This may be acceptable – once.

- Save it to an external drive. Find a printer. Try the library.
- Fix your printer. Change your ink cartridge. Get a better printer!
- Use the Cloud!

If you have to, try them all. And if none work, try something else. Keep trying until you've found a way to print it. But this isn't about homework or printers. It's about developing a "Find a Way" state of mind. It's about understanding that when things go smoothly, it's an aberration. Most of the time, the road will be rough. And it's about not using the unanticipated obstacle as an excuse for not getting done what needs to get done.

It may not seem like a big deal when a homework assignment doesn't get turned in on time. But it is. It is because when students get into the habit of finding an excuse instead of finding a way, it can keep them from achieving goals far more important than turning in a homework paper.

What kind of goals? How about finding a way to…

- get into college
- graduate from college
- get hired
- convince her (or him) to say yes
- start a business
- file taxes on time
- get in shape
- learn a skill

- battle an illness
- help children achieve their dreams

Finding a way also means figuring out things for yourself. In school, students are repeatedly encouraged to ask questions. "There's no such thing as a stupid question," they're told. But this becomes problematic when kids learn to rely on others to tell them what to do whenever they have a smidgen of doubt.

Actually, there is such a thing as a stupid question. It's a stupid question when the person asking it could have figured out the answer without help but didn't even bother to try.

For example, I've heard students ask:

- "Do you want me to put this down?" (a large box being delivered from the office)
- "Do you want me to clean this?" (a mess on the floor, next to their desk)
- "Should I turn in the homework?"
- "So, do you want me to come to class on time?"

What I wanted to say but (probably) didn't:

- "No. Just hold on to it until I have time to open it."
- "No, I'd prefer you leave it for me or someone else to clean."
- "No. I only assigned it to give you something to do last night."
- "Please tell me you didn't just say that."

No, I'm not making these up.

My advice to students - to anyone - about to ask a question is this:

> *Think about it. Do you really need to ask it? Can you find a way to answer your own question? If so, unless an incorrect answer is literally dangerous, go for it! Even if you're wrong, you'll learn a lot more by trusting yourself than by always depending on others to answer your questions.*

**Note:** Finding a way doesn't mean finding *any* way. Obviously, it means finding a *moral* way. Drug warlords find a way to make millions selling their poison. They're smart - but wicked.

If the only way you can find requires lying, cheating and/or preying on the innocent and unfortunate, you found a way. But you found the wrong way.

## Assignment

Find a way to print, in big, bold letters, "**Find a way!**" Put it in a conspicuous place (at the foot of your bed, on the refrigerator, in your locker, on the cover of your binder) where you'll see it and be regularly reminded to use your intelligence and ingenuity to find a way to get it done, no matter what *it* is.

## Fate and Self-Determination

*There is only one way to happiness and that is to cease worrying about things which are beyond the power of our will.*

- Epictetus
(Greek sage and Stoic philosopher)

*God grant me the serenity*
*to accept the things I cannot change,*
*the courage to change the things I can,*
*and wisdom to know the difference.*

- commonly attributed to Reinhold Niebuhr
(American theologian)

Epictetus's message, circa 100 AD, and Niebuhr's "Serenity Prayer," written around 1943, remind me of Eric Roth's 1994 screenplay, *Forrest Gump*. Just before the last scene, Forrest (Tom Hanks) narrates, "I don't know if we each have a destiny, or if we're all just floating around accidental-like on a breeze, but I, I think maybe it's both. Maybe both is happening at the same time."

We need kids to at least be wondering, *How much control do I have over my life?* Even though they'll never know for sure, I hope that, like Forrest, they'll conclude that the answer lies somewhere in the middle.

Babies have zero control over their lives, and it frustrates them. (That's why they're always crying!) They don't get to decide what to eat, drink or wear. This stage doesn't last long, though. When my daughter Kyrra was tiny, I'd dress her in whatever was easiest for me to put on her. Then one morning, at about the same time she was learning to string together enough words to form a sentence, she announced, "Daddy, I don't like these sweats."

Never again would I have a say in what she would wear. From that moment on, my daughter has had more and more control over her life, and I have had less and less. Which is how it should be. Human beings are programmed to be self-determined. Countries don't want to be colonies, and children, no matter how much they love their parents, don't want to be controlled by them.

Most kids haven't thought much about fate and self-determination. They can start by identifying what they *can't* control (fate). For example, they didn't get to choose their...

- parents
- ethnicity
- hair and eye color
- height
- body type
- talents (athleticism, musicality, artistry)
- hometown, state, or country

They can't control the weather, natural disasters, the economy, the evil that others do... It's a depressingly long list that (as the Serenity Prayer teaches) they'll have to learn to accept. Not like. Accept.

On the flip side, the list of what kids can control (self-determination) is infinite, and that should be their focus. As the years pass, fate becomes less a factor. Where you were raised and what your parents did won't matter. Ultimately, it will be up to you to determine where you live and what you do.

A fate/self-determination moment came to me when I was 20. I had just finished basketball practice at Eastern Michigan University and taken a shower. With my hair still wet, I made my way through the bitter January cold to my car, parked in a lot no more than 50 yards away from the gym. After I turned the ignition and my freezing Plymouth coughed to a start, I touched my hair. It had frozen. It wasn't the first time my hair had frozen in the Midwestern cold, but it probably was the fastest. I clearly remember that moment. I sat there thinking, *I hate cold weather. I've always hated cold weather. I'm 20 years old. I don't have to live here anymore!*

The next day I went to the Career Planning and Placement Center. I asked one of the clerks to help me find a summer job in "Florida, Hawaii or California." I ended up working that summer at a camp for blind and deaf kids in Malibu, California, met my wife there and said goodbye forever to the Michigan winters.

Is this a fate story or a self-determination story? Both, right? That's what I want to teach kids. That no matter how much fate envelops us (putting me in Michigan because of my father's job, the exceptionally cold winter weather that day, my future wife choosing the same summer camp…), we still have to act. I had to *choose* to get on a plane that summer and seek a new life.

Still, I was *20*! I wasn't a kid. I was no longer a teenager. Until I was 20, I didn't understand how much control I had over what happened to me. How could I? Nobody ever taught me to think about what I could and couldn't control.

What can't we control? Certain injuries and illnesses. Disabilities with which we are born. True. But legendary UCLA basketball coach John Wooden taught, "Don't let what you cannot do interfere with what you can do." Can we control how people feel about us? Maybe not. But our behavior influences their feelings. Do we have any say over how or when we're going to die? Well, probably not. But if you're obese, drink too much and smoke a pack of cigarettes a day, there's a much greater chance that you'll die prematurely than if you work at your physicality. When you take the time to pause and reflect, you'll find that there's not much over which you don't have at least a little control.

## Assignment

Stop assuming that what happens to you is beyond your control. *Mr. Richards gave me a B-*. No! That sentence should never escape the lips of a student. Mr. Richards did not *give* you a B-! You *earned* a B-! Until fate proves you're not, presume that you, not fateful forces, are in control.

Make a list of what you can't control or take credit for. Some items - your beautiful brown eyes or that you were born into a home with running water and electricity - will be positive. Other stuff – that you are not going to be supermodel-tall or that you love snow but your parents moved you to Miami – may be negative.

Then, turn your paper over and make a list of what you *can* control. But be prepared. You'll be working on that side for a long, long time.

## Major in Success

When I was growing up in Ohio in the 1960's, Cleveland didn't have an NBA team. The Cavaliers hadn't yet been born. Cincinnati, Ohio did have a team – the Royals (now the Sacramento Kings). Their star, Oscar Robertson, "The Big O," was one of my boyhood heroes. A half-dozen times a year, the Royals would play a "home" game in Cleveland. Sometimes I'd get to go.

Back then (and still today), I loved listening to stories about how great sports stars became great. I figured that if I knew what they did – and then did what they did - maybe I could become great, too.

My brother, J.T., told me a stirring story about "The Big O": When he was a child in Indianapolis, Robertson would dribble his basketball to school. He'd play basketball during recess and lunch, then dribble back home. After a quick snack, he'd dribble to the "Dust Bowl," a vacant lot where he'd play past dark. Afterward, he'd dribble back home again, bathe his basketball in the bathtub and take it to bed with him. By constantly having a basketball in his hands, he was able to develop superb ball handling skills. By relentlessly playing the game he loved, he was able to become one of the greatest players, maybe *the* greatest basketball player ever.

So guess what I began doing? I'd dribble my ball to and from school. I'd play basketball during recess and lunch. After school, I'd dribble to and from a nearby court, often getting into trouble for missing supper. I wasn't a bath kid, so I'd wash my ball in the shower before taking it to bed. My mom would come into my room, shake her head and sigh, "Some kids sleep with teddy bears. Mine sleeps with a basketball." Eventually, though, she got used to it.

My wife still hasn't.

That was a joke. No, I don't sleep with my basketball anymore, but I haven't outgrown my desire to study excellence and "major in success." It's a lesson I treasure because it's interesting, motivating and it works. I never came close to playing like "The Big O," but I did improve. So now I teach "Major in Success" to every kid I can. "As you get older," I tell them, "school gets better because the longer you stick with it, the more you can specialize or 'major' in a subject you like. But no matter what specific subject you major in, you should always major in *success*."

Even the greatest leaders majored in success (which may be one explanation for their greatness). Martin Luther King Jr. learned non-violent direct action from Gandhi. Cesar Chavez studied the Montgomery bus boycott model before leading lettuce, grape and table wine boycotts.[19] [20] It doesn't matter who we are; majoring in success is effective.

Although studying Robertson helped me improve my game, it didn't put me anywhere close to his level. However, Super Bowl XXXVII winning coach (and ESPN analyst) Jon Gruden actually surpassed the success of his mentors. (Perhaps because he was studying something that didn't depend so much on natural gifts?) In his memoir, *Do You Love Football?! – Winning with Heart, Passion & Not Much Sleep*, Gruden wrote about the advice he got from his father (also a coach) after he decided he wanted to become a big-time football coach:

> *You want to (start by being) a quarterback coach. If you want to be a major college coach/coordinator kind of guy, you must learn to communicate with the quarterback. And to become the best quarterback coach you can be, you need to learn from the best damn quarterback coaches in the world.*
>
> *Listen to them. Watch them. Study them. Before you're married, while you're young, do whatever you've got to do to*

*get around these kinds of coaches.*

*In 1986, when I was 23 years old, that became my mission in life. I was going to go to the football equivalent of Harvard. I was going to grab hold of a branch on the Bill Walsh tree of coaching knowledge that had grown within the San Francisco 49ers. I was going to practically stalk Mike Holmgren, who at the time was the 49ers quarterback coach and one of the best of the business. I was going to find a way to become a great quarterback coach myself.*[21]

There are three parts to Gruden's story that students must learn:

**Part I:** Gruden knew exactly what he wanted to study – football coaching, specifically quarterback coaching.

**Part II:** He knew exactly which expert he wanted to study – Mike Holmgren. Then he "stalked" him.

**Part III:** Doing this demands work. Figuring out what they want will take thought and research. Finding world-class mentors (in anything) will require time, effort, patience and perseverance.

When kids are unsure about what they want to study (a problem that too often persists into their late 20's and beyond), they need to make a habit of applying Gruden's father's advice by listening to, watching and studying the foremost achievers, no matter what their specialty. Being in the presence of almost *any* great achiever will be beneficial. Sooner or later, though, kids have to choose to study something specific, but the sooner, the better. (They can always change fields of study.) And, like Gruden and his study of quarterback coaching, the more specific the better.

Whenever students encounter *anyone* who is excellent at anything, but especially when it's at something they're even remotely interested in, they should feel compelled to study *how* that person became excellent. And when something is the best, students should feel obligated to study *why* it's the best. Whether it's a superb product, a terrific service or the company (and person) behind the product or service, there's a *reason* why it's successful. Students need to learn what that reason is.

Professional comedians claim that, from a group of kids, they can pick out the future Chris Rocks. When something is funny, most kids will laugh. The student of humor won't. He or she will pointedly remark, "That's funny."

That kind of recognition leads to majoring in success's critical question: *Why is it funny?* More generally, *Why is it good?* It's not difficult to learn *what* is good. Non-athletes can identify skilled athletes. Non-musicians can hear who can really play. Non-dancers can spot the top dancers. Every kid in kindergarten knows who colors best.

Recognizing *what* is good is easy. The challenge is to figure out *why* it's good. This is when serious, focused, rigorous study should begin. When someone or something is successful, serious students learn why it's successful with the obvious motive of applying what they learn to their own passions.

A fundamental part of my writing course curriculum includes teaching students to:

1. identify excellent writing

2. be able to explain *why* it's excellent

Once they know why excellent writing is excellent, they will have a much better chance of producing excellent writing.

It works for just about anything. Wannabe basketball players should be able to explain what makes a sweet jump shot sweet. Wannabe bakers should be able to explain why delicious bread is delicious. Wannabe roofers should be able to look at an expertly installed roof and explain the expertise.

But first they have to have someone to study. Who are the best jump shooters, bakers and roofers? Who are the best dentists, construction workers, plumbers and graphic designers? When students cannot identify the best in their specific areas of interest, there's a gap in their education. It's enormously important for aspiring...

- civil engineers to be able to identify the best civil engineers
- cardiologists to be able to identify the best cardiologists
- cosmetologists to be able to identify the best cosmetologists
- environmental scientists to be able to identify the best environmental scientists
- operating room nurses to be able to identify the best operating room nurses

and so on...

It's not a hard concept, right? Try it out on kids, though. Ask them to name names. With the exception of aspiring actors, athletes and musicians, you won't find many kids who can. I'm not talking about 10 year-olds. I'm talking about the 20 year-old nursing student who can't name five great nurses. I'm talking about the high school math prodigy who has never heard of the Fields Medal (considered math's Nobel Prize), let alone capable of naming its most recent recipient. I'm talking about the 25 year-old electrical engineer who has no idea who the best electrical engineers in the country are. Why not? All it would take is a two-second Internet search.

Whose fault is it? Theirs?

No. It's ours. We require students to learn the names of deceased historical figures - often obscure historical figures – who they will never meet or think about after they leave our classrooms. But we don't insist that they learn the names of the living leaders in their areas of interest – role models they could possibly meet and from whom they could learn. Further, we close off our schools like they're monasteries. *Teachers and students only!* Kids cloistered together in eerie, same-age groups. Where else does this happen? If I walked into a supermarket, and everyone in there was 17, I'd think I was in *The Twilight Zone.*

If we can somehow squeeze some time in between the test prep and the tests, let's get the best engineers, biologists, entrepreneurs, cooks, mathematicians and nurses into classrooms to explain what it takes to be the best. Take a poll. Find out what kids want to be good at. Then find experts in these fields and get these people in front of students, telling them stories about the real world. Because I'm not a millionaire, I can't tell my students how to become a millionaire. But I can get a millionaire to visit my economics class and explain to my students how he or she did it.

Later, teach kids how to do this on their own. Assign homework that requires students to find out who's the best at whatever interests them. Then, embolden them. Encourage them to find a way to meet these people. Mentors aren't fairy godmothers who will magically appear. They need to be actively sought.

Students should be learning from the finest practitioners in their areas of interest, not to become clones - trying to be anyone's double is silly, wrong and impossible - but to soak up the best advice, methods and ideas. Then, they can blend them with their own distinctive talents to create something novel and fabulous.

Success study is complex. There are no easy answers as to how it's attained. Students aren't going to learn it from impromptu, spur-of-the-moment remarks from their instructor or the occasional speech from a "motivational speaker." They need to *study* success with the intensity that advanced math students study calculus.

This means looking for success, recognizing success, observing success, reading about success, interviewing successful people and thinking about success. It means looking for commonalities. If you want to excel at dance, design or entrepreneurship, what do outstanding dancers, designers or entrepreneurs have in common? And don't study only your favorite role model. Seek and study many.

If you play soccer, don't just study Lionel Messi. Study Cristiano Ronaldo, Homare Sawa and Landon Donovan, too.

There's an important scene in the underrated movie *School of Rock*. Dewey Finn (Jack Black) is a substitute teacher. Prior to Finn's arrival on campus, student Freddy Jones hated school. Early in their relationship, Finn asks, "Freddy, what do you like to do?" The obviously misguided Freddy answers, "I don't know, burn stuff?"

Freddy changes when Finn helps him discover his passion (playing the drums). I wish all students would watch the montage when a transfixed Freddy stares at a video of hall-of-fame rock and roll drummers. (That's plural. Finn has him study *multiple* drummers.) For the first time in his life, Freddy is interested in learning something. You can see it in his eyes. It's a look we should see in every student's eyes.

**Minor in Failure?**

One of my brightest students ever, Yale-bound Sonia Wang, suggested that, in addition to majoring in success, we should "minor in failure." Ever since that time when my varsity basketball coach, Ed Klum, prohibited us from watching failure (our junior varsity team), I've avoided trying to learn by studying what *not* to do. It's discouraging, depressing and runs contrary to the benefits of positive immersion.

However, the way Sonia cleverly put it – *minor* in failure – makes great sense. We shouldn't make studying failure our prime focus; we shouldn't *major* in failure. Nevertheless, it would be imprudent to not pay attention to, learn about and study others' failures. We need to be mindful of them so as to not replicate them.

One morning, heading east on the way to work, the sun abruptly arose above the horizon, temporarily blinding a driver in front me. His car lightly scraped against the concrete dividing wall. Sparks flew, but he safely recovered and continued onward. Seeing this, my focus intensified, and I didn't let what happened to him happen to me. Einstein's definition of insanity, "doing the same thing over and over and expecting different results," also applies to repeating others' mishaps, blunders and errors.

## Assignment

Pick three different areas in which you can major in success. Then find experts in those fields to study. Examples:

- Academics – Find and study the student with the best grades in your school.
- Hip hop – Get to know and study the best dancer you've seen.
- Making money – Find, meet and study the wealthiest business owner in your town.
- Making dinner – Carefully watch the best cook in your family prepare a meal.
- Your aspiration – Find and study whoever is great at your interest or passion. Whenever you can, meet these people. When you can't, read about them, listen to them, study them any way you can. Search for them on Google. Look for them on YouTube. Follow them on Twitter… Find a way!

# How To Be Tough

Who's the toughest guy alive? The Ultimate Fighting Champion? The heavyweight champion of the world? The world's strongest or fittest man? Is it the athlete who played through the most debilitating injury? Maybe the toughest "guy" is a girl. The average woman, after all, outlives the average man. So, is the *oldest* person alive the toughest person alive? Or, is the toughest person the one who has been through the most, suffered the most, yet persevered and thrived?

What exactly is toughness?

The best definition I ever heard came from the old football coach, John Madden. During a "success talk" at San Francisco's Cow Palace, Madden shared a story about the times when he was coaching the Pro Bowl (the National Football League's all-star game). Madden confessed that he wasn't all that thrilled about the "opportunity." Until 2010, the Pro Bowl coaches were the two coaches whose teams *almost* made it to the Super Bowl. If you were a Pro Bowl coach, it meant that your team (in Madden's case, the Raiders) was the conference runner-up. You were just one win short of playing for the championship.

Feeling sad and a little sorry for himself, Madden was on his way to Hawaii when he decided to correct his attitude. "Here I was, surrounded by the best football players on the planet," he said, "so I decided to focus on *why* they were the best. What made them special?" Madden was majoring in success.

What he found was that the best players weren't necessarily the biggest, fastest or strongest. "Pro football players," he reminded us, "are all big, fast and strong. The best players," he concluded, "are the *toughest* players." Then he surprised us with his definition of *tough.* "Toughness," he said, "is the ability to accept criticism."

Whereas most players liked to watch film that showed them succeeding – making a block, catching a pass, defending a run or scoring a touchdown, all-star players wanted to watch film that showed them *failing.* When they screwed up, they wanted to know why. They'd ask the coaches to run the film back so they could figure out why they were out of position or made an incorrect decision. Madden's point? *The best football players asked their coaches for criticism.* That's what made them tough.

In *The Little Prince,* Antoine de Saint-Exupéry writes about "The Conceited Man" who wants to be admired by everyone. So, because he cannot bear to hear anything but a compliment, he lives alone on his planet. None of us are completely unlike him. Everyone loves to be complimented. No one loves to be criticized. Criticism carries with it a negative connotation. "Stop criticizing me!" But there's no growth without it. Criticism is absolutely essential to success. Sure, we'd prefer that it be patiently and lovingly offered. Often, though, it won't be. Constructive criticism can be camouflaged by the harsh tone of a parent, teacher, coach or boss, and some of us can't get past that. How do kids normally react when criticized? They get upset. They get angry at whoever is criticizing them. They assume their critics don't like them. "He hates me!" Then they deny, reject, tune out and shut down.

Usually, they're wrong about the hate part. They may do it imperfectly, but most people criticize because they care. A mother sees her two year-old son amble into a busy intersection. She sprints after him. She yanks him up, sets him down and screams, "Don't you ever go into that street again! Look at those speeding cars! One of them could squash you flat! Do you understand me?"

The now terrified little boy bursts into tears. He doesn't like to be snatched off his feet and shouted at. Who would? But did his mother react that way because she hates him?

Consider this scenario: Because you made a series of misguided financial decisions, you and your family are short on cash. You want to start over, only you need $5,000 seed money to start a new business venture. You're at a loss as to where you're going to get the cash when, out of nowhere, your Uncle George stuffs a $5,000 check into your palm and bellows, "Take this! And this time, be smarter and work harder! And after you've turned it around and made the money I know you're capable of making, I expect you to pay me back - every cent - or I'll beat your butt!"

How would you feel? Sure, it would have been nice if the loan had been offered without the vitriol, but, hey, so what? You got what you needed. Furthermore, does Uncle George hate you? No, despite the nastiness, he obviously cares about you.

We must stress to students that criticism, no matter how it's given, is a gift. If it's honest and accurate, then they should seek it. Sometimes they won't like how it's presented, but that's out of their control (the Serenity Prayer). Kids are going to encounter surly teachers and coaches. It's wrong for them to robotically reject criticism just because it's callously delivered.

Sure, sometimes they'll believe they don't need it, but they should accept it anyway. It won't hurt, and constructive criticism is almost always given by people who care and are trying to help, even if they're lousy at giving it. So, kids have to be tough enough to see the humor in the politically incorrect delivery and then use it to get better.

## Assignment

After you've learned what you want to be good at (no easy task), ask people who know what they're talking about to criticize you (Lesson 3 - The Three Questions). Ask your soccer coach to assess your soccer skills, your piano teacher to criticize how well you play or your teacher to evaluate your performance in your favorite class. The more you ask for criticism, the tougher you'll get.

When you think you're ready, graduate to *advanced* toughness. Use Canfield's "Most Valuable Question." Ask your siblings what kind of brother or sister you are. Ask your parents what kind of son or daughter you are. Ask your sweetheart what kind of boyfriend or girlfriend you are. If you're not perfect - and if they're honest, you won't be - ask them what you can do to become a 10.

## Positive Addictions

Homeostasis (Greek for "standing still") is primarily a biological term referring to our body's attempts to maintain equilibrium by continuously changing internally to compensate for any external change affecting it. Simply put, our bodies adapt to and crave the familiar and the routine.

The body has no morals. It doesn't understand values. It adapts to habits. Whatever it's used to, it wants. Whether what it wants is good or bad doesn't matter. It craves what it's used to, what's comfortable. Like fire, homeostasis can improve life or destroy it.

If day after day, week after week, month after month, year after year your typical dinner is pizza, beer and cake, guess what your body will continue to want? If you change it up and start feeding it fruits, vegetables and other healthy stuff, your body (which hates change) will rebel. But only for a while. After it gets used to its new "normal," it will yearn for the healthy stuff. After a year of eating nutritiously, go back to pizza, beer and cake, and your body will rebel against *that*. It will yearn for what it's used to – lean meat, fish, fresh fruit and salad.

The challenge is to become addicted to what's good. If you never exercise, working out is hell. If you exercise regularly, you feel like hell when you *don't* work out. Besides biology, it's physics. Newton's law of inertia says "Every object persists in its state of rest or uniform motion in a straight line unless it is compelled to change that state by forces impressed on it."

So if you sit on the couch too long, you're being double teamed by homeostasis *and* the laws of motion. But if you move regularly, it will be hard to stop. Tell passionate athletes who have been training for years to stop, and they'll go crazy. They'll find a way to do *something.*

The first time most people drink or smoke, they hate it. But drink or smoke long enough and you will "develop a taste for it." The body will get used to having alcohol and cigarettes just as it was used to not having them. Except for babies already born addicted to their mothers' drug dependence, we all get to start without negative addictions. Then, inexplicably, we go looking for them.

This homeostasis effect extends beyond physical responses. Ask students who have never worked hard at their education to buckle down, and it will be brutal – at first. Ask students who always study to stop, and they'll become as frustrated as the injured athlete forced to "rest."

The trick is to habitually strive to improve, serve others, be nice… live the way you know you should. Because if you do the right things long enough, it will be hard to *stop* doing them.

Seems so simple, right? Then why isn't everyone addicted to what's good: healthy food, reading, exercise? Why are so many people addicted to what's bad: junk food, gambling, smoking?

The answer is *it's easier. It's easier* to get used to what's negative. *It's easier* to get used to sugar, salt and fat than fruit, vegetables and lean meats. Thousands of years ago, when humans were fighting to survive, we craved sugar, salt and fat. Our ancestors needed every calorie they could get. Today, even though there is an abundance of food (at least in the first world), our cravings have yet to evolve. We're still drawn to sugar, salt and fat.

For mysterious reasons (Perhaps the payoff is bigger and more immediate?), it's easier to get used to gambling than reading. Obviously, it's easier to smoke and "relax" than to exercise and sweat.

An example of the positive/negative addiction challenge is the battle between natural endorphins and the artificially manufactured high induced by drugs. Which will kids choose? The easy way is enticing, especially when it comes to feeling good. Who wants to work for a high? Yet, that's exactly what we must train children to do.

Endorphins are morphine-like chemicals. They make you feel good. They're manufactured in the brain and spinal cord. They're released in response to physical pain and intense body stress (when you're running or pedaling up hills, for example). Most importantly, they're natural. You don't have to ingest them. But you have to work for them. You have to *work out* for them.

Ecstasy, for example, is a drug that lives up to its name (supposedly, I've never had it). Use it, and your pain threshold increases, your depression decreases, anxiety fades while pleasures are heightened. No wonder people take it.

But it can be addictive. Sooner or later there will be bad side effects. It's illegal. It's expensive. Still, the pleasure it provides – or the pain it masks – must make it worth it. And it's easy. To reach a state of bliss, all you have to do is take a pill.

The Better Business Bureau warns consumers, "If it sounds too good to be true, it probably is." Painted on the wall of hall of fame boxing trainer Freddie Roach's Wild Card gym are three words: "It ain't easy." Roach was referring to boxing, but it applies to practically everything worthwhile, including feeling good. You have to earn your high.

Like a drug, vigorous exercise increases pain threshold, decreases depression and eases anxiety. The only side effects are positive ones. It keeps your weight under control and strengthens your muscles, including the one you can't see – your heart. So why would anyone pay for something with harmful side effects when similar euphoric feelings with positive side effects are available for free?

You already know the answer. *It's easier.* Other than the actual bashing of brains – a boxing workout may be the best workout. Jumping rope, punching bags, push-ups, sit-ups, balance, agility and flexibility drills, working the mitts for hand-eye coordination, long runs for stamina…, it's a complete training regimen that will get you into the best shape of your life.

So train like a boxer - but don't box. (Too many blows to the head will destroy your brain, making your body irrelevant.) Instead, make the fight against *easy*.

## Assignment

1. What bad habits do you want to change? Use the natural laws of science to start and keep moving in the right direction. When I'm cold, when those around me are cold, I like to dance around and shadowbox while repeating, "You've got to keep moving to stay warm! You've got to keep moving to stay warm!"

It's true, right? But it's just as true that, "You've got to keep moving to live well! You've got to keep moving to live well!" Initially, change will be uncomfortable, sometimes unbearably so. Remember, your body despises change. It doesn't want to move (change). It becomes addicted to "the usual." But keep at it long enough (three months minimum), and time - as it was with the Daffodil Principle - will be your ally.

2. Train! Train! Train! Choose a workout. (Why not a boxer's workout?) Breathe hard. Sweat. A few fortunate people feel the endorphin high while they're exercising (but only a few). Most of us feel it afterward. Either way, there's nothing like an earned high. Become addicted to one.

## See the Blue

*You shouldn't be looking for people slipping up, you should be looking for all the good things people do and praising those.*

- Richard Branson

What do you see? What do you miss?

Gene Weingarten wrote a fascinating story for the *Washington Post* about the time when the great violinist, Joshua Bell, posed as a common street musician and played incognito at a Washington D.C. Metro subway station.[22]

Three nights earlier, Bell had performed in front of a packed house in Boston where a mid-level priced seat sold for $100. But on this busy rush hour morning, no one paid much attention to him. Even though Bell was playing timeless, beautiful (and difficult) classical music (Bach's "Chaconne," for instance) using a $3.5 million dollar Gibson ex Huberman violin, handcrafted in 1713 by Antonio Stradivari, the commuters hurried right past him. Most barely gave him a passing glance. Bell had placed a collection plate on the floor in front of him and even seeded it with a few of his own dollars. It didn't help much, though. The world class musician's total take for his stellar performance? $32 dollars.

Interestingly, the passerby that morning who seemed the most drawn to the amazing music was three years old – a little boy named Evan. He must have sensed that he was hearing something special, but despite his protests to stop and listen, his mother hustled him along.

Even when they're tiny, children's ears and eyes don't lie. Some preschoolers, like Evan, are searchers. They scan the world, taking it in. Later, as students, they listen, observe and think before they act. The typical child only reacts. The ones who watch, the ones who search, get it. We need more kids like them.

One way to develop searchers is to teach kids to "see the blue." Start literally. Ask them to find the color. "Look around the room. How many things in here are blue?"

They'll find it. Blue is ubiquitous. But they won't see it until they look for it. "Until I told you to search for it," I explain, "nobody was aware of all the blue surrounding us. But as soon as I told you to seek it, you found it. Now, try to find something blue that no one else sees."

Try it. It's hard! Kids get really good at seeing the blue.

"See the Blue" is a fun game… for five minutes. Then it gets old. The truth is, seeing blue things isn't that rewarding. But there *are* things – if we see them – that can dramatically alter and improve our lives.

If we teach kids to look for these things that - like blue - are everywhere, they can reap massive benefits.

Teach them to look for…

- The good in people - so they can compliment them
- Good things people do – so they can compliment them
- Cool, successful, motivating people they want to meet
- People from whom they can major in success
- Chances to major in success
- What's beautiful – both natural and human-made, big and small
- Kind behavior (so they can emulate it)

- What people are wearing - it's a way to connect

  **Example:** At a teachers' conference, I saw a guy wearing a sweatshirt that had *Samoa* written on it. He looked like he could have been Samoan. I've always wanted to visit Samoa, so I asked him if he had been there. He told me he was born there but had moved to California when he was two. He still had relatives living in Samoa. We had a good conversation that wouldn't have happened if I hadn't paid attention to his clothing.

- Things that are especially good, successful, high class or of superior quality

- Activities that could become passions

- People who are exceptionally good at what they do, whatever it is. They shouldn't overlook the custodian, waitress, fast food worker, receptionist or hotel maid.

- What they do well (Some kids don't recognize their talents, strengths and assets.)

- What they don't do well (Some kids don't recognize their own weaknesses, flaws and failings.)

- Mistakes in their work – writing, for example

- Good uses of time

- *Kefi* (Lesson 7)

- Solutions

- Procedures, rules, policies and laws that need to be created, amended or abolished

- Universal values - so we can bond over our similarities and transcend our differences (Lesson 48)

- Ways to improve the world
- Things in which to immerse (Lesson 11)
- Needs to be filled
- People to add to your Inspirational People List (Lesson 36)
- Things they should be grateful for and appreciative of
- Healthy human contacts (in Lesson 47)
- Lessons they can learn while they're reading, watching movies, listening to music or hearing people talk (or teach)
- Entrepreneurial ideas and opportunities, ways to make money (legally)
- Research, stories and newsworthy items in their areas of interest
- Possible new interests
- Challenges they can undertake, goals they can set
- Positive ways to separate themselves from the masses
- Opportunities to help people
- Opportunities to have fun
- Opportunities!

There are all sorts of quotes, clichés, proverbs, lessons and stories about taking advantage of opportunities. *Opportunity doesn't knock twice.* But "opportunity" is too vague. Unless we teach kids what to look for, most kids wouldn't recognize an opportunity if they were standing in line behind one. They can't hunt one down until they know what they're hunting. So teach them. Teach them, specifically, what opportunities look like. For example, when they see something on the Internet that interests them, have them consider who created it and whether it might be possible to meet or connect with that person.

My favorite movie critic is the *San Francisco Chronicle*'s Mick LaSalle. He's such a talented writer, and I love studying his work because he's exceptionally good at what he does. A while back, he was writing about some movie that, at first, bored him. But after the yawn-inducing beginning, the movie got better. LaSalle wrote, "I was rewarded for listening."

"Rewarded for listening." Don't you love that? If we can teach kids to keep listening because, if they do, there's a chance that they'll be *rewarded* for it, maybe they actually will! And maybe they'll eventually appreciate the enormous value of listening. If we can do that, whether it's listening to music played in a subway station, difficult dialogue in a deep movie or, yes, adult wisdom (even teacher wisdom), we'll be opening up the world to them.

Once kids know what opportunities to look and listen for (just like the color blue), they'll notice them everywhere. Then, and only then, can they take advantage of them.

**Note:** Although blue (at least to me) initially suggests something good, positive and cheerful - blue skies, happiness and sunshine, there's also the "having the blues" kind of blue. Blue can also denote something sad, negative and gloomy. When we begin to see more positive blue – because we've trained ourselves to look for it - does that mean we also notice more negative blue, blue with shades of gray?

Probably. But that's not necessarily bad. Depressing, perhaps, but not bad. Remember, ignorance is *not* bliss. We can't do anything about the world's blue-gray unless we realize it's there.

We've got to be aware of injustice, corruption and evil before we can fight them. When we don't know something is wrong, how can we make it right? Bullying, for example. If we don't see it, why would we even consider addressing it, let alone changing it?

The blue is beautiful, but we have to see the darker shades, too.

## Assignment

Look for people to help. Notice who and what is good. Actively seek new interests, new lessons, new passions, new ideas and new possibilities. When you find them, don't just note them. Act on them. Otherwise, this lesson is a waste of time. It does no good to simply notice the woman struggling to load her child's stroller into the trunk of her car. Politely approach her and give her a hand.

## How to Build Social Capital

*The supreme happiness of life is the conviction that we are loved.*

- Victor Hugo

*Hand me the world on a silver platter*
*And what good would it be*
*With no one to share*
*With no one who truly cares for me.*

- Alicia Keys

*People who need people are the luckiest people in the world*

- Bob Merrill,
Broadway musical *Funny Girl*

That last one is wrong. People who need people aren't the luckiest people in the world. Everyone *needs* people. People who *have* people are the luckiest people in the world. That's why we need to teach kids how to *get* people.

There are infinite reasons why we should get people, starting with the Reverse Daffodil Principle (Lesson 9). You're not going to be able to replace time with people if you don't have people. And you're not going to have people if you're disliked and/or disrespected.

Further, when we are extraordinarily disliked and/or disrespected, our ability to teach, influence or even affect policy diminishes. Near the end of George W. Bush's presidency, Thomas Friedman wrote in the *New York Times* that Bush had said something about the economy that made good sense. But, because Bush's approval rating had sunk so low – in late 2008, only one in four Americans thought he was doing a good job – few people paid attention.

It's wrong, but that's how most people are. When they don't like you, no matter what you say, no matter how brilliant it may be, it will be ignored or dismissed. When they don't like you, no matter what cause you believe in, no matter how worthy it may be, no matter how hard you try to gather support, it will be ignored or dismissed.

Conversely, when people like you, pretty much anything you say will be taken seriously. Pretty much any cause you believe in will be supported. This, too, is wrong. But that's how most people are.

People give to people, not causes, and there are countless worthy causes. So, ultimately, it's not the cause that gets the cash. It's the people advocating for it. If they have lots of social capital, they'll be more successful than if they have little. The Michael J. Fox Foundation has raised over a quarter billion dollars while searching for a cure for Parkinson's disease. Parkinson's research, clearly, is an important cause. But it's not only sympathy for those afflicted with Parkinson's that's bringing in the donations. It's the popular, respected and beloved actor, Michael J. Fox, (and his abundant social capital) who is not only battling Parkinson's, but spearheading the drive to eradicate it.

"Well liked and popular" gets a bad rap, as if being disliked and unknown should be the goal. The truth is, being well liked and popular is only important if you care about being happy and successful. Otherwise, it's overrated.

Seriously, it's distressing for a teacher and heartbreaking for a parent when a child isn't liked. And, obviously, it's devastating for the child. Humans are social creatures. Other humans are the source of our greatest joy. Remove that joy, and kids grow into unhappy teenagers and adults whose goal is to hurt the people they resent. Remove that joy, and there's a possibility that we'll develop kids like Eric Harris and Dylan Klebold, the boys who murdered 12 of their

Columbine High School (Colorado) classmates, then committed suicide.

**Question:** What makes us the most happy?
**Answer:** Other people.

**Question:** What makes us the most unhappy?
**Answer:** Other people.

What can be the best part of our day? What can be the worst part of our day? Again, it's the same answer: our connection with others.

I don't care how smart someone is. I don't care how well he or she can read, write or solve problems. I don't care how impressive a student's GPA or SAT score is. When a child doesn't know what it takes to initiate and build a relationship, he or she is doomed to an unhappy and unsatisfying life.

This is why every child needs to be *taught* how to build the capital more valuable than financial capital – social capital. *Financial capital* is about how much money you have. *Social capital* is about how many people you have – the people in your life you *know* you can count on. When you have social capital, you can build financial capital. The other way around doesn't necessarily work.

It's not enough to merely tell a kid to go make friends. It's hard to make friends! It takes time to make friends. If you want to make friends, there are things you should and shouldn't do.

For over 40 years, from 1953 to 1994, there was a children's television program called *Romper Room.* During many shows, a primary school teacher (my favorite was Miss Nancy) had a "Do-Bee" and "Don't-Bee" segment. Children dressed as good and bad bumblebees would teach their peers how to and how not to behave. "Do be this," Miss Nancy would say. "Don't be that!"

Hoping to come up with a more grown-up version of the "Do be/Don't be" lesson, I asked my students to help me make two lists. The first list would be attractive social behaviors, and the second list would be repelling ones. "What makes you like someone and want to be around them? What makes you dislike someone and want to avoid them?"

**The "Do-Bee" List - Ways to Make Them Love You**

- Have a cause. Care about something beyond yourself. Children? Seniors? The environment? Animals? For what cause are you working?

- Learn how to tell stories. Humans love stories.

- Develop a sense of humor. There are two ways to show that you have it.

- *Be funny*: Self-effacing humor is good.

- *Recognize funny:* Smart, attractive people get jokes. Laugh!

- Verbally compliment or, better, write complimentary notes to a wide variety of people (Lesson 27).

- Give small gifts. Know what people like. If you don't know, find out. Research. Make your gifts personal.

- Master a skill. If you do, right or wrong, people will want to be around you. Human capital (your knowledge, aptitude(s), skills and expertise) leads to social capital.

- Work hard. Hard workers earn respect.

- Become the best listener you know. In one of his novels, Haruki Murakami writes about a gorgeous woman who is considered sexy because of her enormous ears. Her ears are a metaphor for the beauty of listening. Excellent listeners are loved, but they're rare. Be rare. Listen.

- Be an outstanding audience member. Focus, listen, react, respond non-verbally (smile, laugh), ask relevant questions. Whether it's in class, paying attention to the teacher or a classmate, listening to a guest speaker (any speaker!), watching a school assembly or attending a concert, play or movie, great audience members are special and wonderful. They're underappreciated – except by presenters, performers and those sitting near them, who love them!

- Be able to ask people of all ages interesting, thoughtful and (sometimes) even probing questions.
- Give someone the shirt off your back. Literally. The last time I visited my father, he let me borrow his denim jacket. I mentioned to him that I liked it. When it was time for me to leave, I tried to give it back to him but he wouldn't take it. "Keep it," he said. I never saw him alive again. Now, whenever possible, when someone likes something I own, I hand it over. I never miss it. (And I still have and sometimes wear Dad's jacket.)
- Be unpredictable. React differently. When someone falls, don't be like most people and laugh. Instead, help.
- Notice when people are sad or not themselves. Reach out to them. Comfort, or at least offer to comfort those who look like they need comforting.
- When you like something, say so. When you don't, say nothing. People like people who like stuff. "I love that song/movie/TV show/book/sport/food/class/person." Announcing what you don't like, "I hate that song/movie/TV show/book/sport/food/class/person," is often a turn-off, especially to those who like what you just insulted.
- Be curious. Don't be apathetic, insouciant or phlegmatic. Apathetic, insouciant, phlegmatic people are boring.
- Understand what people want or need before they ask for it. When you notice someone needs it, lend a pencil, pen, piece of paper, personal item, a jacket, a sweater…
- "Get it." Don't need long, drawn-out directions or explanations.

- Be able to initiate a conversation. Ask people about themselves. Have a bank of conversation-starters: "Tell me about your family." "Today, if you could have lunch with anyone in the world, who would you choose it to be? Where would it be? What restaurant?" (Lesson 46)

- Stand up for yourself. Have confidence. We respect and like spunk.

- Strive to be innovative. Conformity may be comforting, but creativity is charismatic.

- Let someone cut in front of you, but only if there is no one waiting behind you.

- Offer someone a chair. Maybe even your chair.

- Be open. Be real. Be willing to share your life. Tell the truth. Come clean. Don't pretend to like something you dislike. Don't pretend to dislike something you like.

- On occasion, when you can, pay for the person behind you. Not just at the toll booth, either. Buy something in the vending machine for the person behind you in line, even if you don't know that person. (But first ask what he or she wants.)

- Write more thank you notes. Make them personal and specific.

- Make a snack or lunch for someone.

- Notice when people need help carrying things. Offer to help.

- In a class in which you're excelling, help someone who's not.

- Send or, better, print out a meaningful quote and give it to someone to whom it applies.

- Give someone an appropriate book. (But don't pressure the recipient to read it.)

- Color, draw or paint someone a picture.
- Leave an encouraging, happy, inspiring voicemail.
- Text a compliment and/or an encouraging thought to a different person each day.
- Offer to take a group of underclassmen or newly hired co-workers to lunch.
- Rescue others from embarrassment. When someone's voice cracks or if he or she unintentionally burps, spits or drools, don't laugh. Resist the urge to comment.
- Physically, do the best you can with what you have. We can't all be beautiful, but we can all take pride in our appearance and at least try.
- Make an effort to acknowledge and connect with classmates or co-workers outside the classroom or workplace. That's where bonds are forged.
- Do little things. Close someone's open backpack. Hold the door.
- Notice the small things others do. Let people know you notice and appreciate those things.
- Shake hands (warmly), give high fives, pats on the back and hugs. When done appropriately and properly, the human touch is magical.
- Visit, call or contact an absent classmate or co-worker.
- Be a good judge of character. Immerse yourself in positive activities and surround yourself with positive people (Lesson 11).
- Stand up for and support those who need it. Sometimes this is incredibly difficult, but, if you do, it won't be forgotten.

- Exceed others' expectations. If you do, it won't be forgotten.
- Use people's names when you greet and talk with them.
- Be the first to say "Hello" and "Goodbye."
- Greet or say "Hi" to people you don't know. (Don't worry if they don't respond. That's their problem.)
- When driving, let someone in. If someone lets you in, acknowledge it. Wave a thank you.
- Treat *everyone* well, not just the people you like or think are important. So often we judge people not by how they treat us, but by how they treat others. Remember the old adage about choosing a husband: "Don't evaluate a prospect only by how he treats you. Evaluate him based on how he treats his mother." Don't you love people who show kindness and respect to the people you love? And aren't you deeply impressed by people who treat anyone with kindness and respect? Others notice way more than you think they notice. You're always being evaluated. You're always on stage.
- Learn how to introduce people to an audience. Research their strengths and accomplishments. Then compliment them in your introduction.
- Make matches. Introduce people to each other. Not with the intention of hooking them up romantically, but to connect like-minded, similarly-interested people platonically.
- Be able to talk about pop culture – a movie, a TV show, a sporting event. The more you can talk about, the better.
- Make an effort to talk about the person you're talking to, not just about yourself.
- Become educated. Most people enjoy being around smart people.

- Put the grocery store shopping cart back in the rack. Hardly anybody does it.

- If you hear something nice about people, don't keep it a secret. Tell them what you heard.

- Visit people when they're home sick or hospitalized. They won't forget it.

- Go to people's parties, performances and games. Afterward, give them flowers or gifts.

- Share food.

- When people are doing their job well, let them know. Better, let their *bosses* know.

- Save someone time. Clean, file, organize, run an errand. Time is such an underrated gift!

  **Quick story:** I emailed all the teachers at my school asking if anyone had stereo speakers I could borrow. Six did. "Come by my room and pick them up," they replied. But one teacher had a student deliver them to my room - a small but memorable gesture.

- Forgive someone who made a mistake. Don't hold a grudge.

- When you mess up, apologize. As Randy Pausch taught in his *Last Lecture*, a good apology has three parts[23]:

  Part I: "I'm sorry."

  Part II: "It was my fault."

  Part III: "What can I do to make it right?"

- Apologize publicly. Thank people publicly.

- Offer to listen or help even when the odds are they won't take you up on your offer. Keep in mind how comforting it feels to be offered something, even when you can't accept the offer.

- Whenever you can, when someone offers you a gift, accept it. Avoid saying, "No thank you." Here's why:

  When you accept a gift, the giver feels good. When you don't, the giver feels bad.

  When you truly don't want the gift, take it. Later, give it to someone who will want it. Stop thinking only of yourself.

- Send people links. When you find something you like on the Internet, think about who else might like it. Send it to them. It proves that you know their interests and that you were thinking about them.

- Compliment someone with your question. "How did you get so good at guitar?" "Why do you have such a strong work ethic?" "Who taught you how to be so great at _______?" "How come you're so smart/talented/beautiful?"

- Entertain someone while they're working. Sing. Tell jokes. Just be with them so they won't be alone. Sometimes, your presence is enough.

- Don't interrupt. Teachers are interrupted by students all the time. I swear, when I'm talking to a student, he or she becomes invisible. Other students will walk right up to us and begin a conversation with me. When they don't, when they patiently wait their turn, I notice and respect it.

- Be honest. If you're good at lying and cheating, no one will notice. If you're good at telling the truth and behaving honorably, no one will notice that either. Except you.

- Know when to speak up and when to shut up.

- What else?

**The "Don't-Bee" List – Ways to Make Them Hate You**

Well, maybe not *hate*. That's a little strong. What might cause people to be *annoyed* by you is probably more accurate.

When I was 12, I made the little league all-star team. But I didn't start the all-star game. While sitting on the bench waiting for my chance, our team fell behind. "The reason we're losing is because not enough Orioles are in the game!" I half-jokingly hollered.

My teammates, most of who were not on the Orioles - my regular season team - didn't think I was funny.

"Why don't you shut up?!"

"Yeah, who are you? Shut your mouth."

"If you played as good as you talk, you'd be another Babe Ruth."

Their words struck like stones. They hurt. But I learned (the hard way) that I shouldn't say out loud whatever thought popped into my head. So I stopped talking, finished the game and went home. It's hard for twelve-year-old boys to be humiliated, but that time I was. Luckily, I could take social cues – even the politically incorrect, far from sensitive cues that pre-adolescent boys hurl.

That kind of vile negative feedback was one way I learned how *not* to behave. I don't recommend it, though. It was painful. So painful that more than 40 years later, I clearly remember the details. Still, I learned and adjusted my behavior.

Sadly, some kids don't. They don't recognize even the most obvious social cues. Instead, they keep saying or doing the wrong things, even while their behavior is turning them into social pariahs. To brighten their lives, we need to teach them (and every other kid) these social "don'ts."

If you **don't** want to build social capital, do the following:

- Chew loudly. Chew with your mouth open.

- Brag. Talk about yourself - a lot.

- Take credit for something someone else did.

- Frequently talk negatively about others.
- Talk too much. Dominate the conversation.
- Start every sentence with "I" or "My."
- Don't take anything seriously. Laugh when the mood is serious.
- Talk or, worse, argue about inane, stupid stuff.
- Complain, whine and poison the mood with your pessimism.
- Always look for the exception. Take joy in proving others wrong while missing the point.
- Disagree just for the sake of disagreeing.
- Be condescending. It's bad when an adult talks down to kids. When an adult is condescending toward another adult, it's arrogant and insulting.
- Tell someone how a movie ends or who wins a (prerecorded) game.
- When someone is telling a joke, before they're done, shout out the punch line.
- When you don't get a joke, say the joke is stupid. (More likely, *you're* stupid for not getting it.) After someone tells a joke, say, "That's not funny."
- Disrespect people who have given you no reason to disrespect them.
- Talk and ask a bunch of questions during movies and TV shows.
- Don't say "Please." Don't say "Thank you."
- Without apologizing, interrupt to ask a question or bring up a point that has nothing to do with what's being discussed.
- While with others, wear your headphones.

- While with others, spend lots of time texting or talking on your cell.
- Participate in a conversation only when asked a question (and answer as curtly as possible).
- When teasing others, cross the line.
- Be overly predictable.
- Help yourself to others' food.
- Cuss often and anywhere.
- Argue about facts.
- Consistently be late.
- Always have an excuse.
- Ask unnecessary questions – the kind where you, without help, could answer.
- Ask questions, not because you really want an answer, but to prove how smart you are.
- Sit in someone else's seat.
- Talk to everyone the same way. Make no allowances for your audience's demographic or interests (Lesson 46).
- Complain, but don't do anything to solve or help solve the problem.
- Be closed-minded and argumentative.
- Say you're going to do something. Then don't do it. Do this often.
- Tell people you *almost* did something nice for them, but didn't. As in "I was going to buy you a burrito, but … (you didn't)."
- Compete over stupid stuff, like how *you* are the bigger fan of celebrity X, or how *you* are more depressed, more nervous, more

excited, more stressed or more tired.

- Fail to abide by elevator or public transportation etiquette. (Try to enter before people exit.)

- Fail to abide by "urinal etiquette." (If there are three urinals and only one is being used – the one on the left, for example – use the one on the right. Don't do your business next door! And if you're the first one there, don't choose the middle urinal. Go left or right.)

- Don't lift the toilet seat and miss. Then don't flush.

- Make people feel uncomfortable by watching, noting and criticizing tiny personal habits. "You walk funny." "You eat funny."

- Already know it all. Don't be open to learning anything new.

- When something surprising happens, such as when someone unexpectedly slips or falls, laugh. (Our natural human instinct is to laugh. Fight that instinct.) Note: It's OK to laugh at yourself.

- Pressure others to eat something, drink something or smoke something.

- Litter. Throw trash in the recycle bin. Throw recyclables in the trash bin.

- At a fast food restaurant or movie theater, leave all your trash for "the workers" to clean up.

- Be around too much. Don't give people space.

- Overreact. Make a big thing out of a little thing. "Oh my god! You spilled your drink onto the floor!"

- Underreact. Treat a big thing like it's a little thing. "You just got into Harvard? That's nice. Please pass the ketchup."

- Criticize what others prefer or enjoy (movies, music, magazines).

Rip their personal tastes.

- At the gym, hog the equipment – and don't wipe away your sweat.
- When someone doesn't know something, make them feel bad about it, as in "You didn't know that?!"
- Show no compassion toward (and fail to notice) someone who's having a tough time.
- To get attention, pretend to be sad or hurt when you really aren't that sad or hurt.
- Make fun of old or disabled people.
- Make fun of people.
- Ask or state the obvious. "You're late." "Did you get a haircut?"
- Use *gay* or *retarded* as a negative adjective.
- Only acknowledge or talk to people online or via text.
- When working in a group, don't contribute.
- Act like you're an expert in something you really don't know that much about.
- Be super sensitive. Be unable to take good-natured teasing.
- Don't allow people to finish their thought or story.
- Don't react in any way to people's thoughts or stories.
- Don't take the hint. Don't "get it."
- Ask people to do something illegal or immoral.
- In an attempt to be tough, spit.
- Because you're jealous, negatively criticize people who are

successful and can do (or have done) what you can't do (or haven't done). Professional athletes and entertainers are the usual targets, but people tend to deride anyone who is successful.

- Know that any of the above is annoying someone, but continue to do it anyway.
- Do the opposite of everything listed under "Ways to Make Them Love You."

What else?

## Assignment

As they come up – and they will - add ways to make them love or hate you. Make it a goal to do at least one thing from the Do-Bee list every day. And when you catch yourself doing something from the Don't-Bee list, recognize it and check yourself.

# Have an (Educated) Opinion!

*The hottest places in Hell are reserved for those who in a time of moral crisis preserve their neutrality.*

- John F. Kennedy
(as interpreted from Dante's *Inferno*)

*The only thing necessary for the triumph of evil is for good men to do nothing.*

- Edmund Burke
Irish/British Statesman

A neutron walks into a bar and orders a beer. "How much?" it asks. "For you," the bartender replies, "no charge."

That joke may be the best thing about being a neutron. Other than that, being neutral is bland and boring. Have an opinion!

Not only is not having an opinion uninteresting, it's an exasperating obstacle. In *Good to Great* (Jim Collins's study of what moves a company from mediocrity to superiority), Collins wrote about the CEO's role as an "interrogator":

*Leading from good to great does not mean coming up with the answers and then motivating everyone to follow your messianic vision. It means having the humility to grasp the fact that you do not yet understand enough to have the answers and then ask the questions that will lead to the best possible insights.*[24]

But there won't be any insights if the questions are met with silence, indifference or "I don't know." Somebody needs to speak up! Somebody better have an opinion! So, it's essential that kids be taught that if they don't have an opinion, they need to take the time, put in the effort, educate themselves and get one. Remember, anyone can have an opinion, but some opinions - educated opinions – mean more and carry greater weight.

To make taking class roll more appealing, instead of having students shout out, "Here!" I'll ask each to answer a question. For example, "What do you know more about than anything else?" or "If you had one wish, what would it be?"

Invariably, there will be students who'll say, "I don't know."

That's exasperating.

Or if I ask, "What's your all-time favorite movie?" someone will respond, "I don't have one" or, worse, "I don't watch movies."

Too many intelligent (at least scholastically smart) kids can't formulate or articulate an opinion. Some of the brightest pupils roll their eyes and think these kinds of questions are a lame waste of time.

They're not. Besides preparing them for interviews, social situations, dates and other challenging, inquisitive situations, being able to provide interesting answers to opinion questions will make students more engaging and lead to more social capital. But the ability to express an opinion requires practice.

Most people have opinions, but for a variety of reasons they're afraid to express them. Often, it's because they're afraid of being ridiculed. If you say you like math or piano, some jerk may make fun of you. So why say anything?

Because you should. We can't let kids allow other people to influence what they like or dislike. *They* get to decide. Besides, they can't help it. They like what they like. We all do. We can't force ourselves to not like what we like or like what we don't like. I wish I didn't like donuts, but I do. I wish I did like opera, but I don't.

In the 1990's there was a boy-band named Hanson. As with many pop stars, there was a time when it was cool to like them followed by a time when it was cool to not like them. (Even if you secretly liked them, you couldn't admit you liked them).

One day I asked this roll question: "Who is your favorite singing group?" An 8th grade girl named Casey said, "Hanson."

Her classmates reacted as if she had just confessed that she had spent the weekend selling drugs to third graders. But Casey stood strong. "I like them, and if you don't, too bad." I became a huge Casey fan.

Still, no wonder people are afraid to express their opinions, especially peer-pressured kids. It's so much easier for them to say they like something they don't (if it's popular) or that they don't like something they do (if it's unpopular). So it's vital for students to learn that it's OK to express what they think, feel and believe. Suppressing the truth is toxic. (On the flip side, don't forget that one of the "ways to make them hate you" is to rip other people's tastes.)

Another reason people refrain from unleashing their opinions is they want to be nice. So when they're asked where they want to eat or what movie they want to see, they lie and say, "I don't care." In other words, "I don't want to pick something you're not going to like. Therefore, I'll let you decide." There's nothing wrong with that – except that even though it may be nice, sometimes nice is irritating. Imagine if a waitress asked, "What would you like to drink?" and the customer said, "I don't care."

Most of the time, you *do* care. So don't say you don't. Have some courage. When others ask you what you think or what you'd like, it's refreshing when you tell them. If they don't like your answer, that's their problem. They asked! And what if you really *don't* care? Then, just say something. Anything. If you honestly don't care, it won't matter, right? But it will make life simpler for whoever's asking.

There are times when people really *don't* have an opinion. Or, their opinion is so pathetic that it's embarrassing for them to reveal it. If either of these is the problem, education is the solution. The more you listen, read, learn and think - the better educated you are - the more likely you are to have a meaningful opinion.

Sometimes it's wise to say, "I don't know." Do it too much,

though, and people will wonder, *Why not?* - especially when it's something you *should* know.

## Assignment

Play the "Roll Question Game." When you're with your family or friends, ask each other about their favorites, preferences, wishes and personal histories. Here's a list of 50+ roll questions I've asked. Some are simple. Some are complex. "I don't know," "I don't care" or "I don't have one" are unacceptable responses.

1. Most impactful book, movie and/or play?
2. Best actor/actress?
3. Best fast food restaurant? Best restaurant?
4. Singer (male and female) with the best voice?
5. Favorite ice cream flavor?
6. The best day of your life? The worst?
7. Coolest animal?
8. Celebrity crush?
9. Best Disney film?
10. Disney/Pixar character who reminds you of you?
11. Something you want to learn?
12. Favorite/Least favorite school subject?
13. If you had to choose another name, what would it be?
14. Best year of elementary school?
15. Favorite musical instrument to play (or would like to play)?
16. Favorite instrument to listen to?
17. Teacher/coach/person who taught you the most?

18. State that you've never been to that you want to visit?
19. One week in one place, anywhere in the world – where?
20. Skill/talent you don't have that you wish you did?
21. Best athletic experience you've ever had? Worst?
22. Living person you'd most like to talk with over lunch?
23. An event from history you wish you could change? Historical event you wish you could have witnessed?
24. Do you have any scars? Tell me the story.
25. One positive and one negative adjective that describes you?
26. Country where you'd most want to study abroad?
27. City/State/Country other than where you live where you'd like to live?
28. Song you want played for your first dance at your wedding reception?
29. Type of business you'd start?
30. Fantasy career?
31. What do you do well?
32. College major (if you had to pick it today)?
33. Age you want to get married?
34. In a past life, who might you have been?
35. How many kids do you want? # of boys/girls?
36. Future son's/daughter's name?
37. First crush? How old were you?
38. Best TV show - ever?
39. Favorite sport to play? To watch?

40. Favorite pro sports team? Athlete?
41. Favorite Website?
42. Favorite App?
43. What's your desktop background?
44. If you were a multi-millionaire, how would you spend your money? How would you spend your time? Would you continue to work?
45. Charity or cause you support?
46. The one non-living thing you'd save from your burning house?
47. Place you go to think?
48. Funniest person? (Someone famous and/or someone in your not-so-famous circle of acquaintances)
49. Favorite dog breed?
50. Fantasy pet?
51. Wonder of the World you most want to visit?
52. Favorite number, song, day of the week, crayon color, month, season, president, bug*

*Here's the "bug story": I was teaching a 7th grade English class. I passed out a handout with a list of favorites (much like those listed here). For homework, the students were supposed to fill in their favorites. A boy named Frank lost his paper, so he tried to find a way. As best as he could remember, he wrote down all the favorite categories on a sheet of binder paper and turned it in. For one of the favorites he wrote:

*Bug: bee*

I hadn't listed "bug" as a category, but I loved that Frank had. (And "bee" was a pretty good answer, right?) So, from then on, I always save a day to ask, "What's your favorite bug?" Students think it's ridiculously random – until I share the story.

**Note**: Predictably, the immediate response to the bug question is, "Ewwww! Gross! I hate bugs!" But that's not an acceptable answer. So, when pressed, most of the girls end up choosing a butterfly or ladybug. "Scorpion" is a popular boy answer. Any bug is acceptable, though. Just have an opinion.

## 21 Push-Ups

*Great men can't be ruled.*

- Ayn Rand

Shortly into my teaching career, I learned that there are three kinds of students:

- Group One: Those who do it when it's required.
- Group Two: Those who *don't* do it when it's required.
- Group Three: Those who do it even when it's *not* required.

Most students are in the first group. When an assignment is mandatory, they'll do it. Disappointingly, there are usually a few who fall into the second group. They're the kids who are habitually "looking for easy," often getting into trouble and doing as little as possible. Thankfully, there are students who fall into the third group. The volunteers. The kids who do extra. The ones who exceed expectations.

The adult world is no different. There are three kinds of people:

- Group One: Those who do it when it's required. (most people)
- Group Two: Those who *don't* do it when it's required. (inmates)
- Group Three: Those who do it even when it's not

> required. They're the kind of people we desperately need. The kind of "great men" Rand was talking about. The kind of people who, to quote Bob Marley, "light up the darkness."

*Required* is not quite accurate. Nothing is really *required.* But actions have consequences. Required means that if you don't do it, there will be a negative consequence. A bad grade. Grounding. A fine. Prison.

*It* is the thing you should do – the thing you know in your heart is the right thing to do. *It* is working out when no one is forcing you to. *It* is picking up trash, even when it's not your trash. *It* is volunteering to work with the kid nobody wants to work with. *It* is coming in early and staying late. *It* is being the initiator. Or, what Rand, in *The Fountainhead*, called, the "creator." *It* is raising your hand. *It* is extra credit.

Most people don't even do what's expected. So when students do even a little more than what they're asked, they're part of a sweet minority. That's the sad/happy truth (depending upon your point of view). When dealing with the masses, the competition isn't that tough. Just do what's required, and you'll stand out. And if you do a little bit more than required, you'll shock people.

If I assign a two-page paper, the group-one students will grudgingly do it, yet do everything they creatively can to make it *look* like they wrote two pages without actually writing two pages. They'll use large font, skip lines, write big titles, make their margins a shade wider than they should be… you name it, teachers have seen it.

If group-two students write anything at all, it won't be close to two pages. If I get more than a half page from one of them, I'm secretly thinking *win.*

Group-three students – maybe one or two in a class of thirty – will write a genuine two-page paper and maybe even a quarter-page more.

When I taught martial arts, I'd order my students to, "On your own count, drop and give me 20 (push-ups)." I knew that without me closely watching them, most wouldn't do 20 push-ups. They'd do 17, 18, maybe 19. After the first student stopped, no matter how many he or she did, the others would also stop. Then I'd give them the talk. "Raise your hand if you'll swear on your best friend's life that you honestly did 20 push-ups."

When asked to be, most kids will be truthful, and nearly all of my martial artists would admit that that they hadn't done 20 push-ups. Most hadn't even bothered to count. So after teaching them about the three kinds of students (and adults), I'd teach them the 21 Push-Ups rule:

> "When someone asks you to do something, get into the habit of doing more, even if it's only a tiny bit more. If I ask you to do 20 push-ups, from now on that means 21. When average people are asked to do 20 of something, how many will even *think about* doing 21? Doing more than what's asked is just not in their thought process. Average people don't think, *Do more.* They're thinking, *How can I get away with doing less?* But you don't have to be average."

Not that the longer a paper is, the better it is. Not that the more you do, the better it will be. Quantity doesn't equal quality. But 21 Push-Ups is easily understood by kids and clearly makes the point that it doesn't take an absurd amount of effort to be extraordinary.

It just takes one more push-up.

## Assignment

There are two parts to this lesson:

**Part I:** Decide to be a group-three person. Even when it's not required, do what you know should be done. And when it is required, do it completely – then tack on at least a tiny bit more.

**Part II:** Turn the situation around. When *you* are the leader, don't be delusional and think most people will, on their own, out of their natural goodness, do what you want or need them to do. If you think this way, most of the time you're going to be disappointed. Great people can't be ruled, but most people aren't great. If you want something done, you better require it.

When the retired four-star general and secretary of state, Colin Powell, was advocating for compulsory community service for all high school students, he said, "Back when I was in high school, I didn't volunteer to take algebra. Taking it wasn't optional. And neither should be service. It's at least as important."

When you're the leader, initially, require your followers to do what needs to be done. But while you're at it, teach them 21 Push-Ups. Eventually, hopefully, they'll catch on and no longer need to be required to do what they should be doing on their own.

## Come Clean

*An honest answer is like a kiss on the lips.*

- Proverbs 24:26

"Come Clean" is a song written by lyricists Kara DioGuardi and John Shanks and performed by Hilary Duff.[25] Even though I love its title, "Come Clean" was one of those songs that I heard many times before I paid any attention to the lyrics. Then, on maybe the 22nd listen, I got it.

*I'm shedding*
*Shedding every color*
*Trying to find a pigment of truth*
*Beneath my skin*

Shedding every color isn't easy. In Lesson 20, the perils of expressing an opinion were made clear. Transparency includes coming clean with your opinions – and much more. It means expressing what you sincerely think, not saying what you assume people want to hear. It means explaining your motives and behaviors. It means addressing the elephant in the room. It means confessing your weaknesses. It means apologizing when you screw up. It means speaking out when you know you're right. It means admitting when you're wrong.

Coming clean cleanses the soul. Keeping what needs to be said corked inside is destructive to mental health. True, kids need to be taught when to say it and when to keep it to themselves. Some thoughts should remain unsaid. If we verbalized *all* our thoughts, we'd be despised. Just the same, for the cathartic benefit, some thoughts need to be let loose.

Examples of coming clean:

- **Telling others your religious, political or sexual preferences.** The old adage is to not bring up religion, politics or sex. I agree. You shouldn't. At least not instantaneously. You don't want to introduce yourself by saying, "Hi! My name is Miguel. I'm Buddhist, Republican and gay." That's too much too soon. But if your preferences are important to you (How could they not be?), sooner or later, you'll need to come clean.

- **Being open about what (or even who) you want.** Being afraid to share your ambitions, keeping them secret from the world, makes them less likely to come true. Secrecy is for fantasies.

- **Explaining *why* you truly want what you want.** If you want to go to X college or work for Y corporation because they're prestigious, just admit it. If you're doing it for money, say so, at least to yourself and your confidants. (Maybe not during a job interview.) Declare that you care what you look like. The truth is respected. People may not always agree with you, but they'll respect that you're coming clean.

- **Talking to your parents about your life, telling them about your successes and struggles.** Too many kids live secret lives. Their parents have no clue what they do or think. Whose fault is it? I say both - parent *and* child. Yes, kids need to share more, but proper parenting promotes a healthy "I tell them everything" family culture.

- **Admitting that you don't know.** When someone asks us a question, our proclivity is to answer – even when we're not sure about our answer. Avoid this proclivity! Tell the truth, even if the truth is you don't know.

- **Acknowledge the elephant in the room.** (Those awkward times when there's something everybody is thinking about, but nobody has the guts to say anything about it.) During the 1960 presidential campaign, there were whispers that some Americans wouldn't vote for John F. Kennedy because he was Catholic. Kennedy chose to confront the issue. Less than two months before the election, in a speech to a group of Baptist ministers in Houston, he hushed the whispering. "If this election is decided on the basis that 40 million Americans lost their chance of being president on the day they were baptized, then it is the whole nation that will be the loser."

  After the Dixie Chicks's lead singer, Natalie Maines, publically ripped President George W. Bush during a 2002 concert in London (She was against the Iraq War), the Chicks were scheduled to perform in conservative, red state South Carolina. The concert was boycotted by some, and those who were there sensed the uncomfortable tension - until Maines confronted the elephant. She told the audience that she was going to give them the opportunity to boo her. "One, two, three, go!" she said. Some booed. Others cheered. Then it was over. The elephant had been acknowledged, and the concert continued – comfortably.

- **Confessing that you have a problem.** If you have a problem, whatever it is, first admit it to yourself, then tell someone else about it. Who you tell, of course, is significant. If you're going to bare your soul, you need to confess to the right people. Who are the right people? Trust yourself. You'll know. When you come clean about your problem, you'll feel better and can begin solving it. Boys, especially, have a tough time telling anyone they're struggling with anything, probably because they're afraid it will make them appear less manly. The problem is, men who keep their troubles to themselves will have a harder time resolving them and be more likely to act out in crazy, inappropriate ways.

  Step one of the classic 1939 Alcoholics Anonymous addiction recovery program requires addicts to declare, "I admit that I am powerless over alcohol - that my life has become unmanageable." Key word? *Admit.* Today, nearly all the "Anonymouses" – Narcotics, Cocaine, Overeaters, Debters... recommend coming clean as the first step in healing.

- **Calling people out.** When people are annoying you, it's probably best to endure it - for a while. You don't want to go off the deep end every time someone bugs you. If you do, you'll *always* be in the deep end. But when people persist in upsetting you, you can't ignore it forever. You have to gather your courage and speak out. Even if they continue, you'll feel better because they'll know where you stand.

- **Conceding that you were wrong – and apologizing**. So simple but so hard for so many. Yet, nothing cleans up a social mess as well as a good apology.

## Assignment

What are you hiding? What hasn't been said that needs to be said? Say it! Find the right time, and put it out there. Come clean and you'll feel refreshed!

## Blow the Whistle (Sometimes)

Kids don't call it that. They call it "snitching." Or "tattletaling." Or, back in the day, "squealing" or "ratting." "You rat fink!" Or *way* back, "canary" or "stool pigeon." If words have connotations – and most words do – the connotation of all those is definitely negative. You're just not supposed to "tell on" anyone.

But Upton Sinclair did, and, today, he's considered heroic. So are Bob Woodward, Carl Bernstein and Bill Black. In 2002, Cynthia Cooper of WorldCom, Coleen Rowley of the FBI and Sherron Watkins of Enron were named *Time* magazine's Persons of the Year. The rationale? They snitched. And because they did, the world improved.

In *The Jungle*, Sinclair wrote about the exploitation of the American worker and depicted the filthy conditions in U.S. meat packing factories. Even though the book did not resonate the way Sinclair fully hoped it would (He was probably one of those guys who was never satisfied), his "muckraking" ultimately led to the Food and Drug Administration – which provides Americans with safer food, medicine and medical supplies.

Was Sinclair a hero? I'd say so. When I bite into a cheeseburger, I don't worry about food poisoning. He should get a lot of the credit for that. Was he everybody's hero? Certainly not to the big shots in the meat packing industry. Even trust-busting president Theodore Roosevelt called the left-leaning Sinclair a "crackpot." (If Teddy could have looked into a crystal ball and seen how Sinclair would affect history, would he have felt so negatively about him?)

What if Bob Woodward and Carl Bernstein, the *Washington Post* investigative journalists who broke the Watergate scandal, had sat on their story? How might history have been different if they hadn't told the truth? Because they "tattled," how many politicians have thought twice about cheating? (Admittedly, not enough, but some!) And how many investigative reporters were inspired by them to become today's watchdogs, keeping an eye on would-be con artists?

Cooper, Rowley and Watkins were honored because they blew the whistle on people in sky-high positions, *in their own companies.* Cooper uncovered the phony bookkeeping and cover-ups at WorldCom as did Watkins at Enron. Today, neither company exists. Rowley, an FBI attorney, told FBI Director Robert Mueller that bureau officials ignored her pleas to investigate the September 11th, Al-Qaeda terrorist Zacarias Moussaoui. If they had listened to her, would 911 have ever happened? We'll never know. But, to help prevent it from happening again, we needed to know that her warnings were unheeded.

Throughout our history, from Jacob Riis shocking early 20th century New York City residents with his revealing look at lax police practices and substandard water purification safeguards to William Black divulging the shady dealings at Lehman Brothers, we've depended on morally upright muckrakers and whistle-blowers to uplift our nation.

So why aren't kids being taught to tell the truth, especially when the truth will help society advance? Most kids are eager to make a positive difference, but they don't know how. Whistle-blowing is a concrete way for them to contribute.

Right now, students are only getting it from one side – from their peers, who insist that they "don't tell." Why not balance it out? Why not teach them about real courage by telling them stories about those who "told" and made the world better?

Does this mean kids should always tattle? Of course not. Life is never that simple. There are times to speak up and times to keep quiet. If, one time, the boy who sits next to you borrows your crayons without asking, it's probably best to let him know you'd rather he ask first, but keep it between just the two of you. Nonetheless, if he makes a habit of it, say something. You have to assess how much good (and bad) will come from speaking up or staying silent. Every situation is different.

And don't think for a moment this is a kid issue. It's definitely an adult problem, tragically epitomized by the Penn State tragedy where a revered football coach, the late Joe Paterno, failed to blow the whistle on his assistant coach, Jerry Sandusky, who had been molesting young boys for a decade. Why did Paterno keep quiet? We'll never know for sure, but it's not implausible to speculate that he bought into the "snitches get stitches" culture.

On the other end of the spectrum is WikiLeaks. Founder Julian Assange believes strongly in total transparency. He thinks almost nothing should be concealed. "The goal is justice, the method is transparency," he says. However, there *are* situations when the whistle *should* be swallowed. Again, every case is unique. What kids need to be taught is that, not only is it OK to blow the whistle, it's their *duty* to blow it – but not always. (That's a tough one, right?)

In his *Summa Theologica,* St. Thomas Aquinas wrote about "sins of commission" (doing something we know is wrong) and "sins of omission" (not doing what we know is right). What's disconcerting is that kids don't know (because they're not being taught) that speaking up, raising their voice against injustice, evil and wrong, is right.

We need to change that, starting with lessening the discomfort, embarrassment and awkwardness that accompany blowing the whistle. Whistle-blowing is so often the right thing to do. But, because of the stigma unfairly attached to it, it's a *very* hard thing to do.

## Assignment

Tattle on someone. (Just kidding)

Reflect on a time when you stayed silent. If you had spoken up, would the outcome have been better? Starting now, psychologically prepare for the time when blowing the whistle is necessary and right.

## Seek Sages

When Eric Saperston graduated from San Diego State University, he had no interest in looking for a job or attending graduate school. Instead, he made plans to travel around the United States, following the Grateful Dead.

When he shared his idea with Dr. Tony Smith, his favorite college professor and mentor, Smith challenged him. "Eric," he asked, "what else can you do on this trip that would make it more meaningful? What can you do to provide value, not only to yourself, but to the people you meet along the way?"

Saperston amended his plan. He decided that, while he was traveling, he'd seek counsel from, as he put it, "people at the top of the food chain." He'd invite "some of the most powerful people in the world" out for a cup of coffee and find out from them what it takes to live an extraordinary life.

What he learned he shared on a college lecture tour (My daughter, Kyrra, heard him talk at UCLA) and in a documentary film called *The Journey*. Among the wisdom givers he met were former President Jimmy Carter, congressman and civil rights activist John Lewis, wetsuit innovator Jack O'Neill and his hero, the late Jerry Garcia, the Grateful Dead's lead singer.[26]

What Saperston did is what every student should do: Seek great teachers. Seek mentors. Seek *sages*! They're out there, but they won't magically appear. Students have to aggressively search for them. What would have become of Saperston if not for his first mentor, Smith?

As students mature, they begin to think about college and (too much) the college's reputation. "They have a good business school." Or, "Their engineering department is excellent." What, exactly, does this mean? "Excellent" according to whom? The *U.S. News & World Report*'s dubious college rankings?

They take a hazy look at the institution, paying little attention to the people teaching there. I don't hear students saying, "The reason I'm applying to __________ University is because I want to study under Professor __________."

Why not? Buildings don't teach.

Zoe Lu is an exception. An elite pianist, Zoe left her California home to study music at Ohio's Oberlin College. Once there, despite Oberlin's stellar reputation, she was lukewarm about her instruction. Her primary piano teacher was adequate, but not inspirational.

Then, during the spring break of her freshmen year at Oberlin, she met and connected with Dr. Yu-Jane Yang who did inspire her. Dr. Yang teaches master piano classes in the United States, Taiwan, Singapore and China. She also heads the piano department at Weber State University in Utah. The good news was she wanted Zoe to transfer from Oberlin to Weber State (Utah) and become her full-time apprentice. The bad news was she wanted Zoe to transfer from Oberlin to Weber State and become her full-time apprentice.

Other than Dr. Yang, Zoe knew exactly zero people in Utah. And until she visited Dr. Yang in Ogden, she had never even *been* to Utah. But guess what? She transferred to Weber State.

No, check that. She transferred to *Dr. Yang*, the 2008 Music Teachers National Association "Benjamin Whitten Collegiate Chapter Advisor of the Year" recipient - a teacher recognized as one of the world's foremost educators in piano pedagogy.

Extreme? Maybe. But that's what achievers do. They seek their sages and learn from them, no matter where they are.

When they can't – because they're just kids – they need their parents' help. Schools are resistant about parents requesting teachers, but that shouldn't stop persistent parents. Parents have a responsibility to find out who the best teachers are and then to do whatever it takes to enroll their kids in those teachers' classes.

When our daughter, Kyrra, was five, I heard about a talented kindergarten teacher at a nearby school. There was only one problem. We didn't live within the school's attendance area. So, by rule, Kyrra could not attend Chadbourne Elementary. But there was a loophole. (Find a way, right?) If her *babysitter* lived in the attendance area, Kyrra could enroll. So I called the teacher and asked, "If we can get Kyrra into your school, will you promise to be her teacher?" After she promised, we searched for and found a babysitter, and Kyrra had a wonderful year in kindergarten. Then, every year thereafter until she and her sister completed $8^{th}$ grade, we used our "status" as teachers to get our daughters the best possible teachers.

## Assignment

King Arthur had Merlin. Who's your sage? Make that *sages*. The world is too complicated to have only one mentor. What's your passion? Who can help you master it? If you're a martial artist, who are the best fight trainers? Identify them. Locate them. Meet them. Who are the best trumpet teachers? Who are the best acting instructors? Who are the best vocal coaches? Identify them. Locate them. Meet them.

Meet a master. Make him or her your mentor. Learn and repeat.

## If They Could Do That…

Kids hate history. Occasionally, a few lucky ones will get a Mr. Himler (as I did in 6th grade) who will change their minds. Mr. Himler was one of those rare, charismatic teachers who could reignite turned-off students.

Unfortunately, most kids don't get a Mr. Himler. Instead they get bored. By the time they get to high school, they have little interest in any of the social sciences. For most, history is just a required class, something they have to tolerate.

It's such a shame. Because if history was taught as a story, an "If they could do that…" story, it would be the most motivating subject of all. History is bursting with incredible stories of human achievement. Stories that, if we didn't know were true, would read more like science fiction or fantasy. Stories that *should* make us think, *Wow! If he (or she) could do that, then I certainly should be able to achieve MY goal.*

Consider, for example, the story of the 25 year-old Charles Lindberg's pioneering flight over the Atlantic. The more you learn about it, the more unreal it becomes. I can't tell the story any better than Garrison Keillor did in his May 21, 2007 *Writer's Almanac*:

> *It was on May 21, 1927 that Charles Lindbergh landed his plane in Paris, completing the first solo, nonstop transatlantic flight. He was an airmail pilot, flying between St. Louis and Chicago. It was an incredibly dangerous job at the time. Of the first 40 pilots hired, 31 died in crashes. But in his first four years on the job, Lindbergh flew 7,189 flights,*

*logging almost 2,000 hours in the air, without a single incident.*

*He crossed the Atlantic in a single-engine plane with a large gas tank, which he called the "Spirit of St. Louis." He didn't take a radio, a parachute, or any navigational equipment. He tore unnecessary pages from his flight journal, trimmed the margins from his maps, and only brought five sandwiches for food. The gasoline tank was so heavy that he had trouble getting the plane into the air, and only cleared the telephone lines by 20 feet.*

*From the take-off in New York, he flew north over Connecticut, Rhode Island, and Massachusetts. He reached Nova Scotia and Newfoundland, flew in over the city of St. John's, and then turned toward Ireland. For the next 15 hours, no one would know if he were alive or dead. The humorist Will Rogers wrote in his column, "No attempt at jokes today. A ... slim, tall, bashful, smiling American boy is somewhere over the middle of the Atlantic Ocean, where no lone human being has ever ventured before. ... If he is lost it will be the most universally regretted loss we ever had."*

*After reaching the halfway point of his journey, Lindbergh was exhausted and disoriented. In order to keep himself awake, he flew close enough to the water to feel the spray on his face. He began to hallucinate, and even saw a coastline before his calculations said that he should. When he flew toward it, the coastline vanished.*

*After more than 24 hours, Lindbergh spotted fishing boats on the water. He reached Ireland a few hours later and turned south toward Paris.*

*Lindbergh touched down at 10:24 p.m. on this day in 1927, 33 1/2 hours after he'd taken off. About 150,000 people mobbed the landing strip in Paris, shouting, "Vive Lindbergh!" And overnight, he became one of the most famous men in the world.*

*(Reprinted with permission from The Writer's Almanac, Prairie Home Productions, LLC, to be used and cited as quoted in the permission request.)*

Wow! Right? People all over the world and certainly most educated Americans have heard of Lindbergh and know what he did. But I doubt that more than a tiny percentage have used his story for inspiration. But seriously, If he could do that…

That's how history should be taught.

Here's a small sampling of some incredible "If they could do that…" stories that we all should study:

- The Wright Brothers' first flight (Daring to contradict rather than embrace the "accepted principles of flying" – specifically the wing angles and air pressure data – they succeeded after so many before them had failed.)[27]

- Lewis and Clark (Courage to face the unknown – but not without maximum preparation.)

- Edmond G. Ross (One of the great resistance to peer pressure stories in history. Read the account in JFK's Profiles in Courage.)

- Florence Nightingale (She combined compassion and math – especially statistics – to improve health care.)

## Assignment

Choose someone from history, somebody who did something mind-blowing (and positive), then spend time reading and thinking about it. Work at it! The more you learn, the more real and less fantastical the accomplishment will seem. Plan ways to write your own history. If they could do that…

## How to Overcome Jealousy

Among the multitude of sins that mess up humanity, jealousy is especially dangerous. Not so much in and of itself, but because jealousy ignites destructive behavior.

It's natural to feel jealous. When others have what we want, we're going to envy them. There's no way to fight that. Telling people not to be jealous is like telling them not to be attracted to someone. It won't work. We can't *not* feel something, and we can't *stop* feeling something. Refusing to acknowledge jealousy is a mistake.

The first step in overcoming jealousy is admitting to *yourself* that you're jealous. Don't worry. It's OK to feel what human beings instinctually feel. What's not OK is permitting jealousy to control you and induce spiteful actions against the people you envy.

The second step is to approach the people of whom you're jealous and *tell* them that you're jealous. The best way to do that is to turn it into a compliment.

"I'm so jealous that you sing so well. I wish I had your voice."

"Your hair is gorgeous. I wish mine was that color!"

"I wish I could (dance, run, throw, write, swim…) like you! How did you get so good?"

No one will ever be offended if you approach them this way. Instead, they'll be flattered. Think about it. Turn it around. If someone came up to you and said, "I'm so jealous that you are such a talented teacher, writer (or any of your strengths)," would you be upset or pleased?

So the next time you're jealous, admit it to yourself and then admit it to them. They'll love you for it, and you'll probably make a new friend, one that you obviously admire.

Once that's over, the real benefit kicks in. I don't know exactly why it does, but it does. Maybe it's magic, but as soon as you admit that you're jealous and confess it to the person of whom you're jealous," you won't feel so bad. You'll still wish you had what he or she has, but the angry, bitter, resentful feelings toward that person will dissipate - maybe even vanish. Again, I don't know why this works. It just does.

When my daughter, Kyrra, was about to enter 9th grade, she ran for class vice-president but lost to a girl named Bora. As you would expect, she was hurt and felt resentful. So I suggested she write a letter to Bora, congratulating her on her victory. Initially, she was incredulous. To her credit, though, she grudgingly wrote the letter. Bora, I'm sure, was surprised (but good surprised). Kyrra's jealous feelings subsided, and even though they didn't become close friends, from then on, whenever Kyrra and Bora crossed paths, they were sincerely happy to see each other. There was no animosity between them.

**Note:** Unfortunately, the magic doesn't work with the kind of jealousy attached to romantic love. (When the one you love loves someone else.) It won't assuage your sadness and hurt to tell the girl (or guy) who "got" the person you hoped to get, "I'm so jealous that the man (or woman) I love chose you over me. Congratulations!"

Although it's difficult when your heart is breaking, the only cure for that kind of jealousy is acceptance, time and the faith that there's someone else meant for you.

## Assignment

When someone has what you wish you had – perhaps a talent or skill - tell them! Either in writing or face to face, don't shy away from letting him or her know you're jealous. You'll be pleasantly relieved at the evanescence of the negativity you used to but no longer feel.

## How to Compliment

It started with a note.

An 8th grade basketball player I coached was an all-star in practice but horrible in games. When I talked with him about it, he explained that he wasn't used to referees, scoreboards, formal substitutions and, most of all, crowds. I told him I understood. "Basketball is basketball. The weirdness of a formal game will fade. Give it some time. You'll break through."

Two games later, he did. He scored 14 points, most in the second half, and helped us win. Afterward, I meant to congratulate him but got caught up talking to parents, and he slipped away.

The next day, I scribbled a short note to him on a torn piece of paper. I wrote that I was proud of him. That I knew he could do it. That his basketball future was bright. My teacher's assistant delivered the note, and I didn't think about it again.

Until three years later when my former player had invited some of his high school friends, including my daughter, to hang out at his new house. While he was showing them his room, there, tacked to the wall above his desk – the *only* thing hanging on any of his walls - was a torn piece of paper. My note.

When Kyrra told me this, my first thought was that I should write my notes on better paper. My second thought was that I should write more notes. Compliment notes. And since compliments are so rare and precious – we tend to criticize the bad and ignore the good – there should be some sort of formal instruction on how to give them. Kids should learn how transformative a well-delivered compliment can be for both the receiver *and* the giver. So began the Valentine's

Day Compliment Lesson. It just seems like the right day to teach it. It fits. It also broadens the holiday, allowing platonic love to be shared (Lesson 33).

How to give a compliment in six parts:

**Part I:** Once again, "see the blue" (Lesson 18). Look for people to compliment. Good (even great) people surround us. Yet, unless we're alert, they could walk right by us without us noticing. Then, look for positive features to compliment. They're there. Seek and ye shall find.

**Part II:** Make sure that your compliment is sincere. Instinctively, people will know if you're telling them stuff you don't believe. So don't lie! Find something truthfully good.

**Part III:** Make compliments specific and personal. Compliments like "You're cute and have a nice sense of humor" aren't specific and aren't personal. You could give that compliment to almost anyone. Acid test: You write a compliment for Kristy that accidentally gets delivered to Christine. If Christine reads it and can't tell that it wasn't meant for her, it's a crummy compliment.

Instead, make the compliment special. "You're so adorable! You have the cutest dimple. I love how we laugh at the same stupid stuff. Remember last week when we watched…"

**Part IV:** Naturally, compliments will depend on how well you know the person, but you can compliment just about anyone you meet.

> *Level One:* You don't know the person at all. You can still compliment how a person looks. (Be careful – boys especially. You don't want to come off as crass. But don't worry too much about it. No one really objects when they're told they're attractive.)
>
> You can also compliment people on what they're wearing or what they own. If you like someone's shirt, say so! You may not think that letting people know you like their backpack,

purse, bicycle or car is much of a compliment, but it is. Because, in effect, you're telling them you like their taste, and that makes them feel good. So why keep it to yourself?

*Level Two*: For people you know a little better, you can compliment their accomplishments. "Your oral report today was so good!" "I didn't know you were such an amazing dancer."

Don't make the mistake I once caught myself making during a martial arts class. A police officer was our guest instructor. He had to be at least 50, yet he moved like he was 25. I turned to my friend, Brad, and whispered, "This guy is really good. He moves so gracefully." Then, I thought, *Why am I telling Brad? I should tell the police officer!* So, when I had the chance, I did. When you find yourself talking positively about someone, make sure you let the someone know what you think, too.

*Level Three*: Too often, we don't compliment the people to whom we're closest. Why not? We know them well, so they should be the easiest to praise. So get in the habit of regularly letting them know why we admire them, like them and love them. Compliment their looks, possessions, accomplishments and, since you know so much about it, their character and personality.

**Part V:** Whenever possible, write your compliment. Oral compliments are nice and should be freely offered. But, for the obvious reason that they can be kept (and even hung on a wall), written compliments are better. The less obvious reason is that when you take the time to write it, you can phrase your compliment just right.

Starting the day after Valentine's Day – and every day thereafter until each student in class has had a day - I choose a student to compliment. (By Valentine's Day, we should know each other well enough to be able to write level two or even level three compliments.)

Everyone takes out a nice sheet of paper (which they're required to have). The student we're complimenting chooses a favorite song. Because it creates a contemplative writing mood, I suggest it be a slow song - "the kind you might choose for the first dance at your wedding reception." However, if the "complimentee" insists, it can be an upbeat favorite song. At the song's conclusion, the compliments are collected in a special bag which the complimentee decorated and brought to class for their special day. "When you get home tonight," I instruct, "sit by the fire, put on emotional music, read your compliments and cry."

Compliment days are special days. They put the class in a good mood. Most kids like them a lot. Over the years, many former students have shared that they still have their compliments and read them when they need a self-esteem boost. Yet, if kids only write compliments when it's a class project, they've missed the point. Writing compliments in class is merely practice. In the real world, where complimenting is not formalized or required, it will be up to them to write them on their own.

**Part VI:** If you put time and effort into your compliment, it will show. If you don't, that will show, too. Work hard at writing your compliment. Written words have great power. A well written compliment can lift a mood, maybe even change a life, but not if they look like they were written by someone who's lazy, illiterate or both.

## Assignment

Starting today, form a habit of writing compliments. It will be life changing. Here's why: If you've ever thought writing was boring or unrewarding, it's because you've never written anything meaningful or important (outside of satisfying a required school assignment). To change that, start by working hard - remember all six parts - at writing a compliment to someone special. Make sure it's delivered and read. Do this a few times, and I guarantee that you'll understand and value the power of the written word.

## Stand Out

*Ya gotta believe that I got what it takes*
*To stand out,*
*Above the crowd,*
*Even if I gotta shout out loud.*

- Tevin Campbell
*A Goofy Movie*

It peaks in middle school. Thirteen-year-olds desperately want to fit in. Fortunately, by the time they graduate from high school, they get it. They understand that, although fitting in will always feel important, it's at least as important to stand out. Learning what it takes to stand out in a positive way should be a life-long assignment, and it should begin early. Kids need to know that standing out is good.

Scarcity increases value. Economics 101 says, typically, the less there is of something, the more valuable it is. Both sand and gold are useful, but because you could fit all the gold ever mined inside a high school gymnasium, finding gold is a huge thrill while finding sand is a huge... well, nobody ever looks for sand. If we want our kids to be golden, then they need to be taught to make themselves *scarce.*

Or, to borrow another term from economics, we want kids to develop talents and learn skills that make them *inelastic*. The demand for an elastic product changes – sometimes wildly. When its price drops, the demand for it rises. But when the price rises, the demand for it wanes. Non-necessities – luxury items, expensive gifts, gourmet foods, for example – tend to be elastic.

When the price of an inelastic product rises, the demand for it will fall – but not a whole lot. Necessities - gasoline, medicine, milk and bread, for example – tend to be inelastic. If we can make ourselves inelastic, there will always be a demand for us and our services.

Based on prices and sales, there's a mathematical formula for figuring out if a product or service is elastic or inelastic. When the result is >1, it's said to be elastic. When it's <1, it's inelastic. That's why, I once told a class of 12th grade economics students, "We should all love the <1 symbol. <1 is cool! <1 is inelastic, and inelastic is the goal. Everyone should get a tattoo of <1! If anyone does, I'll give you an A."

I was joking, but one of my students (a C student) took me seriously. A few weeks later, we were in San Francisco on a field trip. At the end of the day, she told me she had a "surprise" for me. She peeled down her lower lip, exposing a "<1" tattoo. I had to give her an A, but I stopped making tattoo promises.

Theoretically, standing out seems like a clear and obvious goal. But, in actuality, it's surprisingly complex. In school, when students stand out for doing well, it's not always a good thing. When one of them earns the highest grade on a test or does more than expected on a project, he or she may be harassed, sometimes playfully and sometimes cruelly. (Which makes "21 Push-ups" a tricky lesson to teach.)

It's an adult world issue, too, especially when there's a perception that there's no incentive to stand out. At a school where I used to teach, the custodians wouldn't do much more than empty the garbage - and if I didn't set the trash can by the door, they wouldn't even do that. They never swept. They never mopped. They had decided that doing anything more than they absolutely had to was a waste of their time. And if one of them did more than he had to? Well, that would only make everyone else look bad. So, just like with kids, there was a ton of peer pressure to *not* stand out.

I don't want my students thinking that way. So I push for and celebrate imaginative thoughts, ideas and behaviors. But only when they're positive and constructive. (History is full of ruthless people who stood out because of their negative and destructive thoughts, ideas and behaviors.)

Thomas Friedman, the *New York Times* columnist, wrote about Harvard labor economist Lawrence Katz's belief that we all must become "artisans:"

> *Everyone today, [Katz] says, needs to think of himself as an 'artisan' — the term used before mass manufacturing to apply to people who made things or provided services with a distinctive touch in which they took personal pride. Everyone today has to be an artisan and bring something extra to their jobs.*
>
> *For instance, says Katz, the baby boomers are aging, which will spawn many health care jobs. Those jobs can be done in a low-skilled way by cheap foreign workers and less-educated Americans or they can be done by skilled labor that is trained to give the elderly a better physical and psychological quality of life. The first will earn McWages [McDonald's equivalent wages]. The second will be in high demand. The same is true for the salesperson who combines passion with a deep knowledge of fashion trends, the photo-store clerk who can teach you new tricks with your digital camera while the machine prints your film, and the pharmacist who doesn't just sell pills but learns to relate to customer health needs in more compassionate and informative ways. They will all do fine.*[28]

Former NBA star turned politician (he was elected mayor of his hometown, Sacramento) Kevin Johnson advised my students to be indispensable. One way to do that is to be an artisan.

Students can be artisans by taking their "job" seriously. If they work hard and excel, they'll stand out. Still, a lot of students work hard and excel. There are thousands and thousands of students who earn A's and score well on college entrance exams. Every school has its valedictorian(s).

But not every school has artisans – students who excel and add something extra. After I told my students that I felt sad because I didn't know them very well, one of them began writing a short fact about herself on the bottom of each homework assignment and test. She told me about her family, her dog, her weekend plans and her favorite books and movies. I looked forward to grading her papers - and I loathe grading papers.

What else can students do to become a positive outlier? I'd offer a list of ideas except for this: When I was in first grade, our teacher led us in an imaginative exercise. She'd play music for us and ask us to close our eyes and allow pictures to form in our minds. Then she'd ask us what we envisioned.

After we listened to some Rimsky-Korsakov, one of my classmates said the music made him think of kids chasing butterflies. My teacher, Sister Marie Marstella, went crazy with praise. She acted as if his answer was the greatest answer ever given to any question. I was jealous.

Two weeks later, we were again listening to classical music. Again, Sister Marstella asked us what we were visualizing. I raised my hand and proudly repeated, "It makes me think about chasing after butterflies."

She gave me a lukewarm, "That's nice" and moved on. I was dumbfounded. Why hadn't she given me the same kind of praise she gave my classmate? Because, I learned way back then, creativity trumps imitation. Kids need to learn how to find new and different ways to stand out.

Whether their goal is college acceptance, a job, a promotion, funding for their project or requited love, kids will discover that competition is the way of the world. So, why would anyone choose you? If there are a hundred applicants competing for one spot, why would anyone select you? What makes you stand out?

**Scarcity footnote, thought and tip:** Whenever there's too much of something, its value diminishes and its appeal regresses. Ever listen to a song too many times? No matter how much you may have liked it, if you hear it too often, you'll grow tired of it.

People can become like that. If we're around too much, we lose our value.

***Modern day high school fable:*** *Girl thinks boy is cute. Boy is attracted to girl. One Monday morning, when the girl is dropped off at school, the boy is there to meet her. The girl is thrilled. As the day wears on, after each class, the boy rushes to the girl's classroom to meet her as she exits and walks her to her next class. The girl is charmed, particularly when after her final period, the boy meets her with a bouquet of violets – her favorite flower.*

*That night, the girl calls her closest girlfriends and tells them everything. They're happy for her.*

*The next morning, the boy is there again. The girl smiles. After each class, he appears. "He's sweet," she thinks.*

*The next day it happens again. And the next day. By Friday, the girl is thinking it's getting a little weird. Then a lot weird, especially when he meets her as she's coming out of the bathroom.*

*By the next week, the girl finds herself hesitating when the bell rings. She's hoping the boy won't be there. When he is, she's frustrated. Then irritated. Then exasperated. Fed up, she finally tells him to go away. She's no longer interested. The relationship that seemed so promising ends.*

Give others space. Give them a break from you. No matter how wonderful we may be, people will grow tired and bored of us if we're always there. Want to increase your value? Develop a sense of when to make yourself scarce. Literally.

## Assignment

Practice being an artisan. Start with schoolwork.

Then think beyond the classroom. Write down what you do that makes you an artisan. What makes you stand out? Unlike your "Three Questions" list, this isn't just a record of your accomplishments. It's a list of what makes you special.

You'll rise above the multitudes if you...

- do "21 push-ups." Again, most people won't do the required 20.
- can write well. Practically no one can write well. (I wrote a book and entitled it *Kids Can't Write!*)
- listen!
- have mastered a constructive skill. Schools educate generalists. We need more specialists.
- are an expert in a subject. Experts in just about everything are needed and sought.
- are well-spoken, especially if you can make an eloquent presentation (Lesson 46).
- are fluent in more than one language.
- are in excellent physical shape. Take a look around. If you're in mint condition, you'll be in a tiny, exclusive club.
- serve in the military. Historically, less than one percent of the United States population does.
- graduate from college. Less than 1% of the world's population has a college degree.
- serve in the Peace Corps. Less Americans have served in the Peace Corps since its 1961 inception (around 200,000), than serve in the smallest branch of the military (the Marines) today.

- volunteer. Most people who can, don't.
- vote. Most people who are eligible, don't.
- pick up trash. Most people don't even think about it, let alone do it.
- work hard. Laziness plagues the planet.
- don't cheat. "But everyone cheats!" No, not everyone.
- are drug and alcohol free. "Everyone does it!" Well, not everyone.
- are faithful. Be exceptional. Remain true.

Study what the majority does and doesn't do. What do most people do that they shouldn't do? Don't be like them. Don't do it! What don't most people do that they should do? Don't be like them. Do it!

# Specialize – and Get Good

Near the conclusion of *The Hurt Locker* (2010 Academy Award - Best Picture, script by Mark Boal) is this compelling scene:[29]

*James looks into his son's unconditionally loving eyes. Something he sees there prompts a confession.*

**James**

You love playing with that, don't you..? You love all your stuffed animals. You love your Mommy, your Daddy. You love your pajamas… You love everything, don't you?

*James playfully spins the mobile. The boy laughs at the whirring color.*

**James**

But you know what buddy? As you get older, some of the things that you love might not seem so special anymore. You know? Like your Jack-in-the-Box.

*The boy touches the Jack-in-the-Box, smiling beautifully.*

**James**

Maybe… you'll realize it's just a piece of tin and a stuffed animal. And the older you get, the fewer things you really love. (beat) By the time you get to my age, maybe it's only one -- or two -- things.

*James pauses. His son continues to giggle and play.*

**James**

With me, I think it's one.

If you've seen the movie, you know that the tragic dilemma was that James, a member of an elite U.S. Army bomb deactivation squad, was passionate about only one thing - deactivating bombs. So, he left his son and wife and returned to his unit in Iraq.

James is right, though. Kids start out loving everything. Like puppies, who'll sniff, nip and chase anything new, they're fascinated by the world. Then, somewhere between sixth and eighth grade when their relationships begin to dominate their lives and supplant their interests, the magic wanes.

If they're lucky, if they're like James, they'll be left with at least one thing – other than their peers – that they love. Is that bad? Is it wrong to be excited about only one thing? What if, like James, their passion is dangerous and takes them away from the people they love? It's complicated, right?

Which is better - know a lot about a little or know a little about a lot? Specialize or generalize?

Orville Redenbacher, the "king of popcorn," had an answer. His maxim? "Learn one thing, but know it better than anyone else." He spent 30 years on a mission to develop the perfect popcorn kernel. I'll bet nobody has ever known more about popcorn than Mr. Redenbacher.

Years ago, on a vacation to Palm Springs, it rained. It's not supposed to rain in Palm Springs, but it did that week. It rained a lot. There's not much to do in Palm Springs when it rains. So when I saw a sign on a shop inviting the public to come in and watch a free film, *The Sex Life of a Date* (date as in the fruit), I was intrigued. I stopped the car.

The film was boring, yet fascinating. It was all about date horticulture. It documented the intricacies involved in growing the tastiest, most succulent dates.

I hate dates.

Still, I thought it was admirable how the guy in the film was so obsessed with dates. He *really* knew dates. He loved dates. You could just tell. He loved learning about them, growing them, selling them and eating them. Orville Redenbacher would have liked the date guy.

"Learn one thing, but know it better than anyone else." Is that the way to go? Just throw everything you have into one obsession? Should we encourage kids to become specialists like Orville and the date guy?

Not at first. Not when they're young. Elementary, middle and early high school students should be generalists. Like diners at an all-you-can-eat buffet, they should be exposed to a wide variety of potential tastes. Kids should try soccer and baseball, scouting and martial arts, swimming and basketball, piano and painting, drama and biking. Ideally, younger students will have inspiring teachers who'll make school so captivating that they'll *want* to study a wide variety of subjects.

The problem is, we take it too far. We expect kids to continue to be good at everything. The student with one A+ and a bunch of C's won't win any academic awards - or admission into a competitive college. (Unless the A+ was in blocking, tackling or dunking.)

Yet history is full of successful people who had a single-subject focus. For Amelia Earhart, it was airplanes. For Martha Graham, it was dance. For the Cousteau family, it was (and is) the ocean.

Sooner or later, like Earhart, Graham and the Cousteaus, kids should choose something and get good at it. Because, if they're good, life will be better. If they're extraordinarily good, all sorts of benefits and special privileges will be heaped upon them. They'll receive special treatment and, fair or not, be able to get away with more than they'd get away with if they weren't good at anything. Being good enables a person to get away with a wide range of behaviors.

Professional athletes, if they can play, can be complete jerks and still be cheered. Great actors and musicians can commit crimes, and their fans will remain loyal. Bosses will look the other way when their best employee messes up.

Fair or not, kids who are good at something get more friends and more respect than those who aren't. Maybe it *is* fair because, except for those born gifted, it requires effort to get good. So encourage kids to specialize in and master something meaningful and beneficial. "Get good at a sport, and you'll have plenty of admirers. If you can act, dance or sing, people will notice and think you're special. Whether it's cars or computers, if you can fix them, you'll be in demand. Get good at creating, building, designing or constructing, and you can contribute to the world. Get good at math, art, business, writing, speaking… Just get good!"

When they do, they'll reap the benefits. They'll find that they've earned themselves a platform from which to speak – and better answers to the three questions (Lesson 3). No matter what they talk about, more people will pay attention to them, accept them and follow them. Their overall confidence will surge. They'll appreciate and value proficiency – which is why all students should be encouraged to specialize in something (preferably something in which they have at least a smidgeon of talent), and then work at it doggedly until they're skilled.

After that, the world can be theirs. They can be jerks, and people will still care about them. And if they're *not* jerks - if they get good and *are* good? If they get good at swimming, they could start a foundation that promotes healthy lifestyles. Michael Phelps did. If they get good at writing computer software, they could start a company, become wealthy and then create a foundation that works to eradicate malaria. Bill Gates did. If they get good at speaking and leading, they could change the world. Abraham Lincoln, FDR and Nelson Mandela did.

And when you're good, people will figure it out. Earl Lloyd taught me that.

One summer afternoon when I was 16, I was playing pick-up basketball at Ann Arbor (Michigan) Pioneer High School when we were told to clear the court. Three of the Detroit Pistons – Erwin

Mueller, Willie Norwood and Jimmy Walker – along with their coach, Earl Lloyd, were there to teach us basketball fundamentals.

I was more interested in playing than listening, but I didn't have a choice. So I took a seat on the bleachers. Earl Lloyd is best known for being the first African-American to play in the NBA. After his playing career ended, he became a coach. Now he was coaching us.

He pointed a finger at Mueller, Norwood and Walker.

"What do they have in common?" he asked.

"They're tall," someone shouted.

"They're all good."

"They hardly ever miss a shot!"

"All true," Lloyd agreed. "But another thing they have in common is they all went to college."

*Here it comes,* I thought, *the standard, cliché, stay-in-school, "get an education," speech.* But then, just as I was about to tune out, Lloyd said something that changed my life:

"It doesn't matter where you go to college. If you're good enough, we'll find you. Look at Willie Norwood over there. He went to Alcorn State University. Does anyone know where Alcorn State is?"

No one did. (It's in Lorman, Mississippi), and that was his point. That if you're good enough, you don't have to play basketball for UCLA, Kentucky or North Carolina. If you're good enough, you can play basketball at Alcorn State, and the pro scouts will find you.

If you're good enough.

If you're good enough, eventually, people will figure it out. They might not figure it out right away, but sooner or later quality gets noticed. I know this to be true with students. At the beginning of the year, some of the shy, quiet ones may get lost in the public school crowd. At first, I may barely even notice them. But, as the school year progresses, if they're good about showing up on time for class each day, taking good notes, producing good homework and completing good projects, I'll figure it out. And I'm not alone. Most people are like me. If you get good, we'll figure it out. We'll notice you, respect you, admire you, maybe even love you.

So, although there are obvious advantages to going to college at Harvard, Stanford or Princeton, in the long run, it won't matter which college you attend. It will only matter if you get good. If you do, like Lloyd said, people will find you.

## Assignment

Make a list of what you do well, even if it's just fairly well. Then make a choice. At which of those would you most like to get *really* good? If you can't come up with anything, dream about what you *wish* you did exceptionally well. Be realistic. If you are, if it's in the realm of possibility, work at it. Use the Daffodil Principle (Lesson 8), and someday you *will* be good.

## The Hard Choice is the Right Choice

Why can't it be the other way around? Why can't the easy choice be the right choice? Why can't donuts be good for you? Why can't sleeping late be a cardio workout? Why can't laziness lead to success?

I like to show my students a scene from Disney's animated film, *Pocahontas.* Pocahontas is at a crossroads in her life. Should she marry and settle down or continue to search and seek adventure?

So she can be alone and think, she paddles her canoe down a river. In due course, she arrives at a fork. One route is tranquil and safe – but dull. It's a metaphor for the easy choice. The other is turbulent and risky – but exhilarating. It's a metaphor for the hard choice. I pause the film and ask my students, "Which path should she take? Which path will she take? Which path would *you* take?"

Whatever the predicament, kids need to know that, when they're faced with a decision, there's almost always going to be a hard choice and an easy choice. One reason why life is so challenging is, way more than it's not, the hard choice is the right choice, and the easy choice is the wrong choice.

Think about it. Should you…

- clean it or leave it?

- help or pretend to be busy?

- save or spend?

- study or slack off?
- push the plate away or have another helping?
- hold your tongue or lash out?
- work for endorphins or resort to an artificial high?
- walk away or fight?
- patiently wait or demand it now?
- get up and exercise or roll over and go back to sleep?
- resist poisonous peer pressure or submit to it?
- stand up for what you believe or feign apathy?
- stay in school or drop out?
- find a way or give up?
- go for your dream or settle for something safer? (Pocahontas, by the way, paddled toward the stretch of the river with the whitewater rapids.)

Even though you know what the right choice is, it's hard to choose it. The easy/wrong choice is excruciatingly tempting.

It's unlikely that anyone will always choose the difficult/right choice. But if you're *aware* that you're making a choice, if you're mindful that one choice is difficult and one choice is easy, that one choice is right and the other choice is wrong, you'll be more likely to choose the difficult/right choice. Not every time, but more often. Educators call it "metacognition" - a scholarly term for "thinking about thinking."

In decision-making, it would work something like this:

*Oh, a text message from Steven wanting help with*

*algebra. Now I have decision to make. I can call him and spend the next 30 minutes (or more) helping him understand the homework. Or, I can ignore his text, and when I see him tomorrow, tell him I went to bed early without checking my phone.*

*The easy choice is to ignore it. I'm so tired! The difficult choice is to call Steven. OK. I'll call him because the difficult choice is the right choice. Besides, if I call him and help him, it will strengthen our relationship, and I'll feel a lot better about myself, too.*

There's a telling story about a personal trainer who prides himself on being up-to-date on the latest fitness methodology. He (condescendingly) asks an old fight trainer why on earth he makes his fighters wake up at 5:00 AM. After all, he argues, fitness research proves that it really doesn't matter when you run. Whether you run at 5:00 AM or 5:00 PM, you'll get the same cardio benefit. So why exhaust your athletes? Why not allow them to sleep longer and get needed rest?

The trainer nods and responds. "That may be true. I don't know much about all that science stuff, but I do know this: The fighter who, at the crack of dawn, can drag his butt out of a warm, comfortable bed is the fighter who, near the end of a fight, will get back up after getting knocked on his ass."

Want to have a happier, better, more successful life? Make the difficult choice more often than the easy choice. Every time you do, you'll be glad you did. Every time you don't, you'll end up regretting it. You'll be disappointed in your weakness.

## Assignment

As you go through a day, keep track of your choices. How many times did you choose the difficult but right choice? How many times did you choose the easy but wrong choice? If you find yourself opting for the easy way too often, own up to your weakness and start strengthening your decision-making muscles.

## How to Earn Respect

*There art two cardinal sins from which all others spring: Impatience and Laziness.*

- Franz Kafka

Getting respect is easy. All you have to do is be born beautiful, talented or rich. And if you're blessed enough to have inherited two or all three of those, jackpot!

It's depressing. It's unfair. But it's true. If you look like a supermodel, if you can run fast, jump high, dance, sing or act well, people will respect you. Ditto if you're wealthy. Donald Trump was paid a million dollars an *hour* to make a speech. Sure, Trump is a real estate wizard. But it didn't hurt that his self-made-millionaire father provided him with a huge head start.

If you're genetically gifted or have affluent ancestors, you're going to have lots of people looking up to you and wanting to be your friend. That's great. Lucky you. You didn't actually *do* anything to earn the respect and admiration heaped upon you, but hey, it must be wonderful to be so fortunate. Appreciate it. Enjoy it.

But what about the rest of us? What about the majority of us in the human race who aren't born beautiful, talented or rich? How do *we* earn respect?

Two words: Work hard. Case in point: Darryl. Big, gangly, awkward Darryl. We met when we were high school sophomores. We both tried out for the junior varsity basketball team. I was surprised when Darryl made it. He was horrible. He could barely dribble. Because of his clumsiness and over-aggressiveness, I was sure he'd foul out in the first quarter. When he shot, I'd feel sorry for the rim. But our coach, Jay Stielstra, kept him, probably because he was big and because he tried.

Darryl hung out with me after every practice and shot and shot and shot. Mostly, he missed and missed and missed. Change, however, is imperceptible at first. No one, including me, noticed that Darryl was getting better. But he was. Two years later, Darryl was better than I was. He became a ferocious rebounder and our most valuable player. When he grabbed a rebound or hit a jump shot (Yes, he developed a solid shot), our fans would howl his nickname, "Duke! Duke! Duke!" Cheers that, two years earlier, had been derisive had become cheers of respect, earned from sweat, not fate.

Darryl earned respect because he got good at something. If you get good at almost anything, you'll get respect. The formula is simple. Want respect? Get good.

The magic of hard work, though, is that even if you *don't* get good, if you work hard, you can still get respect.

Robert wrestled for a high school wrestling team that I helped coach. He was as lousy a wrestler as Darryl was a basketball player. Like Darryl, he worked hard. Unlike Darryl, he didn't have raw talent that, with hard work, would ultimately emerge. Robert was a special needs student who wanted to wrestle even though he got pinned in every match. He wasn't strong. He wasn't athletic. But he tried hard. Near the end of the season, he finally survived a match without being pinned. He still lost, but, for the first time, he made it through all three two-minute periods. The crowd went wild. His teammates acted as if he had just won the state championship. Robert never became a good wrestler. But, because he worked hard, he became a *respected* wrestler.

Hard workers, regardless of the outcome, earn respect. In college, I struggled with a biology class. The pig I dissected looked like roadkill. I studied hard, but I just couldn't get biology. Test after frustrating test, if I got anything above a D, I'd breathe a sigh of relief. After class, I'd trudge upstairs to my professor's office and ask for help.

After the final, I hoped to sneak by with a C. I didn't want a D on my transcript. Imagine my shock and elation when my teacher gave me a B. And I mean that literally. She *gave* me a B that I didn't deserve. The only explanation for it is that she respected me because I tried.

It has been said that girls want to be loved while boys want to be respected. Perhaps that's true, but I'd argue that boys also need to be loved, and girls crave respect. I know it's true that, as girls mature, they're attracted to boys who work hard. (It has got to be some primal female urge to hunt for a man who can provide for her and her offspring – and lazy guys are terrible providers.)

Adolescent infatuation and the "cuteness factor" wear off as women age. Look, girls will always be attracted to cute guys. (I have two daughters.) But cute changes to ugly when the adorable 15-year-old who's always in trouble transforms into the unemployed 25-year-old still living with and off his mother.

Final note to boys: When my daughters were in college, I asked them at separate times, "Other than looks, what's the most attractive guy trait?" I was surprised when they answered in exactly the same way. They both said that the most attractive guy trait is "confidence." (I later discovered that in poll after poll, when girls are asked that question, "confidence" is a recurrent answer. My daughters weren't alone.)

Boys, do you want to impress girls? Then develop confidence. How do you develop it? Work hard.

## Assignment

Want respect? Two words: Work hard. Get into the habit of working hard at everything. We don't have the capacity to "do our best" at everything – there's not enough time for that. But we can work hard at everything we do *while* we're doing it. Start with the little stuff. Work hard at brushing your teeth. Work hard at washing the dishes. Work hard at taking out the trash. Work hard at cooking dinner. Work hard at playing a game of pick-up soccer. Work hard, and respect will come to you.

## It's Whom You're With

Describe the perfect week.

If you're typical, you'll dream about where you'd like to be and what you'd like to do. You'll imagine yourself on a sun-drenched tropical beach, near a serene mountain lake, in the middle of a vibrant city or - if you're six - at a Florida resort, surrounded by Disney theme parks. (Alright, you don't have to be six to love Disney.) You'll envision yourself spending your time sleeping peacefully, eating fabulously and enjoying your favorite activities.

If that's what you did, you fail. You don't get it. But don't worry. I'm going to straighten you out by reminding you about something you intuitively know.

But first, stop stressing about where you are. The grass is always greener, right? I learned that the hard way. I've taught at seven different schools – elementary, junior high and high schools – and I always thought some other school would be better. I've lived in six different places – Ohio, Pennsylvania, Michigan, South Dakota, northern and southern California – and I always thought some other place would be better.

What I learned is that no matter where you are, there's good and there's bad. When it's bad, you think you'd be happier somewhere else. Sometimes that's right, but usually it's not. Because when you move, you'll find the new place has both good and bad.

Second, stop stressing about what you're doing. The opportunity cost will drive you nuts. If you're in Orlando and choose to go to Disney's Epcot, don't spend your time wondering if Disney's Animal Kingdom would have been a better choice. Enjoy Epcot! It's a fascinating theme park. It doesn't have what Animal Kingdom has, but Animal Kingdom doesn't have what Epcot has.

Where you are and what you do is important - but not *that* important. What's most important when designing the perfect week is *whom you're with.* I swear this is true: If you're with the right people, being almost anywhere and doing almost anything can be great. And, if you're with the wrong people (or alone), anyplace or any activity can be unbearable.

Picking up trash – if you're with people you like – can be enjoyable. Sounds crazy, but I know this is true. I've picked up trash in Oakland's Cesar Chavez Park and off the beach in Santa Cruz on California's Coastal Cleanup Day with student volunteers and had a good time. Conversely, spending the day at Disneyland with people you don't enjoy being with can be miserable. (Yes, I've had that experience, too.)

There are people around the world living in horrendous conditions. Their lives appear to be mostly miserable. But people everywhere still have blissful moments - moments spawned by the special *people* in their lives.

Start planning your perfect week by carefully choosing with whom you want to spend it. Whether it's at a beach, mountainside, city or resort won't matter that much. Just pick an interesting place and go. The same applies to what you do. Just do something you think will be fun. Where you are and what you do will be amplified by whom you're with. I'd much rather do something that might seem dull with stimulating people than something that might seem stimulating with dull people.

Back in the real world, stop stressing about which college you're going to attend, where you're going to take your date or what you're going to do with your time. *Start* stressing about whom you're going to spend your time *with*. Be picky. Very picky.

When it comes to planning the perfect week, tell me first about the captivating, inspiring, warm-spirited people with whom you'd most like to spend it. Then I'll know you get it.

## Assignment

A. Describe your perfect day, week, month or year. But be smart and do it in the right order:

1. Decide with whom you'd want to be.
2. Decide where you'd want to be.
3. Decide what you'd like to do.
4. Share your answers with the people you chose!

B. Choose your "cabinet." (The U.S. Constitution allows the president to select a cabinet – a team of experts – to advise him or her.) To whom do you turn when you need advice? With whom would you most want to work on a vital project? Make a list of your cabinet – people with whom you'd most want to (and could realistically) collaborate. Consider people with diverse backgrounds, strengths, talents, expertise and interests. Again, share your answer. Let your cabinet know you chose them.

## The Different Kinds of Love

When my wife told me she was pregnant with our second child, I was concerned. *How*, I wondered, *will I ever love this child as much as I love Kyrra* (our first)? But then, when Kylene was born, I loved her just as much. Not more. Not less. I can't explain why. I just did. I learned that there's enough room in our hearts for infinite platonic love.

Parents understand this. Most mature adults do, too. Children don't. They can't. They can't because they haven't had kids, haven't experienced enough life and haven't been taught this lesson. If they had been, their lives would be so much simpler and happier. I've been around kids long enough to know that platonic love causes major drama:

> "She's supposed to be my best friend, but she's spending the night at her house!"
>
> "I don't know why he invited him to play with us!"
>
> "You're supposed to be our friend. How come you're working in their group?"
>
> "If you let me borrow your crayons, I'll be your best friend."

Jeezo Peezo!

This is why we need to teach kids about love. That it's not all the same. That there are different kinds of love:

**Romantic love:** The kind of love Romeo and Juliet had. The kind of love Mickey and Minnie have. The kind of love the skunk, Pepe Le Pew, has for that cat, Penelope.

I'm no expert on romantic love. Is anybody? But I do have a one-word piece of advice regarding romantic love: *One!* Do everything in your essence to romantically love only one person. More than one romantic love causes relationship implosion.

**Platonic love:** All love that's not romantic (named for the Greek philosopher, Plato, who philosophized about the nature of love).

Platonic love can be divided into several categories:

> **Family love:** The kind of love we have for parents, brothers, sisters, aunts, uncles, grandparents and all the "in-laws." (It should be pointed out to our children that sibling love will usually be the longest-lasting, most enduring love. It's likely that we'll know our brothers and sisters longer than any other human beings. They, more than anyone else, are capable of understanding our intimate personal histories. Therefore, parents should do all they can to ensure that sibling love is nurtured and treasured. The greatest joy in my life is the love that my two daughters have for each other.)
>
> **Pet/Animal love:** The kind of love we have for our dog, cat, horse, guinea pig or whichever animal we fancy. Until we got our puppy, Kihei, I had no idea how powerful this kind of love can be.
>
> **Fantasy love:** The kind of love given to a celebrity (who, most likely, has no idea you exist). Boys feel this for sports stars and hot girls. Girls feel this for hot, successful, famous guys, no matter the profession. Young girls feel it for whomever is the current Justin Timberlake. Young boys feel it for whomever is the current Britney Spears. Fascinatingly, hundreds of thousands of them will be convinced their crush is destined to be theirs

alone. ("He's/She's mine!") Inevitably, all will be anywhere from sad to brokenhearted when reality arrives.

**Friendship love:** The best part about this love is we get to choose whom to love and, as I found out with my daughters, we never run out of platonic love – family or friendship. There's no limit. We never have to say, "I have six friends, and that's it. I'm done. There's no room for more."

Yes, there is! We can have 10 "best" friends and love them all equally. Jealousy should not be a factor when love is platonic. And this is great news because almost all love *is* platonic.

## Assignment

Consider all the people you love and into which category they fit. Understand how ridiculous – and hurtful - it can be to rank platonic relationships.

# The Conflict Between Ambition and Relationships

Relationships, above all else, should be treasured. They are - by far - the most important parts of our lives. They transcend health, trump money and surpass passions. Our relationships set the tone for the quality of our lives. When they're good, they make everything better. When they're bad, nothing feels right.

And of all the kinds of relationships, romantic is the most potent. Especially in its early stages, a romantic relationship is a formidable force.

Nothing feels better than romantic love. We crave it. Without it, there's a hole in our hearts. It, more than anything, makes life worth living.

Yet it can destroy us. Like any other powerful force, romantic love can be very good or very bad. The good is obvious. The bad is not. Because romantic love is so powerful, left unchecked, it can dominate us. It can transform the wisest person into a fool, drive the sanest person crazy. When moving toward romantic love, proceed with caution!

Because once it has its hooks in, there's no such thing as reasonable. That's why it's essential that we teach kids about the conflict between ambition and relationships – especially romantic relationships – *before* they're in one. It might help. Might. I'm not promising anything - such is the power of love.

Most kids have big plans. No child I know dreams small. They all want extraordinary lives. Sadly, what often derails them is their romantic relationships. That's because they haven't learned how to manage the conflict between ambition and relationships.

They need to be taught that, when you're young, before you're married, before you have kids, before you have major responsibilities – ambition has to win the fight. As critical as romance is, it can't be allowed to prevail. If it does, not only will it shatter aspirations, it will eventually destroy itself.

Typical of what happens, a girl has a goal. Say to become a pediatrician. She plans to attend medical school. Then she meets the boy and everything changes. Because she's so in love, studying doesn't seem quite as important. Besides, applying to medical school means applying *everywhere.* If the boy works in California and NYU accepts her, separation is inevitable.

So she settles for nursing school. It wasn't her first choice, but getting into it is easier. It doesn't take as long to complete the coursework. There will be no separation. Nurses can work almost anywhere.

After she denies her doctor dreams, for a time (Five years? Ten years?), she's happy. Eventually, though, the honeymoon wears off. She starts to wonder what she has given up for the guy. When the relationship experiences its inevitable challenges, resentment hacks away at it.

When you're young, ambition must supersede romantic relationships for two reasons. First, choosing to postpone immediate relationship gratification is the ultimate relationship test. If it's real, if it's meant to last, a strong, disciplined relationship will endure separation and withstand the test of time.

Second, you're not going to be young forever. The freedom to chase ambition is fleeting. Once your youth has passed, once you have people depending on you, those relationships – the most important part of your life – take precedent.

How do you teach this? You play the "What will you do if..." game. I used to play it with my martial arts students and, of course, with my own kids. I'd ask them:

- On a field trip, what will you do if you get lost or

separated from your group? (You go inside a public place, find someone who works there and explain your predicament.)

- What will you do if a man tries to drag you into his car? (You punch and kick and scream and, in your loudest voice, you shout, "FIRE!")

- What will you do if your house is on fire? (Go home today and make a plan. Mentally map several escape routes, including at least one from any upstairs floor.)

- What will you do if you have the chance to cheat on an assignment or test – and get away with it? (Tell yourself before this opportunity presents itself that you're not going to give in to cheating. Then, when the time comes – and it will – stay strong.)

- What will you do if you fall in love, and you're tempted to give up your dream in order to be with that person? (Don't do it!)

Will playing the game help?
It might.

## Assignment

Play the "What will you do if..." game. Prepare in advance. Respect romantic love's power. Be ready for it. Don't be caught off guard.

## How to Find a Sweetheart

Kids care about romantic love. Don't delude yourself by thinking they don't. The pull of passion is powerful. Try teaching 17-year-olds about the balance of government power when the balance in their own lives has been derailed by ardor. Not that it's just a teenage phenomenon. Singles, sixteen to sixty, are searching, and that's a problem.

*The Alchemist*, published in 1988 by Brazilian writer Paulo Coelho, has sold over 65 million copies and is already considered one of the greatest novels ever – a modern classic. The story's main character, Santiago, is tempted to sacrifice the life he knows he was destined to live and "settle" for romantic love. He's advised to resist this potent, overwhelming urge.

"No heart has ever suffered when it goes in search of its dreams," Coelho wrote. When you're working hard on your purpose and *not* looking for romantic love – you'll end up finding it. Or, more accurately, it will find you.[30]

Remember, that's exactly how I "found" *my* wife. I promised myself that I'd finish college in California, the place of my dreams. I took that summer job in Malibu at a camp for blind and deaf children (my great purpose). The last thing on my mind was finding a wife. But guess who else was at Camp Bloomfield, pursuing *her* great purpose?

One of my students sent me the "Holstee Manifesto." (Holstee is a company that manufactures products made from recycled materials.) Part of the manifesto declares, "If you are looking for the love of your life, stop; they will be waiting for you when you start doing things you love."[31]

Isn't that Paulo Coelho's message? Wasn't that part of Patanjali's "Great Purpose" message (Lesson 8 assignment)? Isn't this the message kids need to heed when they're sad because they haven't found a sweetheart? And most kids, at some time, will have the romance blues.

When they do, tell them to focus on living well. "Work hard, learn, develop, improve, create, serve. Be the best 'you' you can be. Stop looking for a lover and start searching for a cause. When you find it, lose yourself in it. Improve the world. While you're doing that, out of nowhere, love will magically appear."

## Assignment

Write down your ideal future. What's your big dream? If money was not an issue, where do you see yourself living? How do you see yourself spending your days? Toward what are you powerfully, relentlessly drawn? Put your time and effort into that, and that's when you'll find your love.

# The Inspirational People List

I need my inspirational list for reassurance. Especially today, in a world full of frustrations, who doesn't? My Nicaraguan *amigo*, Chamba, and I were lamenting that, the older we get, the more cynical we become regarding "heroes." Yet, kids need a list, too. Tune into the media. It's dominated by disappointing, disheartening people. They're on fictional television, reality television and they dominate the news. Ignorant, rude, lazy lowlifes are everywhere. Evil people lurk.

It takes effort to fight cynicism, but you can. Instead of focusing on the world's riff raff, immerse in the best of humanity, past and present (Lesson 11). Compile a list of captivating people (with pictures) who inspire you. Start by formulating an initial list. Then, as the years pass, add names. In the sad case that it's necessary, remove names. The list should be fluid - a living document. At first, choose anybody you want, just be able to justify each choice with a description of the person and why he or she was chosen. Later, focus on finding inspiring people who excel in your area(s) of interest - people from whom you can major in success. Student-athletes, check out academic All-Americans. Aspiring entrepreneurs, study the story of the person(s) behind the successful startup. Moms and dads, read moving stories about excellent parents in *Chicken Soup for the Parent's Soul.*

Having an Inspirational People List is an asset. It's a surefire conversation starter. Every person on the list is a story waiting to be told. It gets us thinking about the kind of people we admire (which tells us a lot about ourselves). And it's a powerful document to take to an interview for two reasons. First, if an interviewer is also inspired by someone on the interviewee's list, an instant bond is formed. "Hey! I'm inspired by Cesar Chavez, too. Don't you admire how understated his charisma and power was?" Second, if there is someone on the interviewee's list who the interviewer *isn't* familiar with, the candidate can use this as an opportunity to share. Either way, it's impressive - especially when it's a well-thought-out, eclectic list. An inspirational people list can include people from the past or present. They can be renowned or almost unknown. I've seen lists that include both Nobel Peace Prize winners and grandparents. I prefer lists that aren't loaded with obvious, iconic choices – Lincoln, Gandhi, MLK – but who can argue with obvious, iconic choices?

After you have a list, try to meet the people on it. When you do, it will be an unforgettable moment. Obviously, some people will be more difficult to meet than others, and, of course, some will be impossible to meet. Still, you can continue to learn from them. Search their names. Study their behaviors. Many of the people on my list have social media accounts. Follow them. Immerse yourself in their lives. It will make you feel better about living.

As an example, here's my **Inspirational People List:**

**Alicia Keys:** Gifted singer and lyricist. Classically trained while growing up in the gritty Hell's Kitchen area of Manhattan, she plays seven instruments and writes and performs music that entertains, uplifts and motivates.

**Arthur Ashe:** My all-time favorite athlete. Was way more than a jock. More like a saint.

**Bob Geldof:** In 1984, formed Band Aid to raise funds for African famine victims. Raised incredible amounts of money and started a trend – benefit concerts - that significantly improved the lives of millions of people, worldwide.

**Bob Marley:** Not a perfect man, but wrote beautiful love ballads and incredible social anthems.

**Branch Rickey & Jackie Robinson:** Did as much for integration as the Civil Rights Act of 1964. Both courageous trailblazers.

**Cesar Chavez:** Two words: *la causa.*

**Chamba Acosta & Minako Close:** World Citizens couple builds schools, creates curriculum, organizes communities and spreads hope in El Salvador and Nicaragua. (Close friends, they inspire me to keep returning to Central America.)

**Chris Paul:** Legendary point guard. Legendary *person.*

**Chris Rock:** High school dropout, yet his sharp, roguish, inimitable social commentary is funny, fresh, bold and blunt.

**Cory Booker:** Optimistic, committed U.S. senator from New Jersey. Future president? (We follow each *other* on Twitter. Well, I mostly follow him.)

**Dave Dravecky:** Former San Francisco Giants pitcher. Lost his arm to cancer, but not without an unforgettable fight.

**Desmond Tutu:** Almost God-like human rights activist. Where's America's Tutu?

**Dewey Bozella:** Wrongly convicted of murder, spent 26 years in prison. Used boxing as therapy. After his conviction was finally overturned, emerged from the Sing Sing Correctional Facility without bitterness.

**Don Reed:** His tireless effort to increase funding for stem cell research is an example of what can be accomplished by one person with an emotional attachment to a cause. (Good friend. One of my mentor teachers.)

**Dr. Barry Marshall:** Initially dismissed by the medical establishment as a roguish outsider, the Australian physician/researcher risked his health, stared down the naysayers and proved that stomach ulcers could be cured with antibiotics.

**Dr. Mihaly Csikszentmihalyi:** Author of *Flow*. Pioneering "positive" psychologist. Teaches us how to be happy.

**Ed Klum:** My high school basketball coach. Great coach and man. Modeled for me that working successfully with people means treating them *differently* – according to what each individual needs. I should have appreciated him more when I was 16.

**Enrique Camarena:** Gave his life fighting the Mexican drug lords. Red Ribbon Week is in his honor. He's gone, but the fight goes on... (I was able to meet his widow and son, Enrique Jr.)

**Father Damien:** Spent his life teaching and comforting people with leprosy (Hansen's disease) in Molokai, Hawaii – even though it cost him the ultimate price.

**Fawzia Koofi:** Afghan Parliament member and women's rights activist. Perhaps the most courageous politician in the world. Perhaps the most courageous politician ever.

**Frank Ryan:** My first favorite athlete. Cleveland Browns championship QB was smart and good – a real life, modern day Renaissance man. (Got his autograph when I was nine!)

**Freddie Roach:** Probably knows as much about his craft – training boxers – as any person alive. Overcoming Parkinson's disease. (Got to meet him and work out in his gym!)

**Gary Becker:** Innovative Princeton/University of Chicago trained economist who radically changed the field of economics, making it applicable to social issues. Sacrificed mainstream acceptance but laughed last when awarded the Nobel Prize.

**Horace Mann:** Responsible for the concept of free, public, universal education. Two centuries ahead of his time, Mann believed in educating children of all classes together so they could have a common learning experience – and equal access to success.

**Huey Long:** The politician politicians should aspire to be. Immediately after being mortally wounded by an assassin's bullet, his last words were "God, don't let me die. I have so much left to do."

**Jacqueline Novogratz:** Author of *The Blue Sweater*, a blueprint for how to improve the world.

**Jeff Van Gundy:** Left Yale to pursue his passion – basketball. Proved the doubters wrong.

**Jill Kinmont Boothe:** On her way to the Olympics, paralyzed in a skiing accident. Still became a life-changing teacher and artist.

**Jimmy Fallon:** Brilliant, talented, yet unpretentious comedian. Master of smart humor. All-around good guy.

**John Baker:** Albuquerque, New Mexico track star and P.E. teacher. Died way before his time, but not before leaving a legacy and a school named in his honor.

**Jon Miller:** San Francisco Giants play-by-play baseball announcer. The best there is at what he does.

**Laura and Lisa Ling:** For the kind of people – and sisters - they are. Smart, brave, driven. Their North Korea story is one of the best sibling love stories ever.

**Lyndsey Haraguchi-Nakayama:** With her MBA education she chose to live and work on her family's six generation taro farm on Kauai, Hawaii. The Haraguchi work ethic is admirable – and motivating. (Met her on a Hawaii vacation.)

**Maggie Doyne:** At 18, she skipped college and founded an orphanage in Nepal. She began her great purpose at 18!

**Malala Yousafzai:** Subtitle of her autobiography – "The Girl Who Stood Up for Education and Was Shot by the Taliban."

**Marisol Valles:** At 20, with a baby, she took the job of police chief at a town in Mexico's Juarez Valley, an extraordinarily hazardous region infested with drug cartels. That she was driven out by death threats and emigrated to the United States does not detract from her bravery. It only strengthened others' resolve to fight the cartels.

**Matt Damon:** Intelligent actor with great values. Uses his fame and success as a platform to improve the world.

**Muhammad Yunus:** Nobel Prize winner who introduced the world to the power and magic of microfinance.

**Pat Conroy:** My favorite writer. His book, *The Water is Wide*, convinced me to become a teacher. (A huge thrill when I got to talk to him at a SF Bay Area book signing event.)

**Rell Sunn:** The "Queen of Makaha" lived a nearly perfect, "#2 Life." She surfed and served her community right to the end of her way-too-brief life. Her legacy will live forever, especially on the west coast of Oahu, Hawaii. (Lesson 50)

**Sara Sidner:** Courageous CNN correspondent. Willing to go anywhere, enter the heart of the action and ask the tough questions.

**Shaka Smart:** College basketball coach who is much more than a college basketball coach. I love and admire his intense devotion to his players, program and community.

**Steven Chu:** Nobel winning physicist, brilliant former member of Obama's cabinet (Secretary of Energy).

**Steven Levitt and Stephen Dubner:** The "Freakonomics" guys, who would probably be surprised that they appear here. They do because they ask questions others are afraid to ask and explore possibilities that others don't see. They encourage us to be willing to say, "I don't know."

**Terry Fox:** Cancer research activist. Ran across Canada. Raised millions before succumbing.

**Theodore Roosevelt:** My favorite president. After a sickly childhood, became a badass president who got things done.

**Tom Peters:** Management consultant/author. The guy knows what's important for business success. What he says goes for schools, too.

**Tommy Douglas:** "Greatest Canadian." Fought for and got healthcare for all.

**Tony Robbins:** Overcame problematic childhood. Did not attend college. Became a life-changing teacher, coach, writer and speaker.

**My students:** Not all of them. Some of them. The special ones. The ones who helped me get through tough times. The ones who inspired me to get better.

**My wife, Norma:** Forever the most important person in my life.

**My daughters, Kyrra and Kylene:** My inspiration. My everything.

## Assignment

Make your list. For the rest of your life, add to it. When possible, strive to make real life connections and have at least one true encounter. When you need inspiration, look at your list and be reminded that the world is filled with spectacular people.

# The Ripple Effect

*In our every deliberation, we must consider the impact of our decisions on the next seven generations.*
- The Great Law of Iroquois Confederacy

When the framers of the United States Constitution were majoring in success (Lesson 15) and studying the best government thoughts, ideas and documents, they studied the Iroquois. (The *only* Native Americans they studied.) Considering the impact of their actions on the next seven generations is mind-blowing. Today, it's rare when governments or individuals think about the *next* generation, let alone 150+ years into the future.

When I ask my high school students whether or not they want to have kids, nearly all of them say they do. Then I'll ask, "Have you ever thought about them? What will they be like? What will their world be like?" Most have. It's natural. If it weren't, we would have become extinct millenniums ago.

"What do you think you'll have first, a boy or a girl? What do you *want* first?" I'm not encouraging them to have kids now. Just the opposite. I want them thinking that what they do today will affect how their kids will be tomorrow. That everything they do shapes not only their future, but their yet-to-be-born children and grandchildren's futures, too. And if we're talking seven generations, that includes their great, great, great, great, great grandchildren, too – descendants who will be born long after they die. It's a strange thought, right?

When James Madison wrote the Constitution, the Iroquois

influence was applied right there in the Preamble:

> *We the People of the United States, in Order to form a more perfect Union, establish Justice, insure domestic Tranquility, provide for the common defence, promote the general Welfare, and secure the Blessings of Liberty to ourselves and* **our Posterity**, *do ordain and establish this Constitution for the United States of America.*

The framers weren't thinking only about themselves. They were writing a constitution for future generations - *our posterity*. Today's generation hasn't done a very good job of thinking like that. But, hopefully, we can get our kids thinking like that. We want them thinking big picture. We want children to take care of the planet and push for legislation that will, for generations yet to come, preserve, protect and improve the world.

But it will be easier for them to relate to the small picture. Their personal picture. So, it's realistic to expect kids to understand that what they do will affect their children, grandchildren and who knows how many generations beyond them. If they choose to drink, smoke and/or do drugs, there's going to be an effect (possibly even a physical effect) on their future families.

We need to teach kids that it's selfish to think that their decisions only impact them, because they don't. No decisions do. They have a ripple effect. Whether they decide to be lazy or industrious, whether they're around to see the effect or not, the ripple will be felt.

When Steve Ells started Chipotle, his original goal was to earn enough cash to open a fancy, high-end destination restaurant.[32] [33] He ended up with over 1,400 far-from-high-end fast-food locations throughout the United States, Canada, England and France that are nothing like the sophisticated restaurant he pictured himself owning and operating. Yet the ripple effect of Ells' endeavors is immense: Over 37,000 employees (jobs!), millions of tax dollars generated and an environmentally friendly business plan that supports and promotes healthy, sustainable agriculture practices and animal husbandry. Ells's business model is bound to ripple into other food industry business models.

When something successful starts, the positive ripple doesn't stop. Ells's vision for how his restaurants should be designed will have a lasting effect on Chipotle employees, customers and communities. Additionally, he became a role model for entrepreneurs while changing the way many people think about restaurant food. Ells made people care about how farm animals are treated, how crops are grown and from where and whom they're bought. He impacted the world in ways he couldn't have imagined when he opened the first Chipotle in a former ice cream parlor in Denver, Colorado.

When Welsh rock musician Bob Geldof saw a documentary about famine in Africa, he gathered British pop stars together and formed a group he named "Band Aid." Band Aid recorded a Christmas anthem called "Do They Know It's Christmas?" Proceeds earned from the record's sales were spent on famine relief. Next, Geldof organized Live Aid, a global philanthropic concert. All ticket sales would, again, support his cause.[34] The ripple? Today, decades after Geldof's original, innovative idea, concerts for causes are commonplace.

When Blake Mycoskie decided to create TOMS (shoes for *tomorrow*), a for-profit business that would fund shoes for many of the millions of children around the world who cannot afford them, investors were perplexed. Mycoskie's business plan was to *give away* a pair of shoes for every pair sold. There was no precedent for a for-profit company doing what was considered non-profit work. TOMS set the precedent. Its ripple is the growing trend for for-profit companies to have a strong social mission.[35]

Kids need to know that if they work hard and have a vision like Ells, Geldof and Mycoskie, odds are that the ripple they originate will be positive and beneficial, not only to themselves and to the world, but to their children and children's children. On the other hand, if they're lazy and don't look beyond today, odds are that the ripple they start will be negative and destructive. It's going to break their hearts if, someday, their kids see an advertisement for Disneyland and this exchange has to take place:

> "Daddy, Mommy, can we go to Disneyland, someday? It looks so fun!"
>
> "I'm sorry, Honey. We can't afford it."

Especially if Daddy and Mommy can't afford it because they know in their hearts that they were playing around, constantly pursuing pleasure, living only in *their* moment when they should have been working hard and preparing for a future that included saying "yes" to Disneyland.

We should try almost anything to motivate. This includes asking kids to stop believing that what they do (and don't do) affects only them. Kids are powerful! The repercussions of their actions are powerful. Remind them that the ripple of their words and actions can be powerfully positive – or destructively negative.

## Assignment

Dream, think and plan for the future. The far-off future. What will your children and grandchildren be like? What will *their* children and grandchildren be like? How will what you're doing now, today, affect them? What will their world be like? How will what you're doing today affect it?

## There's No Such Thing as "Happily Ever After"

*For over a thousand years Roman conquerors returning from the wars enjoyed the honor of triumph, a tumultuous parade. In the procession came trumpeters, musicians and strange animals from conquered territories, together with carts laden with treasure and captured armaments. The conquerors rode in a triumphal chariot, the dazed prisoners walking in chains before him. Sometimes his children robed in white stood with him in the chariot or rode the trace horses. A slave stood behind the conqueror holding a golden crown and whispering in his ear a warning: that all glory is fleeting.*

- General George S. Patton Jr.

Immediately after the United States of America won the Revolutionary War, its new citizens celebrated. And with great reason. It was one of history's most implausible upset victories. A country was formed. Its leaders, with their grand vision of what a nation should and could be, were united. The future was full of promise. Only bright days were ahead...

Until the War of 1812 when the happy times vanished. The fledgling republic was confronted with a perilous new challenge – which it met. The sunshine returned. Until, 30 years later when the Mexican-American War darkened the mood and stressed the country. A decade later, the Civil War was brewing...

Real life is no fairy tale. There is no such thing as happily ever after. Maybe Disney should make a movie in which kids get to see Cinderella and Prince Charming arguing over how to discipline their children or who should fire the castle's conniving servant.

Well, maybe not. Let kids have their fantasies. Sooner or later though (When they're 12?), they need to hear "the talk." No, not that one. The one in which we explain to them that there's no happy without sad. That there's no victory without defeat. That *easy = boring.*

The talk is when we reveal to kids one of life's brutal truths – that there will never be a time when they're "there." That every test passed should be celebrated but never exalted.

Nobody ever taught this to me. I wish they had because I thought that, after I graduated from high school, there'd be a happily ever after. There wasn't. So it had to be after college, right? Or after I got married. Or had kids. Or got the job. Or bought the house. Or reached the goal…

Although each success felt good, the good always wore off. Another test awaited. The no-stress life doesn't exist. But that's OK. We need a little stress.

Kids need to know that, ideally, the trend of their lives should be an upward slope. "Keep achieving. Continually improve." But, like the graph of even the best performing stock, a realistic ideal inevitably includes dips and corrections. Most likely, each peak will be followed by some sort of valley.

The great American poet, Robert Frost, understood that the best times – the gold – won't stay:

> *Nature's first green is gold,*
> *Her hardest hue to hold.*
> *Her early leaf's a flower;*
> *But only so an hour.*
> *Then leaf subsides to leaf.*
> *So Eden sank to grief,*
> *So dawn goes down to day.*

*Nothing gold can stay.*

But you know what? The worst times – the fool's gold – won't stay either. Kids need to know that, too.

It's an odd dichotomy: The good times are bad in a "glass half empty" kind of way. Think about it. When you're having an awesome moment, you know that, in the blink of an eye, it's going to be history. So enjoy it. As Patton said of glory, it's fleeting.

Conversely, the bad times are good in a "glass half full" kind of way. When we're at rock bottom, the only way to go is up. Mountaintops aren't far away.

## Assignment

Think and write about the three best and three worst days of your life. Realize that experiencing those extreme Mt. Everest/Death Valley days, along with the daily (even hourly) routine ups and downs, are proof that you're living - *really* living. The no-highs, no-lows, flat------line life may be painless, but it's joyless, too.

## Manhood Training

Ninety-three percent of American prisoners are male.[36] Nearly 60 percent of the bachelor degrees awarded in the United States are earned by females.[37] Nearly one in four women in the United States reports experiencing violence by a current or former spouse or boyfriend at some point in her life. In the United States, the cause of death of at least three women *a day* is relationship abuse.[38] It's not only an American problem. The World Health Organization interviewed nearly 25,000 women at 15 sites in 10 countries and found that rates of partner violence ranged from 15 percent in Yokohama, Japan to 71 percent in rural Ethiopia.[39] Worldwide, one of every six women is a victim of domestic violence.[40] In Afghanistan, in an attempt to escape domestic violence, women and girls set themselves on fire.[41]

What's going on? Why are so many men so messed up? Is there anything we can we do about it? What can we do to produce more than a few good men?

I don't have sons. I have two daughters. That was my initial motivation to develop what has turned into an intense, ongoing interest in "manhood training."

I stole that term from Alex Haley's *Roots*. In 18th century Gambia (Africa's west coast), when boys hit puberty, they were taken from their mothers, grandmothers and sisters and carried off to a special, boys-only encampment. There, they were taught by men how to be men. Good men. Upstanding men. Respected men.

Men like Atticus Finch, the hero of *To Kill a Mockingbird*,

Harper Lee's Pulitzer Prize-winning novel and, according to a 2012 National Public Radio poll, the third favorite teen novel of all time[42] - after the *Harry Potter* and *The Hunger Games* series. When I taught that book, I used Atticus as an example of the kind of man my high school boys should aspire to be. But before we looked at what makes him so worthy of emulation, I gave my sophomore girls an assignment: "Other than good looks, what makes someone romantically desirable? Given a choice of 50 partners, all of whom are equally good-looking, what qualities would make one of them stand out?"

The next day the girls wanted to share their answers, but I wouldn't let them. I had to give the boys their assignment. They thought I was going to give them the same assignment I had given to the girls. They were wrong.

"Boys," I said, "before we hear what the girls consider attractive guy traits, try to predict what they said. Make a list of the qualities *you* think the girls are attracted to."

Initially, not only were they reluctant, they thought it was stupid. I disagreed. I told them that it only made sense to learn what qualities - beyond physical attractiveness - a future partner might seek. That, frequently, in *Men's Health* (a magazine to which every guy should subscribe!), women wrote about this sort of thing. I insisted that it makes good sense for a man to learn what a potential romantic partner might find attractive *and* repelling.

One of those 16-year-old boys wasn't buying it.

"This is so dumb, Mr. Richards. I feel like a fool doing this," he insisted.

"OK," I shot back. "Tell me. Do you have a girlfriend?"

"No."

"Well, maybe this is why! You need this lesson. What do *you* think the girls said? What do they find attractive?"

"I don't know."

"Besides good looks, what do girls look for?"

"I don't know. I haven't thought about it."

"Think about it now."

"Uh… big balls?"

Astonished, the girls erupted with revulsion. "Ewww! Gross! Mr. Richards!"

"See," I said. "This is why you don't have a girlfriend. You seriously need this lesson!"

He's not the only one. There's a reason romantic comedies are popular with women. The men in those movies (ironically, not always the actors playing them) are good guys. Maybe not perfect guys. But good guys. The kind of guys the women in the audience wish they had. Men might want to pay attention to what those guys say and do.

So, what did my sophomore girls say appealed to them?

"Funny."

"Open-minded."

"Motivated. I don't like lazy boys, even if they're cute."

"Honest."

"Compassionate."

"He has to be interesting. I hate boring guys."

"Committed."

"Determined."

The most entertaining answer came from Jenna: "I don't know. Whipped?" (Translation: a guy who would take orders and submit to her – completely.)

So, other than English teachers pointing out male role models in classic books, romantic comedy screenwriters and women straight up telling guys what qualities are attractive, who's conducting manhood training in 21st century America? It ought to concern everyone that the answer is *nobody* (at least formally), even if you aren't a dad with daughters.

The United States used to have a form of formal manhood training. When there was a draft, all healthy men were required to serve in the military. There, surrounded by older, mentor-type men, a lot of boys grew up. Not that it was a perfect "school." The mission of the armed forces has never been "to create good guys." Still, when 18-year-olds from Philadelphia to Portland, representing diverse religions, ethnicities and income brackets were forced to work together, a lot of positive socialization occurred. If a guy acted like an idiot, he was swiftly set straight.

I observed and experienced this. Even though I entered the Air Force a decade after the draft was abolished, I saw lots of formal and informal manhood training. Once, as my squadron's executive officer, I had to visit a sergeant's repugnant on-base house. The guy and his young family were living in filth. In a polite but "get your act together or else" way, I had to order him to put his house in order. How did I find out about his pigsty? His disgusted peers had reported him.

I was mentored in the military. Formally, by a series of commanding officers and informally by lots of older, wiser guys. Once, while playing pick-up basketball, this jerk was trying to hurry us off the court because his team had volleyball practice.

"Get off our court!" he squawked.

Livid, I started a fight. (I wasn't yet 25. Guys' brains and decision-making skills aren't fully formed until they're 25.) It was quickly broken up, but that made me fume even more. I threatened the guy and told him that we should "take it outside." (So mature, right?) That's when an older, non-commissioned officer set me straight. "Lieutenant, let it go. You have nothing to prove. Just go home." Calmed by his calm, I did. If he hadn't been around, if I had gone after the guy, I would have ended up in all kinds of trouble.

Where do young, angry jerks (like I was) who aren't in the military get that kind of mentoring? (Less than half a percent of Americans – some of them women - are on active duty.) Where do today's boys get their mentoring? Beer commercials? (Pathetically, in some cases, yes.)

Ideally, of course, a boy's mentor should be his father. But guess what? Worldwide, a quarter to a third of households are headed by a single parent. In the United States, more than a third of families are single-parent families (highest in the developed world), and over 80% of those single parents are women.[43] Too frequently, there *isn't* a father!

And even if a father exists, it doesn't mean a father is present. Having a lousy father is worse than having no father. There is a huge difference between being a father and contributing sperm. Our world has a shortage of fathers and a surplus of guys motivated only by their biological urge to reproduce. Having a technical father in the home isn't the same as having a real father in the home.

So what about all those boys who don't have good fathers at home? What about them? Who teaches them? Scoutmasters? Maybe. But somebody has to push boys into scouting and, again, just because you're in scouting, doesn't mean it's automatically good. So much depends on the quality of the scoutmaster(s), and that's a crapshoot.

The same is true with athletics. If a boy wins the coaching lottery and ends up with an Eric Taylor from the fictional (unfortunately) television series about high school football in Texas, *Friday Night Lights* (best TV program ever!), he's set. He's going to learn what it takes to be a man. But how many Eric Taylors are there in real life?

What about school? Should we add "manhood training" to the curriculum? I wish. After all, since boys have to be in school anyway, why not take advantage of it? While they're there, teach them how to be good men. Why blow the chance to impact them before they reach that limbo age (15 – 25) when, if they haven't been taught, there is little chance they'll ever be taught?

Even if manhood training was formally taught in school, chances are women would be teaching it. (Not necessarily a bad thing – plenty of single mothers raise superior sons, as do grandmothers. Still, there's something inimitable about *men* teaching boys.) No doubt, though, schools are dominated by females and female teachers. Bryan Nelson, founder of MenTeach.org, reports that in the United States (as of 2012) just 42.7% of secondary school, 18.6% of elementary/middle and, alarmingly, only 1.9% of early education teachers are men. Nelson's mission: Change this. Get more men into classrooms.

It's important that he succeeds. But he's up against three formidable hurdles:

1. The perception that men aren't nurturing. Not only can this prevent men from getting hired, it can turn into a self-fulfilling prophecy.

2. The stigma that if men are teaching children, especially young children, they must be creepy child molesters. Would you enter a profession that has people thinking that way about you?

3. If #2 isn't bad enough already, teaching (at least in America) is still a low-status/low-pay profession.[44] [45]

Even if Nelson succeeds and convinces more men to teach, that alone won't guarantee boys will be successfully taught how to become the kind of men the world needs. Getting more men into the classroom is a start. What they teach after they're there is more important.

No matter who's teaching it, what, precisely, should a manhood training curriculum include?

A lot! But it has to start with two fundamentals: hard work and urge-control. Lazy, uncontrolled boys don't magically morph into men. They turn into dangerous old "boys" (not *men*) who, at best, because of their lost potential, fail to contribute anything good or meaningful. At worst, they poison us with violent crime.

Hard-workers earn respect, and if there is anything a man craves, it's respect. Men who aren't respected confuse respect with fear and go looking for ways to instill it. Boys need to learn that women – adult women – not only respect hard-workers, they're primordially attracted to them. (It's part of their primal desire to mate with a good provider.) Unless they're born with incredible looks, talent or fortune - and maybe even *with* those blessings - there's only one real way to earn respect: Work.

Two-year-old boys are taught they can't pee wherever they want. Peeing anywhere other than in a toilet is not an option. Except for Oakland Raiders fans, most guys get that. (Just kidding! Sort of.) Six-year-old boys learn they can`t pee *whenever* they feel like it. My first grade teacher wife has to break it to her students that, since they are no longer in kindergarten and because there's no bathroom in her classroom, they will only be allowed to use the restroom at recess and lunch. They will need to learn to manage their urinary urges. Similarly, despite some guys' arguments to the contrary, it's possible to control burps and farts. A 15-year-old boy eating lunch next to his crush will find a way to suppress a burp or fart in her presence.

If we ate everything that looked good, we'd all have zero packs and health issues. It's hard to walk away from a plate full of brownies.

We shouldn't say every thought that pops into our heads. If we did, we'd be hated, sued, beaten, jailed or dead. No matter how badly we want to, we can't punch people in the face. If we did, we'd be hated, sued, beaten, jailed or dead.

Men need to learn that they can't have every woman they desire. It's a hard lesson and many guys will never get it or accept it. Hence, we get song lyrics like this from Travis (Travie) McCoy and the Gym Class Heroes:

> *They look so good in their Seven Jeans*
>
> *Want you to be the one and my only*
>
> *I wanna be faithful but I can't keep my hands out of the cookie jar...*

I'll give McCoy this: He and the rest of the "Heroes" are transparent. They said (sang) what most heterosexual men feel. But women aren't cookies. If a guy really wants a "one and my only," he shouldn't devastate her by trying to figure out how to get with every hot girl he sees. If he loves her, he should be a man, stay strong and resist his primal urges. Yes, we're animals, with animalistic impulses. But we're supposed to be superior animals, not lowlifes who snap at every lure.

The difference between a man and a boy is urge control. The list of male urges – from knocking someone out to knocking some girl up – is a mile long. Boys don't control their urges. Men do. The ultimate manly urge control story is the Jackie Robinson story. Perhaps because it's a sports story, it's not part of the official United States history curriculum (even though it should be). Yet, every kid should know that in 1947, when Robinson became the first African-American to play major league baseball, he resisted the overwhelming urge to lash out at his haters. Robinson wasn't passive by nature, but when Brooklyn Dodgers owner Branch Rickey told him he couldn't fight back, that he'd have to turn the other cheek to the ruthless taunts he was bound to hear from the bigots, he complied. It must have doubled his blood pressure, but he somehow controlled his urge to pummel his tormentors. Beyond the fact that he changed history by proving that professional sports could and should be integrated, he became the ultimate role model for urge management. Every eight-year-old boy ought to be presented with a framed photograph of Robinson.

What makes a man a man? Not his age. There are 15-year-old men and 50-year-old boys. Not his strength. Some of the greatest men are physically frail, some wheelchair bound. Not his income. That would eliminate social workers, most clergy and pretty much every guy in the military. What makes a man a man is his ability to manage his urges. The better he is at that, the better man he is.

What else do we need to teach boys?

When I asked one of my female students (a high school senior) exactly that, she said, "Teach them how to be hygienic."

I laughed. Then I thought about it and realized her answer was a great one. Hygiene – good or bad – is an indicator of something deeper than just how a guy presents himself physically. Good hygiene takes discipline and effort. The point is, we need to *teach* boys, and, at first, it doesn't matter a whole lot *what* we teach them. Because whether they're learning good hygiene, self-defense, how to make a tackle or how to bake a cake – how to do *anything* well - they'll need discipline and effort.

Teaching most *men* is practically impossible. Too many of them think they already know it all. Successful men (think famous jocks and celebrities) believe they can do whatever they want. Failed men (think inmates) take out their disappointments on their wives, kids and anyone else unfortunate enough to be around them when they're feeling frustrated.

So we better reach boys when they're young. We better instill in every boy the importance of becoming a better father, son, husband, brother, uncle or grandfather. Am I wrong? If you're a man, self-assess. How good a guy are you? Are you done developing? Do you know all you need to know?

You know how we argue about athletes: Who's the best quarterback, center fielder, point guard or coach? Instead of arguing about who the best athletes are, at least every once in a while, let's turn our attention to who the best *men* are. Instead of touchdown passes and batting averages, let's compare faithfulness and fatherhood. Who has never cheated on his wife? Who's most devoted to his kids?

Let's program our boys so they become obsessive-compulsive about improving. Not just improving their bench press, sprint time, skateboarding or guitar skills. Let's teach them to get better at being boys. Let's teach them to brush their teeth and take a shower, even when they're not "in the mood."

Let's teach them to drink less and read more. Let's teach them to play video games less and write more. (Most women aren't attracted to gamers anyway. They'd rather see a guy *play* basketball than pretend to play basketball.) Let's teach them to talk less and listen more. Let's teach them to fight less and love more. Not more women. More people. Let's teach them to make more friends.

Let's teach them to be kinder. Let's teach them to help each other and serve little kids and seniors. Let's teach them to select and commit (despite the temptations). Let's teach them to be open-minded and empty their cups (Lesson 1) despite their egos. Let's teach them to show respect. To people. To cultures. To institutions. To the environment. To themselves. Better yet, in addition to teaching them, let's *show* them. We need parents, extended family, youth leaders (religious and secular), teachers and coaches to demonstrate to boys what it takes to be a good man.

"A good man." What exactly is that? More importantly, for teaching purposes, *who*, exactly, is that? The obvious answer is you know them when you see them. Atticus Finch, for example. We need to teach boys *why* he's a literary role model and why Jackie Robinson is a historical role model. Exactly what do we admire about them? More importantly, what can we learn from them? Boys need to learn about Atticus's uncommon courage. They need to hear about how he stood up to a mob and fought for what's right even when his stance wasn't popular. Boys need to learn about Robinson's legendary self-control. Boys need to study Cesar Chavez who, while spending his life working to improve the lives of exploited farm workers, wrote:

> *It is my deepest belief that only by giving life do we find life, that the truest act of courage, the strongest act of manliness is to sacrifice ourselves for others in a totally non-violent struggle for justice. To be a man is to suffer for others. God help us to be men.*

Boys need to learn what character traits make men admirable. They need to be taught what's to be admired and emulated - and what's not to be. Because of "the blur," it's tricky. Gandhi is a classic example of the blur. The man is revered, and for a lot of reasons he should be. He was one of the greatest leaders ever. He organized an improbable, non-violent resistance that freed India. Still, reportedly, his relationships with women were strange. Very strange. He wasn't perfect.[46]

Who is? Boys, especially, don't get that most "heroes" aren't perfect. When they admire some aspect about someone – athletic ability (particularly), on-screen charm, rapping skills - they blur that talent or skill with *everything* about the man. So, even though the athlete's work ethic and competitive spirit can and should be admired, it doesn't mean his cockiness and rudeness should be seen as assets, too. Just because boys laugh at the comedic actor, it doesn't mean they should worship all aspects of him. Just because the rapping is worthy of respect, it doesn't always follow that the rapper is worthy of respect.

Boys need to be taught to look at the *whole* man, not just the cool part. (Although we need to point out what *really is* the cool part.) In addition to hard work and self-control, what else do (should) boys respect? For the simple reason that they can't replicate them, let's help boys move beyond the veneration of talent and gifts. They'll never have LeBron James's athleticism, Ryan Gosling's looks or Eminem's way with words. But they can admire all those guys' drive to succeed.

It's complicated, though. It's not as simple as identifying a certain character trait as desirable and then instructing boys to cultivate that trait. Loyalty is a good trait. But too much loyalty can be bad. Over-the-top sports fans are exceedingly loyal. But when they threaten, beat or shoot someone because they don't like the color someone is wearing, they're not loyal. They're thugs. Bryan Stow, a San Francisco Giants fan wore a Giants jersey to a Giants-Dodgers game in Los Angeles. For that, and because he dared to support his team, he was brutally beaten. A "loyal" University of Alabama fanatic maliciously poisoned a pair of revered oak trees that had been growing for over 130 years on the Auburn University campus (Alabama's archrival).[47] Gang members are extraordinarily loyal. Too much national loyalty caused World War I.

A sense of humor is good, but not when it wounds others. Being outgoing is good, but not when it becomes domineering. Being a good listener is good, but not if you *only* listen and never speak. Standing up for yourself is good, but not when it's taken to extremes and you're ready to fight at the slightest slight. Boys need men to explain those slippery nuances.

Why not women? Because boys' situations and experiences are just different. A guy needs to learn the difference between chickening out and wisely avoiding a fight. A woman's perspective isn't the same. No matter how brilliant her advice may be, the boy is going to be thinking, *You just don't understand.* And he'll be right.

Not just about loyalty and fighting. About friendship, fatherhood and romantic love. About education, careers, goals and success. Sometimes, a boy learns best from a good man. They're out there. Before it's too late, we need to teach boys that it's vital that they find them.

## Assignment

Seek sages (Lesson 24) – in this case great men. What makes a great man? What qualities? How do *you* want to be perceived? What kind of man do *you* want to be? Then name names. Take a close look at the men on your Inspirational People List. Why are they there? Is it because they are especially talented and good at something considered popular and attractive? (i.e. It gets them women.) Sports, music and acting, for example. Or is it because of their character? Have they been especially courageous, ethical or kind? Have they revealed exceptional creativity or demonstrated superior urge control?

If we admire in others what we hope to see in ourselves, the question is this: What, specifically - what precisely - do you want to see in yourself? Make a list.

## Evolutionary Motivation

Instead of primitive motivation, we need to advance to evolutionary motivation. By the time they enter high school, kids are fed up with operant conditioning. (Even if they don't know what that is.)

Operant conditioning is primal, rewards and punishment motivation. On a basic level, it works. After all, we're all motivated by the same two forces:

1. We do something because, if we do it, something good will happen. (Rewards motivate.)

2. We do something because, if we don't do it, something bad will happen. (Fear motivates.)

There's a lot of number 2, right? Too much of it. If most of what kids do is motivated by the fear of negative consequences, they'll have a cruddy life. Yet, sadly, that's how a lot of them (and a lot of adults, too) live. *If I don't show up for school, complete this assignment or practice the piano, I'll get in trouble. So, OK, I'll do it.*

Number 1 is better. But it, too, is primitive. *I'll eat because food tastes good. I'll sleep because it's satisfying. I'll work so I can be rewarded. If I do it, what will you give me?*

This low-level, carrot and stick motivation is used to train dogs, horses and rats. Yet, sadly, sometimes, it works for humans (especially kids), too.

Evolutionary motivation – human-only motivation – is the motivation taught by American author Dan Pink. (For a wonderful and creative presentation of his theories, search online for "RSA Animate – The Surprising Truth about What Motivates Us.")[48]

Pink points out that for simplistic tasks – mowing lawns, washing clothes, cleaning the house – primitive motivation works. "If I do it, I'll get my allowance. If I don't, I won't."

But when it comes to high level tasks – tasks that require vision, ingenuity, innovation and problem solving – we need evolutionary motivation. The kind of motivation that won't work for a dog, horse or rat, but will work wonders for aspiring, intelligent human beings. The way to motivate those kind of people is to tap into their human desire for autonomy, mastery and purpose:

**Autonomy:** Whether it's one person or an entire country, people crave control. We want and need to be responsible for our own destinies. Our parents may be better at choosing a romantic partner for us, but we still don't want them to do it. First graders want to choose their own crayons. Twelfth graders want to choose their own colleges. At every age, the more we get to choose for ourselves, the more motivated we'll be.

So we need to find a way to give kids more choices. Real, relevant choices. This is a tough one. Lots of times, kids don't even know what they want. So, why let them choose? Simple. The more adults make choices for them, the less motivated kids will become. Further, if we don't allow them to make independent choices, they'll never learn to make good ones. We've got to give them the "opportunity" to screw up and make bad ones. So, starting small, starting slowly, if we want kids to be intrinsically motivated, we've got to give them the gift of autonomy.

**Mastery:** Human beings want to be good at stuff. "Would you rather be good or bad at dancing?" "Would you rather get an A or F?" "Would you rather be a good friend or a bad friend?"

The answers are obvious, yet, often, we treat kids like we think they don't want to excel. To motivate, we have to show reasonable trust. We have to trust that, if we let go of the contingent, carrot and stick motivators, kids will still want to work hard to get good. Natural laws say they will. Indeed, they won't be able to help it. Their nature is to shine.

So that they'll be crystal clear about what it looks like, let's immerse students in success. Whenever they celebrate failure by making jokes about their lousy performance, lack of effort or poor grade, call them on it! Pathetically, it's not unusual when, outwardly at least, underachievers laugh off their underachievement. "What? My project got a record low score for incompetence? Cool!" Let's insist that kids seek success and major in it, not hunt for failure and celebrate it. No normal kid is going to choose ineptitude over accomplishment. Mastery will be preferred almost every time.

**Purpose:** More specifically, *higher* purpose. Beyond basic, extrinsic motivators, we want to have a reason for getting up in the morning. We want to contribute. We want to make a difference. We want what we do to mean something. We want to matter.

So do kids. When they know that what they're doing is important, that it's meaningful and that it matters, they'll be motivated. When what they're assigned is perceived as busy work with no true benefit or value (and kids are more perceptive than lots of adults think), well, would *you* be motivated to excel? Real work, real projects (Search "Project Based Learning"), real responsibilities are evolutionary motivators. When students understand *why* they need to learn what they're being taught, when they recognize the purpose for studying what they're assigned, that's evolutionary motivation. When they're told to learn something because it's "part of the curriculum," "in the standards" or, worse, "because I said so" that's primitive motivation. Just as a salary isn't the only motivator for adults, a grade isn't the only motivator for kids. When the reward is an A and the punishment is an F, that's primitive.

It's time to move beyond that.

## Assignment

Whenever an instructor teaches or assigns something, and you don't understand its purpose, raise your hand and ask, "Why are we being taught/assigned this?" It's your responsibility to your classmates and to yourself to insist that this question is answered. Teachers should be able to provide you with a reasonable explanation. When they can't, maybe they'll think and ask themselves, *Why am I teaching this?*

It's worth a try, right?

## Selective Settling

If we keep getting the same advice over and over (such as Confucius' now overused recommendation to "Choose a job you love, and you will never have to work a day in your life"), boring or not, we probably shouldn't blow it off.

> *You've got to find what you love. And that is as true for your work as it is for your lovers. Your work is going to fill a large part of your life, and the only way to be truly satisfied is to do what you believe is great work. And the only way to do great work is to love what you do. If you haven't found it yet, keep looking. Don't settle. As with all matters of the heart, you'll know when you find it. And, like any great relationship, it just gets better and better as the years roll on. So keep looking until you find it. Don't settle.*
>
> - Steve Jobs
> 2005 Stanford commencement speech

When I was studying to be a principal, I was part of a cohort that was taught a lesson I won't forget. It was memorable because it extended way beyond its original focus – hiring teachers.

The set-up was this: "You're a principal with a bunch of brand new teachers. As we know all too well, once teachers receive tenure, it's difficult to get rid of them. So, at the conclusion of their first year in the classroom, prior to offering them an opportunity to return for a second year, using a 1-10 scale, what's the lowest 'score' you would consider 'passing'?"

**Note:** In many districts, the only teachers who can be easily and immediately terminated are first-year teachers.

A lot of us said 7, 6 or even 5. Our thinking was that brand new teachers, with time and training, could improve and become 9's or even 10's. However, our professor made us feel foolish.

"Do you mean to say," he scolded, "that you'd settle for a 5, 6 or 7? Brand new teachers, who should be doing everything they can to impress, should be better than a 6 or 7! Look, with teachers, it doesn't take long to figure out which ones are excellent or potentially excellent. So, are you going to settle for mediocre teachers in the hope that, in time, they'll rise to a notch or two above mediocrity? How many kids' education are they going to ruin while you're hoping for something to happen that's not likely to happen?"

Oh.

I left that class thinking that when it comes to hiring teachers, don't settle. But I was also thinking, *What else is like that? In what other areas shouldn't we settle?*

The obvious answer was *everything. Never* settle.

It sounded smart then, but it's not realistic. There aren't enough hours in the day to *never* settle. Sometimes I (we) have to settle for a house that's not perfectly clean, a wardrobe that's not currently fashionable or a homework assignment that's not perfectly completed.

Lisa Quinn's book, *Life's Too Short to Fold Fitted Sheets*, is about exactly this. We don't have to make everything perfect. We can't. So, in some areas – how well we fold the laundry or dust the furniture – we *should* settle.[49]

On the other hand, there are areas where we shouldn't. Starting with our romantic partners. Not long after I learned the lesson about not settling when hiring teachers, I asked my seniors, "When choosing a future husband or wife, on a 1-10 scale, what's the lowest overall rating you'd accept?"

My students were a little pickier than we (the prospective principals) were – but not much. A few said 7. Most said 8 or 9. My favorite answer, though, came from Patrice.

"Eleven," she said.

Which is the way it should be with that category. When I met my wife, Norma, she was unquestionably an 11 – much too good for me. We've been married over 35 years. It has been a wonderful marriage, but not without angry arguments and trying times. During the first five years we were married, because of my Air Force commitment, we had to spend four of them apart. If, on our wedding day, we had thought the other was a 7, 8, or even a 9, we would have split up a long time ago.

As much as we can, we shouldn't settle on work that's just "good enough." I once heard Debbi Fields, the founder of Mrs. Fields Cookies, speak at San Francisco's Cow Palace. (The best arena name ever, by the way.) While we all waited for the matronly Mrs. Fields (our preconceived image of her) to tell us the story of how she built a multi-million dollar cookie business, an attractive blond approached the microphone, apparently to introduce Mrs. Fields. Surprising those of us who had never seen her (the majority of us), she introduced *herself* to us. "Hello everyone," she began. "My name is Debbi Fields, and I'm here to tell you my story."

After waiting for us to regain our composure and push up our dropped jaws, she shared. An important part of her story was not settling. She told us about the anxiety she felt about franchising. She was a perfectionist. Her cookies had to be baked just right, with the highest quality ingredients. How could she entrust anyone else to make *her* cookies? So she adopted and implemented her business philosophy:

*Good enough never is.*

When she'd visit one of her Mrs. Fields cookie stores and notice a batch had been under or over baked, she'd insist that it be tossed in the trash. When it came to her business's reputation – *her* reputation - Debbi Fields refused to settle.

What else? Ultimately, it's a personal choice, but you might seriously consider not settling when it comes to…

- **your life's work**
  As Jobs inferred, one ingredient in the recipe for an unhappy life is to work at something you're just not that into. Finding work you love sounds simple, but it's far from easy. Due to life being life, you may have to take jobs you don't like, and that's OK – as long as they're temporary. Ultimately, though, you've got to find work that's a reason to get out of bed in the morning.

- **your integrity**
  You want this part of your reputation spotless. Lie or cheat once and you're done. Years ago, I taught a kind, fun, friendly freshman. Sadly, halfway through the school year, I learned she had cheated on at least one test and maybe on a bunch of them. Three years later, when she was a senior, she was in my class again. We got along except that I could never see or think about her without remembering that she had cheated. I tried to get past it but never could, even though I both liked and respected her. The point? Even the smallest stain on your rep is likely to be permanent.

- **your friends**
  In our finite amount of time on earth, why settle for a second-rate support group? We're born into a family. We don't select our parents, siblings, aunts, uncles, cousins or grandparents. Good, bad or both, we're stuck with them. Friends, on the other hand, aren't fate. The best part about our non-family relationships is we get to choose them. So choose wisely.

- **your use of free time**
  It's not really free. In economics, there's debate as to whether or not time is a resource (since everyone gets the same 24-hour days and 365-day years), but there is a cost to not using it well. Nonproductive activity is a cheap use of time. Productive activity is

a valuable use of it. Who decides what's nonproductive and productive? You. But have high standards. Don't settle.

- **your health**
  You have one body. One life. If you can help it, don't settle for being overweight. Don't settle for being in lousy shape. Don't settle for a lousy diet. Don't settle for feeling fatigued all the time. Don't settle for being addicted to cigarettes, beer or any other destructive drug.

- **your faith**
  It doesn't matter which one you follow. (Well, I don't believe it does.) Just don't settle for one you don't trust or doesn't uplift you or provide solace and peace. Keep searching until you're content.

## Assignment

It's up to you to decide when settling is an acceptable option and when it isn't. The important thing is to have an awareness. If you're going to settle, at least make settling a conscious decision. If you do, you might think twice about it, and that can only be good. Consider the areas of your life when you'll allow yourself to settle and when you won't. Perhaps living with a B or C in a class or two will allow you more time to work on your passion, spend more time with family and friends or exercise consistently. If settling for a lower grade is not an option, settling for less than what you'd like in some other area will be necessary. "Never settle" is a worthy goal, but it becomes unrealistic when we try to apply it to *all* our goals.

## The Answer is Work

What's fulfilling?
*Work.*

What's uplifting?
*Work.*

What makes life worth living?
*Work.*

What will earn me respect?
*Work.*

What can cure (or at least diminish) depression?
*Work.*

What's my purpose?
*Work.*

The answer is *work*. No matter what the problem is, the answer is almost always work. Work is good.

Kids don't think that. They think work sucks. It's the enemy, something to be avoided.

On the last day of school one year, I had a heart-to-heart with my students. I wanted to know what I needed to do to be better. How could I reach more of them?

One student, hinting that my expectations were unrealistically high, told me the truth. "Mr. Richards, all anyone at this school cares about is getting the highest possible grade with the least amount of work."

The class agreed. I didn't argue because I knew they were right. But I don't think this attitude was just at our school. I think it's at most schools. There's more incentive to get a grade than learn a lesson.

It's so wrong! It teaches kids the exact opposite of what they need to know about work, happiness, fulfillment and gratification. They need to know that easy isn't good. When all kids care about is getting the grade, they'll hunt for easy. It'll become a game. To score well, to look good (but not necessarily *be* good), they'll do whatever it takes. They'll even cheat – as long as cheating doesn't demand too much work.

What schools should be teaching – but don't – is that happiness doesn't come from easy A's. It comes from challenging work. Getting a good grade without the hard work is about as gratifying as defeating a preschooler in a game of checkers. Easy eliminates gratification and strips satisfaction.

Happiness, research shows, practically proves that working at anything (cleaning, weeding, mowing, dusting, filing, exercising, completing a project, studying for a tough test) boosts our mood, and working at something meaningful supercharges it.

Want to feel happier? Work.

Not happy. Happier. Happy is fleeting. Happy can't be the goal. Happier is the goal. More satisfied. More content. More fulfilled. More gratified. But never totally there.

Happy is the mountain peak. The trouble is, if you make it up there, it's only cool for a little while. Then you've got to scale another mountain. You've got to keep climbing. Remember, "There's No Such Thing as Happily Ever After (Lesson 38)."

If we could get this across to kids, if we could convince them that work will not only make them more successful, it will make them happier, maybe they'd cease the search for easy. If kids learn this, it will be a huge breakthrough that will serve them well for the rest of their lives.

Ironically, I was reminded of this simple but powerful truth while spending a winter break vacationing on the island of Kauai, Hawaii. On Kauai's north shore, in the town of Hanalei, sits a gorgeous taro field operated for over six generations by the Haraguchi family. Taro is an underrated food. Most people associate it with poi, and most people gag at poi - probably, I learned, because they incorrectly try to eat it straight. (It needs to be mixed.) But taro is used to make all kinds of good tasting, nutrient rich, gluten-free foods.

I tried something called pa'i'ai, which means "fresher than poi." It was, too. And better tasting, even though the only "seasoning" on it was fresh coconut shavings. Our petite tour guide, Lyndsey Haraguchi-Nakayama, told us that when she was experiencing a difficult pregnancy, a taro diet rescued her. She stopped feeling nauseous, and after giving birth to a *nine-pound* baby boy, her doctors were bewildered. "What have you been eating?!" they wondered.

Lyndsey also told us the story of how five generations of the Haraguchi family had worked the family farm. Continuing the tradition during her two pregnancies with generation six, Lyndsey slogged through the fields, doing all she could. I was captivated by the exceptionally strong Haraguchi work ethic. Boys and girls, kids and adults - everyone pitched in. Lyndsey was driving a tractor when she was six. Her uncle was in charge of pest control when he was eight.

The crucial question is this: How do you instill the kind of simple, powerful work ethic that's seemingly innate in the Haraguchis? Should we get our family involved in highly-intensive, interdependent agriculture? Probably not. Even if that was a surefire way to inculcate kids to appreciate the panacea that is work, it's obviously unrealistic. Less than 2% of Americans make a living farming.

How about getting everyone working for the family business? Maybe. But what if there is no family business? What then?

Then how about this? Whatever the work, model the work ethic.

It's not enough to work hard. Kids need to see it and be included in it. Lyndsey watched and modeled her parents and grandparents. Then, after she went off to the University of Hawaii and Hawaii Pacific University where she earned, respectively, a BA in tropical agriculture and a Masters in Business Administration, she returned home and started a family. And now her kids will get to watch and model her. I'd bet that they're hard-working kids who will grow into hard-working adults.

The obvious enemy of work is laziness, and the sneakiest kind of laziness is "disguised laziness." Disguised laziness is a crafty way of making people think you're working when you really aren't or finding a reason not to work that is more rationalization than explanation. For example, you "can't" do the hard work because you "have" to do something easier or you had some other "responsibility." Hey, you're not fooling anyone! Especially yourself.

Examples of disguised laziness:

- *"It's creative."*

  No it's not. It's lazy. (Maybe.) Creativity requires work. Modern dance doesn't (or shouldn't) mean you just move to music in any way you want, call it "creative" and expect compliments. Just because something is strange doesn't mean it's creative. Don't slop something together in six minutes, call it "abstract art" and tell me I "shouldn't judge." Guess what? People recognize effort (and the lack of it). You're not fooling anyone.

- *"I'm not helping my students (or children) because I want them to learn/grow/think for themselves/do things for themselves."*

  That might be true. But it could also be disguised laziness. After all, it's a lot easier to have them do it or figure it out for themselves than for you to get off your rear end and help them.

- *"I'm not going to go to that class...complete that assignment... listen to that teacher because it's stupid...a waste of time... he/she annoys me..."*

No. You're rationalizing...looking for excuses...disguising your laziness.

- *"I'm quitting because... I don't have time...have other interests and responsibilities...I'm injured, sick, tired, stressed..."*

  Perhaps. But is that really the reason you're quitting? Are you being completely honest with yourself? Or is your quitting disguised laziness?

- *"I can't practice now. I need to finish (something else, something easier) first."*

  No you don't. Get your priorities right. Practice comes first. The only reason you're "finishing" that other thing is to rationalize not doing what you know you should be doing - practicing.

- *"I didn't do my homework because I had to drive my girlfriend to work."*

  That was nice of you, but you could have driven your girlfriend to work *and* done your homework. It would have been harder to do both, but you could have and should have found a way.

- *"I don't believe in (whatever)"*
  *(buying holiday presents, for example)*

  Is that really your belief, or does believing mean more work? If it does, it's probably disguised laziness.

- *"I'm not good at (whatever)"*
  *(wrapping holiday presents, for example)*

  Is your claiming not to be "good" a way of getting out of doing it? If it is, it's disguised laziness.

- *"I didn't go work out because my sick friend needed me to be with him."*

  Liar. You just used that as an excuse to not exercise because visiting your friend was easier. You could have found a way to do both.

- *"I'm not interested enough in learning (Spanish, ukulele, coding...) so I'm not going to bother with it."*

  If that's really true, fine. But maybe you're not being honest. Maybe you really *are* interested, but you just don't want to put in the work. Maybe it's disguised laziness.

- *"I can't because I'm injured/sick/old."*

  Only you know if this is true or if it's disguised laziness.

- *"I'm going to make this simpler and easier for you."*

  Are you? Or are you making it simpler and easier for yourself?

- *"I'm going to break that rule or law because I'm unconventional, a rebel, a nonconformist, a change agent."*

  Sometimes breaking a rule is the right thing to do. Martin Luther King Jr. said, "One has not only a legal but a moral responsibility to obey just laws. Conversely one has a moral responsibility to disobey unjust laws."

Marcus Buckingham and Curt Coffman wrote a best-selling business book called *First, Break All the Rules* in which they claim "Great managers share one common trait: They do not hesitate to break virtually every rule held sacred by conventional wisdom."[50]

All of which is fine – great even – as long as the rule breaking isn't disguised laziness. It should be hard to break a rule. It should be stressful to break a rule. If breaking the rule is easier than following it, breaking the rule is probably disguised laziness. When King broke a law, he was marching in the streets or being hauled off to jail. He wasn't lying on the couch, sipping a beer. When great managers break a rule "held sacred by conventional wisdom," it's not because it's easy. It's because they believe it's necessary, right and it will result in the most success. They take the risk and bear the criticism because they trust that the direction they're headed is the right direction, even when it's on a brand new path.

## Assignment

Next time you're feeling unfulfilled, dejected, depressed, disrespected or purposeless, don't do something easy. Before you collapse on the couch, turn on the TV or surf the Internet, do something that's difficult. Do some work. When you're done, *then* relax. You may not feel blissful, but you'll feel better. It will be hard, but remember that line from Jimmy Dugan (Tom Hanks) in *A League of Their Own*, "It's supposed to be hard. If it wasn't hard, everyone would do it. The hard is what makes it great."

## The Notebook, Ideas and the Life List

If I were in charge of teaching teachers, a required "textbook" would be Steven Johnson's *Where Good Ideas Come From: The Natural History of Innovation.* We need to teach teachers how to teach students to come up with world-improving ideas. It's clear from reading Johnson that the best ideas don't mystically emerge. They come after observing, listening, reading (yes, students, *reading*!), questioning, collaborating and thinking. They come as a result of being immersed in groups of great thinkers who share their thoughts. They come after considering those thoughts, writing them down, studying them, synthesizing them and presto! A new idea is born.[51]

Teachers in all subjects in all grades must insist that their students write down notes, thoughts and ideas in a notebook. Laptop, tablet, mobile phone or old-fashioned spiral, it doesn't matter where or in what form. If no note-taking device is handy, write your idea on whatever is available – in a book margin, on a piece of scratch paper, or even on a napkin.

Regardless of where or how notes are written, make sure kids get the message: *Note taking is critical to success.* Leonardo da Vinci, considered by scholars to be the most intelligent, most accomplished man *ever*, lugged his notebook around Florence, Italy with him. In it, he'd write down and sketch his ideas. He sketched the original idea for a parachute in the margin of his notebook in 1438. In 2000, an exact replica of da Vinci's parachute was constructed and tested. It worked!

*Leonardo da Vinci carried a notebook with him at all times*

> *so that he could jot down ideas, impressions, and observations as they occurred. His notebooks (7,000 pages exist; most scholars estimate that this is about one half of the amount he left to Francesco Melzi in his will) contained jokes and fables, the observations and thoughts of scholars he admired, personal financial records, letters, reflections on domestic problems, philosophical musings and prophecies, plans for inventions, and treatises on anatomy, botany, geology, flight, water, and painting.*[52]

When kids question the value of a notebook, I remind them that if it worked for the smartest man in history, it could work for them, too.

Johnson refers to the "commonplace book" – a form of notebook (Lesson 46) - and how it was used by European enlightenment era thinkers to record lessons and thoughts (their own and others') that sometimes grew into the next great idea, even if the idea took time to percolate and come to fruition. Charles Darwin, Johnson points out, speculated about natural selection (in his notebooks) over two decades before it was formalized in *The Origin of Species.*[53]

Another example of the power and magic associated with writing down an idea took place at 2:00 AM on the morning of October 31st, 1920. A young Canadian doctor named Frederick Banting lay awake. Restless from preparing a lecture he was to deliver that day to physiology students at Ontario's Western University, he had just finished reading a professional journal article on carbohydrate metabolism when an idea came to him. In Banting's words, "I got up, wrote down the idea and spent most of the night thinking about it."[54] Banting's idea (that the pancreas secreted a substance that affected blood sugars) resulted in the discovery of insulin which drastically improved and saved the lives of millions of children and adults suffering from and dying of diabetes. Banting's predawn speculation, written in his notebook, was one of the great medical discoveries in history.

Again, if thinkers such as Darwin and Banting wrote down their ideas, why not insist that thinkers such as our students write down theirs? Their ideas could be world changing, too. When we don't require a notebook, we're underestimating our kids and not pushing them to their potential.

Still, simply telling students, "Start and maintain an Idea File," is too vague. "Ideas about what?" kids will want to know. To get them started, *require* that they create and maintain a file (sorted by categories) that stores their best ideas on how to live an extraordinary and impactful life.

**Note:** Make no mistake about it, coming up with an idea and writing it down is not the hardest thing to do – the work (an incredible amount of it) comes later. Still, without an idea, there's no work to be done.

The core of the Idea File is the Life List. (I prefer to not call it a "bucket list" - things you want to do before you "kick the bucket" - because, *A*, that term is horribly depressing and, *B*, it suggests desperation.) A decade ago, it was unusual to have even heard about such a list. Today, even though the concept isn't fresh (*The Bucket List*, a major motion picture starring Jack Nicholson and Morgan Freeman, was released in 2007), a lot of people - probably most people – have never taken the time to create one. Prior to me assigning it, the vast majority of my students didn't have a life list. But they should, so I assign it. They need one. We all do. We all need hope. An Idea File that includes a Life List is the antidote to hopelessness. Ideas electrify the future. *Everyone* should have at least one! Seriously, we need to teach kids to make a conscious effort to come up with ideas, record them (like da Vinci, in words and/or sketches), then work at converting them from dream to reality. Not only do ideas make life more exciting, they give us a reason to live.

I'm skeptical when motivational speakers preach that writing down goals and hanging them up in a conspicuous place is magical - as if that's all we need to do to make our dreams come true. There are conflicting studies about whether or not writing down goals does any good. Still, I'm in love with the concept of formalizing and organizing ideas and goals, and it sure can't hurt. Writing down ideas forces us to think about them.

Therefore, the first and most important item in the Idea File should be a Life List bursting with aspirations including:

- Places you want to go
- People you want to meet
- Things you want to do or try
- Things you want to learn
- Things you want to start, change, fix or eliminate
- Things you want to buy
- Things you want to achieve
- Things you want to do for others

A Life List is essentially a list of goals and resolutions. Gretchen Rubin, in *The Happiness Project*, draws an important distinction between the two. "You *hit* a goal, you *keep* a resolution."[55] A goal is typically a one-time event. Once you accomplish it, you can check it off your list. It may be repeated, but often it's not. "Complete a triathlon," "Visit Florence," "Earn a bachelor's degree" are examples of goals. Resolutions are ongoing, such as establishing (or breaking) a habit or improving your lifestyle. "Exercise," "Write in a journal" and "Watch inspiring videos" are examples of resolutions.

When I first learned about and became interested in YouTube, I showed my non-techie wife one of its most watched videos - "Charlie Bit My Finger." She liked it. So, a few days later, I called upstairs to her.

"Honey, come watch this!"

"What is it?"

"Something I found on YouTube."

"I've already seen YouTube!"

I was thinking resolution. She was thinking goal.

Goals and resolutions can be big or small, short or long-term. Some, such as tasting an exotic or bizarre food (chocolate-covered ants), aren't overly difficult or excessively expensive and can often be done almost immediately. They don't require tremendous effort. For example, riding the world's tallest Ferris wheel - the 630 foot New York Wheel being built in Staten Island, New York – won't require work. Courage, perhaps, but not exertion. Getting there - affording a trip to New York City - may require time and effort, but riding the New York Wheel won't. Goals such as skydiving, bungee jumping or swimming with dolphins fall into this category. They're fun, exciting and worthy life list ideas, but they don't demand the stress, labor and commitment it takes to run a marathon, make a million dollars or stop drinking. The best Life Lists include a balance of "fun" and arduous goals and resolutions.

Although creating a Life List is entertaining and engaging, it's only a prelude. In order to turn an idea into reality, we have to change what we're doing and sometimes how we're living. If doing something on the Life List doesn't require focus, planning and, most of all, *change*, it doesn't belong on the list. If, in the normal course of events, we can achieve our goal or resolution without changing, without *improving* our thoughts or behaviors, it's a crummy goal or resolution. The purpose of the Life List is to push us, to lift us a notch above our current practices and routines. Goal attainment and sticking to a resolution should be challenging.

But not too challenging. Balance, right? (Lesson 2) If an idea for a goal or resolution is too fantastical, if *we* don't believe it can happen, it won't. So no crazy "Become the next LeBron James" or "Cure cancer in my spare time" ideas. We should push ourselves, but not to the point where our goals and resolutions are fantasies.

Life Lists should be specific. The more specific the better. "Travel" isn't specific. "See Sydney, Australia" is. "Do better in school" isn't specific. "Earn a 3.5 grade point average this semester" is. "Learn another language" isn't specific. "Learn conversational Spanish" is. "Exercise" isn't specific. "Work out at least five days a week" is. We need to be able to visualize our goals and resolutions, and it's hard to visualize generic ones.

Life Lists should only include goals and resolutions that *we* can make happen. Whether or not they are attained should be mostly up to us and not depend on some lucky twist of fate. The first time I asked my students to write down goals and resolutions for improvement, their naivety taught me that I needed to do a better job of teaching them how to do it.

I shouldn't have said, "Write down what you want." It's not that easy. What worthwhile activity is? Students wrote down non-challenging goals such as, "Graduate from 6th grade." Others wrote what they might request if a genie granted them three wishes: "Be the next Joe Montana" one non-athletic boy wrote. (It was 1990.)

And one confused student announced…

"Mr. Richards, I want to get a new bike!"

"Great," I said. "How do you plan on earning the money to buy it?"

"I'm going to ask my mom to buy me one for my birthday."

No! Life Lists are not about wishing and hoping and depending on someone else. Yes, part of it is learning how to ask for help, but most of it is about making things happen ourselves. It's about deciding what we want, devising a plan to get it and then working hard (sometimes for a very long time) to get it. Goal setting and resolution making are about self-determination, not fate.

One way to avoid turning the Life List into a wish list is to include a deadline, or at least an approximate deadline for each goal listed. For resolutions, state when you plan to begin (preferably immediately). Don't just write "Quit smoking pot." Write "Quit smoking pot today!" Don't just write "Bungee jump in New Zealand." Write "Bungee jump in New Zealand before I turn 30." When goals and resolutions aren't tied to a timeline, they fall into the dangerous "someday" category. When we say we're going to do something "someday," we might as well just admit that we're giving it such a low priority that, chances are, it's not going to happen. A deadline adds stress but increases possibility.

Goals on the Life List are enhanced when they're illuminated with activities and specific details. "Go to Hawaii" is a good goal. "Surf in Hawaii" is better. "Start a business" is a respectable goal. "Start a business that makes millions, employs hundreds and includes social branding" is a great one. "Meet someone on my Inspirational People List" is cool. "Buy lunch for (that person)" is cooler.

Life Lists should include goals and resolutions representing all aspects of our lives. Refer to the Leading Life Indicators (Lesson 10).

We should include goals that enhance our...

**Physicality**

- *Weigh 180 pounds with less than 12% body fat*
- *Bench press my weight*
- *Stop smoking*

**Family, friend and romantic relationships**

- *Call my sisters at least once a month*
- *Celebrate New Year's Eve with my friends in Times Square*
- *Learn how to cook my partner's favorite meal*

**Passion**

- *Publish a book*
- *Earn a blackbelt*

- *Get up an hour earlier to work on (my passion)*

**Education and/or career**

- *Become fluent in Spanish*
- *Study for a master's degree in Education*
- *Start my own (fill in type) business*

**Money**

- *Sell my company for five million dollars*
- *Pay for my daughters' college education*
- *Save money using the "Daffodil Principle" ($100 dollars every week, for example)*

***la causa***

- *Build a school in Nicaragua*
- *Start a foundation that provides art, athletic and music tools to the disadvantaged*
- *Teach someone a skill you've mastered – writing, coding, guitar playing*

**Spiritualty**

- *Read a (specific) spiritual book e.g. Siddhartha, The Chronicles of Narnia*
- *Visit a (specific) spiritual place e.g. Lourdes France, Mecca*
- *Research spiritual beliefs e.g. A specific religion (Buddhism) or a general idea (reincarnation)*

I first heard about a Life List while listening to sports talk show host Jim Rome's radio show. He was interviewing Internet pioneer (AOL) and sports franchise owner (Washington Wizards and Capitals) Ted Leonsis. Rome asked Leonsis about his list – 100 things he wanted to do in his life (which included making a million dollars and owning a sports team). Leonsis's goal at the time was to play a one-on-one basketball game against Michael Jordan who was then playing for the Wizards.

Instantly, I fell in love with the list idea. That day, I shared it with my freshmen and seniors, proposing that all of us make a Life List with at least 25 goals and resolutions on it. "Surprise me," I said.

They did. I'm embarrassed to admit that when I gave them my original guidelines, it didn't occur to me to include examples of what is now a principal reason to have a Life List – humanitarianism. When that first group of students turned in their lists, almost half of them included at least one selfless aspiration:

- Buy my mom a car
- Adopt a child from a 3rd world country
- Collect shoes for inner city elementary school students
- Work at a homeless shelter during the holidays
- Make my parents proud

I felt like a jerk. Why hadn't *I* thought of noble, altruistic goals? *Oh well*, I thought, remembering a lyric in the Rodgers and Hammerstein Broadway musical, *The King and I*. "From your students you'll be taught." Now, starting with my own, I insist that every life list include at least one unselfish goal or resolution.

Like the Inspirational People List, Life Lists are fluid. Ideas come and fade. Sometimes they change. When a goal is completed, cross it off the list - but then add a new one. (When Leonsis completes a major goal, he celebrates.) It's OK to change your mind. When a goal is no longer relevant, desirable or feasible, replace it with one that is. When a resolution, for whatever reason, doesn't work out, either recommit or try something else. Not every idea pans out.

Once the list is created, decorate it. Make it look special. Then hang it someplace where you'll see it often. That alone won't help you achieve what's on the list, but it will remind you to live purposely.

A supplement to the Life List is the Vision Board. Again, I'm not sure I believe a Vision Board is magical or if it will enhance the chances that a goal will be reached or a resolution kept. But why not try it? They're fun to look at, and they make us feel good. They lead to interesting conversations, and who knows? They could work! A lot of people – Oprah, for one - swear by them.

A Vision Board is a place where you post images that represent your goals. If you want to visit the Sydney Opera House, cut out and hang up a photograph of the iconic Australian landmark. If you want to learn to surf, draw a picture of yourself riding a wave. Turn your Life List into a motivational collage.

In the years leading up to Apollo 11 and the United States landing astronauts on the moon, the scientists at NASA covered an entire wall with a colossal photograph of the moon. The mission was clear to everyone.[56]

In my classroom, one large bulletin board is our shared Vision Board. In September, each student adds an image that represents one of his or her goals. The conditions are that it has to be specific, challenging, realistic, self-determined and can be achieved by the end of the school year. On the last day of school, students take down their images and share with their classmates and me whether or not they were successful. (I participate, too.)

If they were, it's a time to celebrate. If they weren't, it's a time to contemplate. "Why weren't you successful?" I ask. "Did you not want it badly enough? Did you not work hard enough for it? Was it *too* challenging? Was 'by the last day of school' an unrealistic deadline? Even though the school year is over and the rest of us may never know if you accomplish it, do you still want it? Will you still go after it?"

## Assignment

Start your Idea File! Online or on paper, create a file filled with your thoughts, questions and ideas, including your Life List. If you already have one, update it. Once your list is complete (try to come up with at least 25 goals and resolutions), make it look good. Make copies. Put one inside your locker, on your bathroom mirror, on your bulletin board, anywhere where you'll see it frequently. Then, using your Life List as your blueprint, create a Vision Board. You get an A if there is an image for each item on your list.

Dream of reaching your goals and sticking with your resolutions. Most importantly, work on them. If you aren't working on a goal right now, select something from your list and get to work. Turn your best thoughts and ideas into something concrete and real. But, first, make that list! Then, if you're ever asked, "What are you working on?" you'll have at least 25 answers from which to choose.

# The Good Fail

There's nothing like learning the hard way. Even though it's agonizing, the hard way is a powerful and effective teacher. Like most American kids, I grew up hearing "If you want something badly enough, if you work hard enough for it, you can be/have whatever you want."

Too bad it isn't true. But I didn't always know that. I used to believe the "nothing is impossible" fantasy.

I grew up wanting to play in the NFL or the NBA. It wasn't until I was 16 years old, sitting near the floor of Detroit's Cobo Arena watching the Detroit Pistons with Dave Bing play the Phoenix Suns with Dick Van Arsdale when it became clear that I would never play in the NBA.

I wasn't fast enough. What separates levels of athletic excellence - whether it is amateur/professional or grade school/high school/college/pro – isn't so much size and strength (although these are obviously contributing factors). No, the biggest filter is speed. It's all about quickness and speed.

The higher the level, the faster the athlete. Speed is a gift. Like height, you either have it or you don't. You can enhance it, but you can't spawn it. Not only were the pros bigger and stronger than I was, they were lightning fast. I wasn't even thunder fast. I never would be, either. It became clear to me that night that playing in the NBA was an unreachable goal. It wasn't realistic.

So I set a new goal. I would earn a college basketball scholarship, play college ball, then maybe teach and coach. All I had to do was work hard enough and believe in the dream, and it would come true.

It would begin to happen during my senior year.

It started promisingly enough. We won most of our games. I played well. Then we lost some important games, and I didn't play well. I sprained my ankle. I tried playing on it but without much success. My last high school game was in the first round of the Michigan single-elimination state tournament. It was a disaster. We lost to a team we had beaten earlier in the season, and I stunk. I made just two of the fifteen shots I attempted, was pulled from the game and ended my high school basketball career on the bench.

Devastated, I hurried out of the locker room into the frigid winter night. Not only was I forlorn, I was bewildered. Hadn't I done everything right? Hadn't I worked hard? How many other players had stayed after practice as long as *five hours* trying to perfect his jump shot? None!

Yet, I had failed. No college coach would be offering me a scholarship. The goal I had worked for would not be realized. I was depressed for months. But years later, I would see a silver lining. I failed, but it was a good fail. Don't misunderstand. A fail – even a good fail – still stings. I don't wish one on anyone. But in a world where happily ever after is a fantasy, failure is inevitable. So we might as well make our failures good fails.

What's the difference between a good fail and a bad fail?

1. A good fail is an effort fail. You try hard. You give it all you have. But you don't get what you were working for. Example: You spend hours in a study group then stay up all night studying – and end up with a grade you didn't want.

   A bad fail is a lazy fail. You don't try hard. You don't deserve to succeed. Example: You don't study. Not surprisingly, you bomb the test.

2. A good fail is when you learn something. The education may not assuage the immediate disappointment, but it

> will ensure that the effort was not in vain.
>
> A bad fail is when you screw up and then make the same mistake again. A bad fail is when, after the fail, you're no smarter and no better off than you were before the fail.

**Note:** 1 and 2 are not mutually exclusive. A good fail is an effort fail *and* a learn-from-it fail. The only thing you learn from a bad fail is that you should have tried harder – not exactly rocket science. Bad fails don't teach specifics.

Near the tragic conclusion of the film, *Camelot*, a distraught King Arthur asks his teacher and advisor, Merlin, one of humanity's great questions, "What's the best thing for being sad?"

Merlin's timeless advice:

*Learn something.*

Learn something. When we fail, we feel sad. The way to feel better is to learn something.

From my basketball failure I learned that, although I had tried hard, I had worked on the wrong things. Rather than just shooting the basketball repeatedly, I should have spent more time improving my athleticism. So I stopped feeling sorry for myself and got back into the gym. I lifted weights and improved my strength and quickness enough that I was able to play a year of college basketball. It was the best, most rewarding basketball season of my life.

My semi-happy ending, however, doesn't guarantee anything. I had a chance to walk onto my college basketball team. What if I hadn't had that chance? What if I never went to college? What if I never got to use what I learned? It happens.

Two of the best failures ever were Michelle Kwan's "fails." I use quotation marks because winning a silver and bronze medal in consecutive Olympics can hardly be considered failures. But Kwan, who dominated women's figure skating from the mid 1990's to the early 2000's, was far from satisfied with second and third place finishes. One of the saddest, most painful-to-watch Olympic moments was her performance at the 1998 skating medalists' exhibition. Anticipating only one result – a result that would never transpire - she skated to Sting's "Fields of Gold."

Although heartwrenching, Kwan's fail was an epic effort fail. Her preparation, her training, her coaching – everything she did seemed perfect and right. Yet she "lost." What did she learn? I speculate two things:

1. That because she *did* prepare so hard, because she didn't succumb to laziness, she could live with the result. There was nothing else she could have done. That has to be comforting.

2. That people would identify, love and respect her because she had put body, mind and spirit into her gold medal quest.

Still, why even bother working hard when we're more likely to fail than succeed? After all, one of life's great truths is that to do something well, it's going to be harder, take longer and be a lot more complicated than we think. In his Cracked.com column, "How the Karate Kid Ruined the Modern World" (a must-read for anyone 12 or older), Jason Pargin (a.k.a. David Wong) says that finding meaningful and lucrative work will be massively more difficult than we anticipated it would be when we were growing up and studying our way through school. To get what we want, we will have to push past more and greater obstacles than we ever imagined. And even if we have enough grit to keep pushing, unless we catch a few breaks, experience good fortune, have dumb luck or be blessed by providence, we're probably *still* going to fail! [57]

So why even try?

Simple. If, even when we work incredibly hard, the odds are we won't achieve our dreams, what are the chances for success when we *don't* work hard?

Zero. Or close to it. Effort *guarantees* us nothing. But it does increase the odds that we'll be successful. And if we want it badly, that's no small thing. Moreover, if we fail with a good try, it will be a lot easier to live with than if it's a bad try. There will still be regrets, but they'll be tolerable.

## Assignment

Give it a try. An effort try. If you don't try, you won't succeed. Guaranteed. If you do try, you'll have a *chance* you'll succeed. A chance. That's all.

This may not be as rousing and (misleadingly) reassuring as "If you want it bad enough, if you work for it hard enough, you'll get it." But it's realistic.

## Solving the "What should I do with my life?" Dilemma

The norm is for high school graduates to have no idea what they want to do with their lives. Which is understandable. After all, they're 17 and 18-year-old kids. Yet, when *college* graduates are clueless about how to spend their post school lives, it's scary.

When high school grads are unsure about which direction to take, we practically celebrate it:

"Don't worry. You'll figure it out."

"You're young. There's plenty of time to decide."

"I didn't start (my career) until I was 30 (or 40, or 50).

"That's what college is for."

Maybe.

But maybe not. When kids don't know what to do with their lives, let's stop dismissing it as normal, natural and no big deal. It is a big deal! Having no clue about what you want to do is *not* OK. Not when you're about to graduate from high school. Or, worse, college.

I'm not advocating locking into a career at 18 or 22. I am advocating encouraging or even requiring graduates to at least know which direction to head. If they're directionless, it's not all their fault. It's the system's fault. It's their school's fault. It's their teachers' fault. We do a haphazard job of helping students discover their ambitions. We teach kids academic subjects that many master without making a connection between what they're being taught in the classroom and how they'll use it when they leave the secluded walls of academia. The goal is succeeding in the class - "Study. Get an A. Get out."

Then what?

Sophomores in our district, Fremont Unified (California), have a "career unit" thrown at them for a few days. They'll take an aptitude test and/or complete a career interest survey that may reveal valuable insights. But there's little follow-up and not enough of a link between what they learn about themselves and what they're learning in school.

What needs to change?

First, most of all, the isolation. Schools are one thing. Reality is another. The disconnect between the two is startling. When what goes on inside school virtually contradicts what goes on outside it, it's destructive. No wonder so many kids have no clue about what to do with their lives. No wonder so many kids quit school.

Ideally, twice a week, starting in middle school and continuing throughout high school, students would be taken from their classrooms out into the world where they'd be required to study people at work. They'd have to look, listen and question. They'd learn how school is connected to work. They'd realize that what it takes to succeed in school – a strong work ethic, for example – is not different from what it takes to succeed in the non-school world. More importantly, kids could pinpoint what they find fascinating and what they don't.

Regrettably, with few exceptions (some private and charter schools?), this isn't realistic. What *is* possible is for teachers to invite "guest teachers" into their classrooms. These real world people would tell stories, teach lessons and share their outside-of-school lives. This can't compare to actually transporting students from school to offices, factories, hospitals or laboratories, but it's as close as we can realistically get. Guest teachers could include doctors instructing science classes, engineers teaching math classes, writers sharing ideas with English classes, government workers (elected and appointed) firing up social science classes, and entrepreneurs inspiring economics classes. It should be mandatory for students to invite "the most successful people you can find" into the classroom so they can "teach us how to succeed professionally and live well."

Who is successful? What is success? Students can and should determine that - they'll know it when they see it. The idea is to get people who are content with their careers and happy with their lives into the classroom so students can begin forming ideas about which direction they might want to head.

When the guest teacher arrives, students can practice making an introduction and providing hospitality (offering a chair or providing bottled water). During the talk, they should be forced to ask interesting, relevant questions and, to prove they're listening, meaningful and probing follow-up questions. If a speaker claims, "Life gets better after high school," and leaves it at that, someone better ask, "Why? What will make it better?" Afterward, students should handwrite and snail mail a sincere thank-you card.

What else can kids do to See the Blue (Lesson 18) and get a clue about what to do with their lives?

1. **Channel their "I can do it better!" rage:** When we care enough to get emotional about the way someone is performing his or her job, it's a pretty good bet that we care about that job. One reason I became a teacher is that I had a lot of terrible teachers. *If I was teaching this class*, I'd think, *I'd do it so differently – so much better!* I almost became a principal for the same reason. I never felt that way about my doctors, landscapers, mail carriers or electricians. I didn't even feel that way about the cops who have pulled me over. When kids get angry about an adult's job performance, it's good. It may mean that, someday, they'll be doing that adult's job - but they'll be doing it better.

2. **Be aware of "the moment":** If we're aware of it, a single moment can launch our destinies. There's a scene in the movie *Charlie Wilson's War* (based on a true story) when Texas Congressman Charlie Wilson gazes out over the squalor and horror of an Afghan refugee camp in northern Pakistan. At that moment,

he resolved to find a way for the U.S. to back the Afghan freedom fighters who eventually defeated the Soviets.

If students are taught what a *moment* is – a freeze frame of an extraordinary, life-directing, life-changing snippet of time - they'll have a better chance of recognizing, capturing and taking advantage of one when it comes. For example:

- the kid who fractures his femur has a moment during his recuperation and rehabilitation when he decides to become a physical therapist. He realizes that instead of being the patient, he could help the patient.
- a girl coerced to meet her father's work colleagues finds herself in a fascinating conversation with an environmental lawyer and decides that she, too, wants to study environmental law.

A teacher might teach a lesson that speaks to something deep within – if a student is tuned in enough to grasp it. A single moment can change everything. Trouble is, we don't usually recognize the moment while it's happening. There's a scene in *Field of Dreams* that depicts exactly this. Doc (Burt Lancaster), once a youthful baseball prospect but now a timeworn retired family physician near the end of his life, reflects on the only major league baseball game in which he appeared. He was inserted into right field in the top half of the ninth inning. No balls were hit to him. In the bottom of ninth, he didn't get a chance to bat. So, because that was his only major league game, he *never* got a chance to bat.

> *It was like coming this close to your dreams, then watching them brush past you like a stranger in a crowd. Then, you don't think about it. We just don't recognize the most significant moments in our lives while they're happening. Back then, I'm thinking 'There will be other days.' I didn't realize that that was the only day.*

Is it possible to recognize "the moment" when it comes? Perhaps not. But perhaps. If we're attuned. If we see the blue.

**Side story**: Even if a moment doesn't lead to a vocation selection, recognizing one while it's happening can still be life-enhancing. My daughter, Kyrra, was a three-year member of the UCLA dance team. Two months before her graduation, her little sister, Kylene (then a UCLA freshman), planned to try out for the following year's team. On the evening before the audition, Kyrra, now working at an LA dance studio, opened its doors so she could help Kylene prepare.

My wife and I had planned to take them to dinner afterward. But when we arrived at the studio, they weren't finished. So we had a seat and watched. It was a Saturday night. Only the four of us were there.

The rehearsal was hard. There was a lot of sweat. And when Kylene couldn't get it right, tears. But there was laughter, too. And joy. And satisfaction.

As I sat there in that dance studio next to my wife, watching my daughters do what they both loved and despised – their passion - I was mindful of the moment. It was perfect. My family. My daughters, dancing together. Kyrra helping Kylene. It was, I thought, a moment I'd likely replay in my mind the moment I take my last breath.

3. **Ask "How can I help the most people?" or "How can I help people the most?":** Sometimes it's as simple as that. Assuming that many or, hopefully, most kids believe their purpose is to contribute to the world, this gives them permission to apply what they're best at.

Or not. Often, an appropriate reason to learn a skill - to develop a specific aspect of human capital - is because you can use that skill to help people. You may not *love* the gritty details of dentistry, plumbing or roofing, but mastering any of these vocations will not only make you a living, it will enable you to improve others' lives. Dentists can enter impoverished areas and perform free or reduced rate dental work on children who may never otherwise see a dentist. Plumbers can help build and rebuild homes or volunteer to work in third-world countries bringing running water into the homes of families who'll believe (rightly so) that modern plumbing is magic. And when the roof is leaking, there's no one more important, valuable or life-enhancing than the expert who can repair it.

Get good at almost anything, and you can help. Warren Buffett was good at making money. By doing so, by providing jobs, paying taxes, investing in companies and offering investment advice, he made a lot of people's lives better.

But that's Warren Buffett. What if kids are good at something that *won't* make them rich? Hairstyling. Cooking. Preschool teaching. Guess what? They can still help. And if helping is their main motive, they're likely to be content using their strengths to improve the world. Maybe they won't be super wealthy, yet there is the potential for entrepreneurship. When people like what they're doing and know that their lives matter, not only will they be good at what they do, they'll be looking for ways to innovate their profession. Sometimes innovators are financially rewarded with book deals, speaking engagements and consulting opportunities. But even if they aren't, they'll be OK. If they get to use their talents to make others' lives better, they'll be rewarded in other ways. Nicole Edwards-Masuda, an attorney for Hawaii's Domestic Violence Action Center, introduced me to the term "psychic income." She could probably make more money – a lot more – practicing a different kind of law while working for a commercial law firm. But in exchange for a larger salary, she'd have to sacrifice her psychic income – the good, incalculable feelings that come with helping victims of family violence.

The world needs contributors who are great at what they do, even when what they do won't make them Warren Buffett rich. When you need a barber, butcher, carpenter or mechanic, don't you want them to be an exceptionally good barber, butcher, carpenter or mechanic?

**4. Allow "the big picture" to motivate:** Trisha didn't especially like biology. She wasn't crazy about chemistry or physics, either. The truth was, Trisha didn't like studying *science*. Yet, Trisha wanted to be a doctor. And if you want to be a doctor, you *have* to study science!

But she could push past that problem by focusing on the big picture. She knew that she wasn't studying biology, chemistry or physics because she was fascinated by the course material. She didn't want to be a researcher or teacher. She didn't even think she would love "doctoring" that much. What she did love was helping people, and she was certain she'd love *healing* people. So, despite the science, she's enrolled in a pre-med program at the University of California, San Diego.

You don't have to love every part of what it takes to reach your goal. You just have to love your goal.

**5. Try to achieve "The Engineer's Dream":** A talented, content (and rich) electrical engineer told my class that the engineer's dream is to "build something that millions of people will use and feel they can't live without."

You don't have to be an engineer to dream that dream. Many of us aspire to create or produce something coveted by the masses. A recipe. A blueprint. A plan. The question for kids to ask themselves is "What do I care more about and know more about than anything else?" Once they can answer that, they can start planning ways to share it with the world.

**6. Attend symposiums, lectures and workshops:** Listen to guest speakers and campus visitors. (Parents, teachers and principals - get those speakers there!) When someone's life interests students' lives, they should recognize it as a signal that they might like to pursue a similar life. Simple, right? What's complex is getting kids to attend symposiums, lectures and workshops!

7. **Tour possible places of employment:** I spent a summer touring three state-of-the-art, high-tech companies:

- Piazza (piazza.com), a Palo Alto, California start-up that allows college students to collaborate online.
- Zappos (zappos.com), the online shoe and apparel shop located in Las Vegas, Nevada (acquired by Amazon but operating as an independent entity)
- Google (google.com), headquartered in Mountain View, California

My intent was to learn what it takes to work for these kinds of companies. What are they looking for in their new hires? (I found out they're looking for people who have mastered the lessons in this book.) While there, I felt like I should have dragged along my students. They are the ones who should be touring businesses, asking themselves if they'd like working there and whether or not they would be a good fit for the company.

Ideally, schools would plan field trips to businesses, government and non-government organizations. (Don't count on this anytime soon, however. Sadly, at many schools, field trips are becoming increasingly rare. They're expensive and burdened with stifling regulations by administrators more concerned with litigation than education.) On the other hand, there's nothing preventing high school students – seniors especially - from arranging their own tours to work places that interest them.

8. **Read!:** Two books, *The Water is Wide* by Pat Conroy and *The Other Side of the Mountain* by E.G. Valens, convinced me to become a teacher.

9. **Watch movies and television:** Silly? Maybe. But a surprising number of people who love their jobs became interested in those jobs because they saw someone performing them on film. The

police chief who used to watch *Dragnet* and the optical engineer who first became fascinated by lasers after seeing them in a Chinese sci-fi movie were both guest speakers in my class.

**10. Examine your Life List:** It's full of clues about what interests you and what kind of life you hope to lead. If it's loaded with exotic places you want to visit, you probably should look into a job that allows you to travel the world (or pays you enough to afford it). If there's a lot on the list that involves helping people and serving society, a philanthropic career should be explored.

**Personal Example:** I was able to go to Nicaragua to help build a school. ("Build a school in a third-world country" was on my life list.) As a teacher, I had the chance to lead a student group there during my summer break, and all expenses were paid.

**11. Write a mission statement:** Practically every business, school and organization has one. For example:

**Google:** *Organize the world's information and make it universally accessible and useful.*

**Cisco:** *Enable people to make powerful connections - whether in business, education, philanthropy, or creativity. Cisco hardware, software, and service offerings are used to create the Internet solutions that make networks possible-providing easy access to information anywhere, at any time.*

**Facebook:** *Give people the power to share and make the world more open and connected.*

**Myabetic:** *Transform the image of diabetes, encouraging people with diabetes to control their health with style, not shame.*

**Bloomingdale's:** *Not a store, but a destination.*

**Apple:** *Committed to bringing the best personal computing experience to students, educators, creative professionals and* *consumers around the world through its innovative hardware, software and Internet offerings.*

**Chipotle:** *Food with integrity.*

**Nike:** *To bring motivation and originality to all athletes worldwide. If you have a body, you are a sportsperson.*

**Varian:** *Focus energy on saving lives. Our goal is to help save millions of lives around the world every year. To meet this challenge, we equip the world with new tools for fighting cancer, taking x-ray images, and protecting our borders.*

**Eastern Michigan University:** *Inspire, educate, and prepare professionals to be outstanding educators, leaders, and scholars in urban global and diverse educational and community settings.*

**UCLA:** *Creation, dissemination, preservation, and application of knowledge for the betterment of our global society.*

**San Jose State University:** *In collaboration with nearby industries and communities, SJSU faculty and staff are dedicated to achieving the university's mission as a responsive institution of the state of California: To enrich the lives of its students, to transmit knowledge to its students along with the necessary skills for applying it in the service of our society, and to expand the base of knowledge through research and scholarship.*

**Kiva:** *To connect people through lending for the sake of alleviating poverty.*

Shouldn't people have mission statements, too? Shouldn't we all identify and articulate our purpose for existence? Why are we here? What do we hope to accomplish and contribute?

Here's mine:

> *Learn what it takes to live an extraordinary life, live one, and teach what it takes to others. This will be accomplished by studying great lives from the past and present, applying their wisdom to myself and sharing what works with as many people as I can.*

Mission statements should be concise, specific and personal. No two should be the same. Generic mission statements – the kind anyone could have - *Live a happy life; Be the best person I can be; Make the world a better place...* are a waste of time. They aren't distinctive. They don't tell the world why you're here – or give you a clue as to why you *want* to be here.

**12. Write a Personal Constitution:** States and countries have them – detailed plans outlining and structuring what they stand for and how they want to operate. Use the United States Constitution (a successful one) as a blueprint. Once again, review your Leading Life Indicators (Lesson 10). For each indicator, like the Constitution, include an article and the necessary sections for how you plan to manage that part of your life. (Ten in all, remember? -- Physicality, the three Relationships, Passion, Education/Career, Money, *la causa*, Hope and Spirituality). Once you've thoroughly thought through how you intend to live, you'll have a better idea of what you want to do for a living.

**Note:** Your mission statement should be your "preamble."

**13. Understand the "crap factor":** Every job has it. Even the fantasy jobs. Two of my daughter's college friends made the NFL – one played for the Green Bay Packers, the other for the Chicago Bears. It was their dream come true. Yet both found parts of the job – meetings, morning workouts, living far from home in a strange city – tedious and difficult. No job, no career is free from the crap factor. So stop searching for fun-all-the-time, perfect work. It doesn't exist.

**14. Know when you can compete:** Just as I had a "welcome to reality" moment when I was 16 and realized I would never be good enough to compete with NBA-caliber athletes, I had the opposite experience while listening to Jack Canfield speak (the *Chicken Soup for the Soul* creator). This is in no way meant to be disrespectful to Canfield. On the contrary, he's one of the great writers, speakers and motivators of our time, and that's why this was such an enlightening moment for me. I hope this doesn't come off as arrogant, because that's not my intent. But after having read his book and listening to him speak, I thought, *I can do this. I'm at least as good. I can compete with Jack!*

Obviously, I'm not even in the same galaxy as Canfield when it comes to overall success and influence. But at that moment, I believed I *could* be. I wasn't there yet, and I'm still nowhere close. But deep in my soul I believed I could be a world class writer and speaker.

What do you want to do? Find the best practitioners in your areas of interest and ask yourself:

- Can I do this, too?
- Am I or can I be at least as good?
- Can I compete with them?

If your answers are "yes," you may have figured out what you want to do with your life.

**15. Examine your free-time thoughts and behaviors:** When you have real, pure free time, what do you find yourself thinking about and doing? If you doodle, what kind of things do you draw? What are you trying to learn? What are you trying to teach yourself? These are your real, pure interests. Is there any way you can make money with these interests?

**16. Do something:** The worst thing you can do is sit around, trying to figure it out. As soon as you can, preferably as an intern, preferably while you're still in school, try some job - any job. If you do, you'll begin to develop a clearer picture about what you want and don't want. Maybe you'll fall in love with your work. Maybe you'll fall in love with some aspect of your work and veer off in that direction. Or maybe you'll detest your work and decide to pursue a completely different path. But you won't learn anything about your true interests if all you do is wait around, thinking your destiny will miraculously reveal itself to you.

## Assignment

Until you figure it out, try them all. Try all 16 tips for figuring out what to do with your life. Take this seriously. Finding your purpose - your destiny - is difficult, but make it mandatory. When someone says there's no hurry, that in time you'll "figure it out," don't be too comforted. A lot of people *never* figure it out. They're still waiting for it to magically come to them. Don't let that be you.

## How to Talk

Since most kids aren't formally taught how to be strong conversationalists, it's not surprising that many of them suffer from weak conversation skills. They aren't able to answer questions interestingly or ask them adeptly. They're unable to get people talking or keep them talking. This is a shame because some of life's best, most exhilarating moments stem from talking. Whether they're funny and lighthearted, deep and intense or enlightening and thought-provoking, meaningful, elevated conversations can radiate an endorphin-like high.

There's a difference between simple, low-level conversation and meaningful, elevated conversation. Unlike typical talk, the latter energizes. It leaves us feeling smarter and better. It gives us a *kefi* conversation high. But it requires work. And intellect. Uneducated people don't engage in many meaningful, elevated conversations. So we have to teach kids how to talk. It starts with teaching them how to answer questions, especially the kinds of questions that can be answered with a yes/no or with only a word or two. Questions such as:

- "How are you?"
- "Are you hungry?"
- "Where would you like to eat?"
- "Did you like the movie?"
- "What's your all-time favorite movie?"

Typically, a kid will answer:

- "Good"
- "Yes" (or "No")
- "McDonald's" (or, worse, "I don't care.")
- "Yes" (or "No")
- "*The Lion King*" (or, worse, "I don't know.")

Acceptable answers? Maybe - if you're a small child. Once a student reaches high school, it's not even close to cute to answer monosyllabically. Ever have one of those one–way conversations that begins with you asking a question that gets a too short and too terse answer? So you follow it up with another question that is, again, answered as if words are hidden assets, only meant to be used in emergencies. It's exhausting.

Better answers would have been:

- "Pretty good. This (good thing) happened today." Or, "Great! I'm looking forward to watching/going to/seeing _______ tonight."
- "I'm starving. All I've eaten today is half a donut. How about you?"
- "Can we please eat at In-N-Out? I'm craving a chocolate shake and a double cheeseburger."
- "I loved it! My favorite part was when …"
- "I guess I'd have to say *The Lion King* because it made me both laugh *and* cry."

Obviously, the answers in the second scenario are light years more interesting. They're conversation starters, not killers. They invite the questioner to do more than fire off questions. They encourage him or her to participate in the conversation, not be responsible for it.

Jean Faust is our high school's direct line to colleges. She's responsible for sending transcripts to admission offices all over the country. She has a good gauge on who gets accepted into college and who doesn't, especially to the most competitive schools. She has found that it's not always those with the best GPAs and highest test scores who are accepted. Many times it comes down to the personal statement (sometimes called the college entrance essay).

What's a game-changing personal statement? Jean tells the story of a University of California, Berkeley admissions officer who told her that if a personal statement stimulates him enough that he'd want to have a cup of coffee with the student who wrote it, it's a good one. And a rare one. "Not many make me feel that way," he said.

The same admissions officer also instructed a handful of prospective UC students to, "In ten seconds, tell me about yourself." Each who tried struck out – most without swinging. After an uncomfortable pause, most stammered and stuttered and offered nothing beyond clichés. Even if conversational skills are not officially evaluated or a part of most colleges' admission formulas (Which begs the question, *Why not?*), they matter. They matter a lot.

And what if a student *does* get to have that cup of coffee with a college admissions official? What then? (This is part of the application process at many private and even some public universities' special programs. Both my daughters were formally interviewed prior to their acceptance into UCLA's dance program.) Or, if not with a college admissions official, what about the make-it-or-break-it meeting with the potential employer, business partner or client? Will he or she be prepared? Will he or she be ready to talk? Will he or she be any good at talking?

Usually not. Not without...

1. a healthy respect for the importance of developing top-tier conversational skills

2. a conversation plan - discussion topics and ideas

3. plenty of practice

The first and third are obvious. The second is what most students aren't taught. I teach "commonplacing." The "commonplace book" (as discussed by Steven Johnson in *Where Good Ideas Come From*) became an important part of teaching in 17th Century England. John Locke and John Milton "commonplaced." Later, at Harvard, Ralph Waldo Emerson and Henry David Thoreau were expected to produce a commonplace book - a place to store (in a common place) an array of thoughts, concepts, lessons, quotes, photographs, letters, poems, proverbs, plans and designs. The commonplace book is a personal accumulation of its writer's interests, knowledge, ambitions and ideas depicted in words, images, charts and graphs. It's a scrapbook of life.

For many courses, I require students to create a commonplace book that includes the most important lessons they learn in my class. Some lessons, such as the Personal Constitution, Leading Life Indicators, Inspirational People List and Life List are required. But the majority of their commonplace entries are electives – *they* decide what lessons are most personal, interesting and relevant to them.

Armed with a commonplace book, almost anyone can initiate a conversation – formal or informal. A commonplace book is packed with a wealth of meaningful topics to discuss. Think about the depth of a conversation you could have about someone on your Inspirational People List. Wouldn't it be something you'd love to share? Who's on your list? Ask your conversation partners whom they have on theirs.

I had a chance to ask a school board member who he would put on his list. When he mentioned Cesar Chavez, I told him about the time that Chavez's grandson, Anthony Chavez, all grown up and carrying on his grandfather's work, taught a lesson to my fourth period government and economics class.

With or without the tool that is the commonplace book, skilled conversationalists have mastered the ability to answer *and* ask questions insightfully. Prerequisites for both include empathy, wit and practice.

**How questions should be answered**

Don't make conversing with you painful. When answering questions, be aware that *Why is understood.* When someone asks a question that can be answered with one word, don't answer with one word!

Save your conversation partner from awkwardness and embarrassment by including *why* in your answer, even if it was not directly asked. For example, if you're asked "What's your favorite sport?" don't simply name a sport. Explain *why* that sport is your favorite. You could distinguish between your favorite participatory and spectator sport. Tell a story about when, why or how you got hooked. When did you first realize your sport was appealing? Why is it still appealing?

Talk should be comfortable and pleasant. If you answer questions with only a word or two, then a conversation with you is uncomfortable and unpleasant. You become that mind-numbing, exhausting person most of us once endured but now avoid.

**How questions should be asked**

Even though YOU know the *why* is implicit, most people won't. So, chances are, you'll have to tack *why* on to your question. But don't do it right away. Give people a chance. If they mess up (expect that they will), then include the "*Why*?"

"What movie has had the greatest impact on you?"

"*Titanic*"

"Why?"

"If you could have lunch with anyone in the world, with

whom would it be?"

"*Ellen DeGeneres*"

"Why Ellen? Why is she your choice?"

There are two types of questions: *initiators* and *follow-ups*:

**Initiators:** Initiators get people to *start* talking. But be careful. If you ask an initiator with no context, it's awkward. Imagine you're sitting among a group with no one talking when, out of nowhere, you blurt, "So, who has the best singing voice of all time?"

That would be weird. But not if you lead into it. For example, "Yesterday, my teacher asked us who we thought has the best singing voice of all time. Who do you think does?"

Or, "My daughter thinks Christina Aguilera has the best singing voice in the world. What do you think? Does she? If not Christina, who?"

If you can find a way to make your questions contextual, you'll be a conversational genius. So be ready with a set of interesting interrogatives and imperatives.

Here are some ideas for starting feel-good conversations:

- What are you working on or toward?
- What was your worst loss and greatest victory?
- What are you struggling with right now?
- If you had to switch lives with someone, with whom would it be?
- What do you wish you could do that you know you'll never do?
- What award, medal or trophy have you won that means the most to you?
- If you could win any award – Nobel Prize, Academy Award, Grammy, Super Bowl MVP – which would you choose?

- With what could you use help? (How can *I* help you?)

- Tell me about someone who used to be in your life that you really miss.

- Tell me about three things and three people you're especially grateful for having in your life.

- What do you wish you could redo?

  **Rule:** You can't say, "Nothing, because everything I did has made me into the person I am today."

- What's legal that should be illegal? Rudeness? Meanness? Laziness? Playing "Marco Polo" in swimming pools? (A personal pet peeve – it drives me nuts!)

- What's illegal that should be legal? (Drinking a beer when you're a 20-year-old army sergeant? Coming to a "complete" stop at a four-way stop sign when there's not another car within a hundred miles?)

- How did you meet your husband/wife? How did your parents meet? (It's surprising how many kids *don't* know.) Tell me about your kids. Do you have any pets?

- What were you like when you were our age? Were you wild? Did you rebel? Were you ever a teacher's favorite? What was your favorite and least favorite subject?

- Why do you do the work you do? Is this what you ultimately want to do? Are you "there"? If not, what's next? What's the goal? If you could no longer work at your job, what would you do instead? What was your childhood dream job? What's your fantasy career?

- If you were to start a non-profit organization or NGO, in what area of need would it specialize?

- What do you think is fun that others might *not* think is fun?

- What *don't* you think is fun that many people think *is* fun?
- What are the best parts of your job? The worst?
- At work, if you were "the boss of everyone" and could change anything you wanted, what change(s) would you make?
- Would you want to be the King (or Queen) of the World? If you were, what would be your first decree?
- Fiction or nonfiction? What's the most impactful book you've read? Who's your favorite author?
- Would you rather be a principal or a teacher? (The real question: Do you want to be a manager, overseeing others or in the trenches, doing it? Hospital administrator or doctor? Police chief or police officer? Coach or player?)
- Would you rather affect a small group of people in a large way or a large group of people in a small way?
- Would you rather know a little about a lot or a lot about a little - generalist or specialist? Which describes you best right now?
- What do you most want us to learn from you and teach to others?
- What don't you own that you want to own?
- What angers you?
- Tell us about someone you love being around and why you love being around him or her. (You can use his or her name.) Tell us about someone you can't stand being around and what he or she does that annoys. (Please don't use his or her name.)
- My teacher requires us to create and maintain a list of people (famous and not so famous, living or historical) who inspire us. Who would be on your list?

- Did/do you have a mentor? If you could be mentored by anyone in the world, who would it be?
- What wasn't taught to you in school that you wish had been taught?
- What was the most valuable lesson a teacher taught you?
- What was the most important *academic* lesson you learned in school – one that you still use today as an adult?
- Did you learn your most important life lessons inside or outside the classroom? (e.g. basketball court, family, club, band, church...)
- How did you learn social skills and develop your considerable social intelligence? *This is an example of a complimentary question (Lesson 19).*
- From whom, where or what did you get your motivation?
- Can you think of an example when your success in one part of your life transferred to another part of your life? If so, how?
- Describe UOP's "One Word Project." Ask about theirs. Share yours. (Every entering student at the University of Pacific has to pick one word that best describes him or her. Examples: *Warrior, Comic, Innovator.* Their choices appear on the UOP website.)

What else? What do *you* want to ask?

*In addition to these, play the favorite/question game described in Lesson 20. Those can be conversation starters, too.*

**Follow-ups:** Follow-up questions require that we listen, think and then ask a logical, relevant question based on what the speaker has *already said.* Asking a high-quality follow-up question is more challenging and takes more perception and intelligence than an initiator. Either way, whether it's an initiator or a follow-up, it's important to sincerely care about the speaker's response. Why have a discussion when we are apathetic about the content of that discussion?

We should care about our conversation topics and practice talking about them. Like with almost anything, the more we do it, the more we work at it, the better we'll get. The problem is that not many in the upper echelons of the education policy-making hierarchy recognize how critical it is for kids to master communication and interpersonal skills. They must consider them fluff. If they didn't, learning how to carry on a conversation would be at least hinted at in some state or national standard. Because it's not, it's not taught, which means it's not practiced and not tested. Therefore, it's not learned.

What about those afraid to talk - those whose introversion is in their DNA? Author Susan Cain, in her much-viewed TED Talk, outlines the positive attributes of introverts. During their alone time, Cain claims, introverts formulate ideas that can change the world. Cain cites Gandhi, Buddha and Lincoln as introverts. They preferred *not* to speak, especially in public. Yet, because they needed to communicate their messages, they *forced* themselves to talk. They understood that their wisdom, born during time spent, as Cain puts it, "in the wilderness," had to be "taken out of the suitcase" and shared.

The point? We are not the destiny of our nature. When the cause is great, we can fight our natural (but detrimental) inclinations and defeat them. Introverts are often creative geniuses. But they aren't doing anyone any good (including themselves) when their great ideas are kept inside, hidden from a world that desperately needs them.

**Formal Presenting**

I taught at a high school where leadership students visited third-period classrooms twice a week to update us on school events - many of which the leadership kids themselves had planned. Theoretically, they were supposed to motivate their peers to participate.

They didn't. Most of my students tuned them out, and it wasn't a mystery why. The presentations were usually read from the presenters' cellphones. The speakers would stare down at their devices, ignoring their audience. Again, these were *leadership* students.

At many high schools, a class in "public speaking" used to be required. The thinking was that, no matter what the profession, the ability to present well was an essential ingredient for success. Today, however, public speaking can't compete with the Advanced Placement courses seen by many college admission officials as the primary measuring stick for acceptance.

No wonder so many kids and adults are woefully inarticulate. Speaking takes practice. If students aren't expected to speak intelligibly, if they aren't evaluated on their ability to present effectively (The New Report Card), we shouldn't be surprised when they're no good at it. Why work at what isn't valued?

Yet, it *is* valued. Maybe not by college admission officials but by just about everyone else. And because it's valued by real life professionals in almost every possible profession, students who can make a genuine, high-quality oral presentation (not a condescendingly praised one as in "That was good - for a kid"), will differentiate themselves (Lesson 28).

Since I don't foresee public speaking classes making a comeback anytime soon, we better find a way to teach kids presentation do's and don'ts. If we don't, whether they're presenting to a classroom full of peers or to a corporation's board of directors, they'll be as boring and ineffective as the leadership kids who visited my classroom.

Kids need to understand that no one *has* to listen to them, especially after they leave school. It will be their task to persuade even reluctant audiences to *want* to listen to them. To do that, they'll need to know that a high-quality presentation includes the following:

- *A strong opening and a powerful closing*
  Great writers labor over how to begin and end a piece. So should great speakers.

- *Huge consideration for the audience*
  Every radio station on the dial has a target demographic such as *teenage females, women ages 18–34*, or *men, ages 25-54*. The station program managers make a concerted effort to broadcast to their listeners' tastes, interests, maturity and intelligence. Speakers should do the same.

- *Minimal reading*
  It's acceptable for a speaker to refer to notes or read short passages. But it's not acceptable to read an entire speech.

- *Multimedia*
  Pictures, video clips, sound bites, music, charts, graphs and/or diagrams. Audiences want to see and hear something besides the speaker. (I particularly like to include poignant and motivating movie scenes.)

- *Acknowledgment of the elephant in the room*
  When the unexpected isn't addressed, instead of paying attention to the message, the audience will be focused on the distraction. Experienced speakers don't ignore the sudden disruption, even when it ruins their rhythm. The unanticipated entrance/exit, unforeseen audience reaction, or the embarrassing voice crack should be briefly recognized (and quickly dismissed). Only then will the audience let it go.

- *Substantial preparation*
  It takes great effort to make a presentation appear effortless. The more important the presentation, the more preparation is necessary. Relentless planning diminishes tension while fortifying confidence.

- *Care!*
  If you don't care, if you're not enthused about what you're presenting, not many people will be interested in listening to you. Audiences aren't easily moved – or fooled.

- *The basics*
  Public Speaking 101 fundamentals that used to be taught and practiced, but now rarely are: appropriate voice tone, assertive body language and audience eye contact.

## Assignment

There's no way around it. The only way to get good at conversing is to converse - often. Reading this chapter and studying these techniques will give you a clue about what to do. But reading, alone, won't help. You've got to practice. Building relationships can be fun, but it entails work. Especially if you're an introvert, seek chances to chat. When you do, you'll be rewarded with improved communication skills and, sometimes, with a conversation high.

A fun, effective technique for achieving that high is the "walk-talk." Invite someone to go for a walk, preferably (but it doesn't have to be) in a naturally beautiful, relatively quiet place. Before the walk, plan. Have in mind topics to discuss. The conversation doesn't have to be *only* about those topics, but you'll find it advantageous to have walk-talk objectives.

## What to Think About at the End of the Day

**Final thoughts before sleep:**

**Option #1 – The Day's Accomplishments**

Review the day, focusing on successes. What did you get done? What's the best thing you did? Second best? I'm not referring to the best thing that *happened*. That's fate. It may be exciting, but you can't count on it. Or control it. What were the best things *you* did? Things you controlled (self-determination).

Refer, once more, to the Leading Life Indicators:

- **Physicality**
  Did you work out? Eat well? Did you get a haircut? A manicure? A massage? Buy any new clothes? Cosmetics? Take your medication? Resist recreational drugs/alcohol/cigarettes? What did you do for your body so you look and feel better?

- **Relationships** (family, friends, romantic)
  How were they strengthened or nurtured?

- **Passion**
  What did you accomplish regarding the development of your passion? Did you practice? If you're a writer, did you write? If you're a musician, did you play? If you're a painter, did you paint? Did you study your passion? Did you watch it? Read about it? Interview experts in it? Did you have a successful moment in one or more of your passions today? What was it? I've drifted off to sleep

while re-experiencing successful jump shots and well-surfed waves.

- **Education/Career**
  What did you do to augment it? Enrich it? Study particularly hard for a test? Ask your teacher (or a capable student) for help? Get an A on a test? Sign up for a class? Complete a job? Work extra hard on a project? Make a new contact? Meet a new prospect? Make a sale? Come up with a profitable idea?

- **Money**
  Did you earn any? Did you figure out a way to earn more? Did you pay off a bill? Did you make a wise investment?

- ***la causa***
  Did you help anyone? Contribute to society? What did you do? How is the world better off because of what you did today?

- **Spirituality**
  Contemplating life's spiritual/theological purpose can be comforting. But did you live your beliefs? What is the point of having spiritual beliefs or belonging to an organized religion if we don't live what it teaches and preaches? Did you do unto others as you would have them do unto you?

- **Hope**
  What's next? What are you looking forward to tomorrow? Next week? Next month? Next year? Next decade?

Is it necessary to be relentlessly striving?

I say yes. That's why we're here. To continually push ourselves. To make a difference. To get things done. To have a positive impact.

Can you have a good day, or even a great day, without accomplishing anything that falls under the Leading Life Indicators?

Of course. Maybe your goal for the day was to catch up on your favorite TV show, relax and have fun. If you did that, your day was purposeful.

But that shouldn't be the goal *every* day. If your goal every day is to rest and relax, you're going to be miserable. Remember the difference between pleasures and passions (Lessons 4 & 5)? You need something from which to rest and relax! Too much resting and relaxing results in restlessness and remorse.

What if you realize at the end of the day that you didn't accomplish anything? Then what?

Then fall asleep planning how you'll improve tomorrow.

## Option #2 – Healthy Human Contacts (HHCs)

### A. Seeking HHCs

When I was a kid growing up near Cleveland, my parents would take us on outings to northern Ohio's metropolitan parks. On the way, we'd drive past the "the hermit's house." On the edge of the woods lived a man who rarely ventured out into the world. He lived alone. As far as we knew, he didn't speak. As much as we could tell, he avoided human contact.

He was a curiosity. As we drove past his small, single-story home, we'd stare out the car window, hoping to get a glimpse of him. Humans, by nature, are social. Because the hermit wasn't, because his solitude and isolation was so strange, so alien, we were frightened and fascinated by him. Sightings of him were rare but strangely thrilling. "There he is!" we'd whisper loudly.

Looking back, the hermit story saddens me. I never found out why he lived alone and shunned people. How long had he been that way? Was he born with a social disorder? What was he like as a kid? Had he endured a great tragedy? How does someone end up being branded "the hermit"?

He couldn't have been happy because, whether they last five seconds, five minutes or five hours, the quality of our human contacts determines the quality of our day.

Ever walk past someone who smiles and says "Hi"? That small, probably forgotten acknowledgment momentarily lifted your mood, right? When I was a high school freshman, if I got a smile and a "Hi" from a "fine" (my generation's adjective for today's "hot") girl, I'd brag about it to my friends. It would make being a fifteen-year-old boy a little more bearable. Ever go for a run and come upon someone running in the opposite direction? Your eyes meet. As you pass, you acknowledge each other's presence (and travail), and your spirit is lifted. You feel a jolt of energy. You pick up your pace.

These kinds of uplifting ephemeral meets, along with warm moments spent with family, friends and/or our romantic partner are Healthy Human Contacts (HHCs). They make us feel better. Happier. They're the antithesis of what we've all experienced too many times - unhealthy human contacts. The more "HHCs" we have, the better our day. The better our lives. We want them and need them, so we should seek them.

Often, we don't. Sometimes we're afraid to take a social risk. After all, no human contact beats an unhealthy one. But no human contact eliminates any chance for a healthy one. We can't afford to take that kind of risk with our health, nor with the quality of our lives.

Sometimes it's deeper, more complex and not necessarily a matter of conscious choice. More than one out of every 15 Americans suffer from Social Anxiety Disorder (SAD). The onset of SAD is usually age 14-16, but 35% of the time it occurs before age 10. Girls are more likely to have it than boys. A shocking 50% of those diagnosed with SAD don't finish high school, yet only 5% with SAD get treatment. Fifty percent of those with SAD also have another psychiatric disorder, especially alcohol abuse. (Is it because they crave human contact but don't feel comfortable communicating *without* alcohol?)[58] [59] [60]

Adults and children with SAD (also referred to as a social phobia) will avoid human contact. They're terrified that they'll be judged, ridiculed, bullied or rejected. So, instead of looking for an opportunity to feel better, they look for ways to *not* connect with others.

They won't answer the door or their phones. When they see

someone coming, they'll head the other way, even if it's the longer way. To evade eye contact, they'll look down or away. To avoid being approached, they'll pretend to text or talk on their phone.

We need to teach them not to do this! We need to teach kids to move *toward* people, not away from them. Or, at the very least, allow natural encounters to occur. We need to teach kids to collect HHCs, not dismiss them. They need to know that, at the end of the day, even if they only talked to the mail carrier for seven seconds, they'll be happier than if they talked to no one. And when they reach the point where they're capable of engaging in an extended, enriching conversation with a bright, inspiring person, they'll become addicted to HHCs.

Besides fleeting meetings and long talks, HHC interaction can include texts, emails, online and video chats, even old fashioned telephone conversations (remember those?). But there's still no replacement for a real, face-to-face human interaction. As long as it's genuine and elevating, it qualifies as an HHC.

What *doesn't* qualify as an HHC is when the store/business employee offers a token (and probably required) "Hello" when we arrive and a "Have a nice day" when we depart. An HHC has to be real, not forced, contrived or rehearsed.

Each day, kids should wake up and search for the blue. In this case, the blue is composed of Healthy Human Contacts. Kids should make it a priority, even a daily goal, to meet and talk to people. When a social encounter makes them feel good, they should add it to their daily HHC tally. The more HHCs accumulated, the better the day.

### B. Being the HHC

Kids' lives are enriched by Healthy Human Contacts. So why not teach them to enrich the lives of as many others as they can?

Only searching for HHCs is selfish. Kids should be taught and encouraged to be on the other end, too. Smiling and saying "Hi" is a start. Initiating a meaningful conversation is even better. When kids consistently practice the behaviors on the Do-Bee list (Lesson 19), others will be thinking about the HHC they had with *them* as they fall asleep at night.

*Which is more important – accomplishments or Healthy Human Contacts? The answer is they're equally important. Option #1 and #2 could have been reversed. Some days will be productive days. Other days will be people days. The best days will include a heavy dose of both.*

## Assignment

While lying in bed at the end of the day, sort through your achievements. Use the Leading Life Indicators as a checklist. On which indicator(s) was your day spent? On which do you need to focus tomorrow? Which indicators earned a high score? Which need work?

Then, if you're having trouble falling asleep, don't count sheep. Count HHCs. If you drift off before you're able to count them all, regardless of what else happened, it was probably a good day.

## Universal Values – and Flaws

At the beginning of each chapter of her autobiography, *The Favored Daughter: One Woman's Fight to Lead Afghanistan into the Future*, Afghan Parliament speaker and human rights activist Fawzia Koofi writes a letter to her two daughters, Shaharzad and Shuhra, then 12 and 10. Because she knows her life is in danger each time she leaves her home (at only 37, she has already survived two assassination attempts), she wants to leave a written record of her hopes and dreams for them.[61]

Her first letter focuses on her educational aspirations for Shaharzad and Shuhra:

> *After you graduate from eighth grade, I want you to continue your studies abroad. I want you to be familiar with universal values. The world is a big, beautiful wonderful place and it is yours to explore.*

Polarization plagues our planet. Divisiveness is everywhere. It's there, between countries and within countries. Cities, states and municipalities can't seem to elude it. Dissention and discord among factions are found in corporate boardrooms and school cafeterias. That's why, more than ever, we need to teach what we have in common and not dwell on our differences.

Let's be clear. Universal values are not *unanimous* values. Not everybody buys into them. But a *lot* of people in a *lot* of places do, and that's what gives us hope.

I've seen universal values work. I've watched while values such as our will to win and our respect for hard work diminish differences. Experiencing kids from different religions, ethnicities or social classes blow off their dissimilarities and focus on achieving something larger than themselves is profoundly impressive. I've coached basketball teams that included (among others) African-American, Asian-American, European-American, Indian-American and Mexican-American kids who practiced (among others) Buddhism, Christianity, Islam and Hinduism. But none of that mattered when they played.

All they cared about on the basketball court was performing well and experiencing *kefi* – two universal values. It doesn't matter if it's basketball, dancing, math or playing the ukulele, kids want to be good at what they do and experience joyful moments while they're doing it. And adults aren't any different. When we're working toward a common goal – feeding the hungry, healing the sick, running a business – similarities trump our dissimilarities.

What other universal values trivialize our differences? There are obvious ones – health, honesty, justice, security, peace, the natural rights (life, liberty, the pursuit of happiness), the Golden Rule... but Koofi also writes about less obvious but equally important ones:

- Dignity for all people, regardless of their position in society

- Family, love and loyalty - Koofi describes the nuances of sibling relationships and how important they can be.

- Our belief in the value of change (along with our reluctance to embrace it)

- Education, even if we don't make clear distinctions between effective, less effective, ineffective and detrimental education e.g. radical madrassas that teach hate and violence

- The rule of law

- A respect for intelligence
- Patience
- Self-sacrifice
- Humility
- Kindness
- The opportunity to pursue our dreams
- The ability to prepare food for loved ones (Koofi writes that this is a *woman's* value. Is it only a value for women?)
- Volunteerism, charity and charitable giving - Donating time and/or money to the disadvantaged and unfortunate (psychic income)
- The desire to celebrate - Universally, we celebrate birthdays, coming of age ceremonies, graduations, marriages…
- A longing to marry the person of our dreams
- The duty to protest and/or rebel against tyrannical authority
- Perseverance - The "Don't give up!" spirit
- The importance of taking action and making things happen (as opposed to waiting around for someone else to do it)

The list of universal traits Koofi hopes to instill in Shaharzad and Shuhra's core value system is extensive, but not all-encompassing. She could have also included:

- Sportsmanship (winning and losing with grace)

- Respect for and appreciation of beauty, nature and the environment.
- A sense of humor – laughter, smiles
- Attachment to others - the pain of goodbye
- *Kefi*. Around the world, people find moments of joy.
- Harmony, peace - Cliché, yes, but cliché for obvious reasons.
- Caring for children - Seeing that their needs are met. Putting them first.
- Pets! There are animal lovers everywhere.

Every school's curriculum should include an intense study of the universal values because, far too often, we let our minor differences divide us. If you don't think that people are essentially alike, consider that genetic scientists claim that human beings share 99% of our DNA with chimpanzees, 98% of it with gorillas and 97% with orangutans![62] The point is, if we resemble the great apes that closely (at least with regard to DNA), just think how alike any two *people* are! Even that annoying politician, neighbor or classmate is way more like you than unlike you.

It's hard to get past those differences, though. It must be human nature to detect and dwell on what we *don't* have in common. What we search for, we'll find. If we look for what unites us, we'll find it. If we look for what divides us, we'll find that, too.

Not everything that connects us is positive. Just as there are universal values, there are universal flaws. Alcoholism and drug addiction are universal. So is cruelty. Thieves are found all over the world. So is litter. Damaged relationships and broken families exist in all hemispheres. By nature, we're all tempted to be lazy. We look for easy when the easy choice is usually the wrong choice. We can all be impatient. We share a tendency to be selfish, self-absorbed and egocentric.

We have a dangerous and irrational need to "clan up" and choose sides in an "us vs. them" rivalry. Countries, states, cities, neighborhoods and neighbors consider themselves the good guys and their "rivals" the bad guys. If you're a Boston Red Sox fan, you "have" to despise the New York Yankees and their fans.

Why? I'm pretty sure the Boston Red Sox players don't despise the New York Yankees players (and vice versa) as much as their fanatics despise each other. Except for team allegiance, a Red Sox fan and a Yankees fan could have been best friends or even soulmates. If that didn't happen just because of a uniform they worship, it's stupid. Rivalries are stupid.

Knowing that we all share certain weaknesses can help us understand, tolerate and connect with one another. Jealousy, for example, is universal. If we acknowledge this, we'll be less likely to boast about our accomplishments or brag about our assets. Realizing that people get jealous - and knowing that jealously hurts - can keep us humble. Frustration is universal. The only antidote for it is time. If we're aware of this, we'll be more apt to give frustrated people their space while they defuse.

If we can't accept that people are imperfect, we'll end up bitter and resentful. Acceptance and forgiveness are rarely easy, but they're nearly impossible when we're expecting perfection. Fortunately, acceptance and forgiveness are universally valued.

## Assignment

Use your knowledge of universal values. Understand that the way you think probably isn't much different from the way most people think. Not only is this comforting (you're not alone!), it can help you build your social capital. If, for example, you're humble, kind and you persevere, expect to be well-liked, respected and included. If your actions are contrary to what's universally valued – if you're arrogant, mean and you give up easily - don't be surprised when you feel the wrath of humanity.

Understanding universal values can also help you make money. Sometimes, lots of it. Here's an example:

> In the summer of 1951, while driving with his wife and five children from Memphis to Washington D.C., Kemmons Wilson faced a dilemma. Either he could exit the highway, drive into a large city and pay top dollar to spend one night in a fancy hotel, or he could save money at the cost of subjecting his kids to an evening spent at a seedy roadhouse. He was also frustrated and upset when he learned that some hotels charged an extra $2 dollars per child.
>
> *Why not*, he thought, *build a clean, comfortable, safe, family-friendly hotel complete with air conditioning, an on-site restaurant and a swimming pool, all in plain sight, right off the highway exit?* Wilson was wise enough to assume that other families had similar needs. He trusted that he wasn't alone in his thinking. So he acted.

The result? The Holiday Inn hotel chain that has not only served millions, it made Wilson millions.[63]

The lesson? Trust that if you feel strongly about something, others will feel that way, too. If you like something, the odds are that there will be other people who like it. If you dislike something, the chances are that other people will agree with you.

If you come up with an idea, plan or business proposal that seems great to you, trust that it will seem great to a lot of other people, as well. Then do what Kemmons Wilson did. Act!

And when you feel a need to raise your voice, to say what needs to be said, to make a change, to blow the whistle, to protest, to rebel, to improve the world, remember you're not the only one feeling that need. Others are with you, waiting for you to lead them. Waiting for you to act.

## The Warrior's Weapons

For eight years, I attended St. Barnabas and St. Timothy Catholic schools. During that time, I found fault with them. Too many silly rules. Not enough freedom. Yet, along the way, I was inculcated with values that still define me. Chief among them (even though I probably bombed the tests on them), were the "seven deadly sins" and the "seven heavenly virtues." The sins – lust, gluttony, greed, sloth, wrath, envy and pride could be countered by the virtues – chastity, temperance, charity, diligence, patience, kindness and humility. The sins and virtues, I realized, were at war. And so were we. Among us and within us. But despite my Catholic upbringing and the religious connotation of sins and virtues along with hell and heaven, this isn't a religious war. It's a universal war. We're all battling the sins. We all need the virtues.

There's a generally unheralded and largely underappreciated syndicated television program called *Eco Company*. Here's how it's described on its website:

> ***About Eco Company:***
>
> *What does it mean to "go green" as a teen? More and more young people want to know the answer to that question. Now there's Eco Company, a national TV show on a quest to find answers. Eco Company is hosted by a dynamic group of teens who combine their natural curiosity with their enthusiasm to preserve the planet they inherit.*
>
> *Eco Company explores all aspects of being green and*

> *understanding how we impact our world. From reporting on the latest technologies in energy, recycling, conservation and organics to sharing the stories of young people making a positive impact on the environment. In addition, every week Eco Company provides a practical tip that teens and people of all ages can use in their daily lives. Eco Company is designed to be an interactive program from finding out what's on the minds of teens by talking to them wherever we find them to providing a forum on this website for teens to share their own videos about going green.*

The teenagers who host the program are impressive. They're smart, well spoken and committed to improving the world. Watching *Eco Company* is positive immersion (Lesson 11). The hosts lift your spirit and give you hope.

But for every *Eco Company* kid, there is an "I don't care" kid. Each school day my classroom is flooded with teenagers, many the same age as the Eco Company teenagers. In the front of my classroom sits a trash can and a recycle bin. Even though my students have been taught practically from birth to recycle and "save the planet," each day I find stuff that can be recycled (paper, bottles, aluminum cans) in the trash can and trash (used tissue, apple cores, chewed gum) in the recycle bin.

Not a big deal? I say it *is*. It's a big deal because, in a small but obvious way, it epitomizes the war - the battles between:

- good and evil
- effort and sloth
- selfless and selfish
- intelligence and stupidity

Good people take care of the world. Evil people ruin it. Improving the world takes effort. Making it worse doesn't. It's difficult to be selfless. It's easy to be selfish. Smart people understand the importance of the green movement. Undereducated people don't.

To improve the world, the good, hardworking, selfless, intelligent people must battle the evil, slothful, selfish, undereducated people. The latter, the looking-for-easy offenders, toss their cigarette butts on the ground. The former pick them up and dispose of them properly.

"Looking for easy" is both a positive and negative human propensity. The result of our continuous quest to find an easier way has been revolutionary technological innovation. For example, mixing concrete and cement by hand is difficult, backbreaking work. So, in 1905, a construction company entrepreneur named Gebhard Jaeger designed and built the first concrete mixing machine.[64] On the other hand, "looking for easy" contradicts one of the tenants of this book (Lesson 42). The easy way is rarely the gratifying, rewarding or right way. "Looking for easy" leads to cheating, crime, depression and drug abuse. "Looking for easy" can harm humanity as much as it can help it.

**Side note:** If ever there was a metaphor for what's wrong with humanity, it's the cigarette butt in the street. It was produced by a company that, lusting for profit, creates addicting poison. It was consumed by someone with little sense, no self-discipline and with no regard for…

- his or her health
- the ripple effect of the inevitable health care costs associated with cancer and other smoking-related diseases
- the harmful effect that secondhand smoke has on others
- the potential dangers stemming from throwing a cigarette butt on the ground: possible fires, land and water pollution, animals mistaking it for food…

- the "I'm incredibly lazy, apathetic and "someone else will clean it" message it sends to everyone, but especially to kids

- the opportunity cost - The money spent on cigarettes could have been used to help someone, not squandered on toxin tossed onto the street

If we didn't have environmental warriors battling the environmental destroyers, the earth would already be doomed.

We need warriors using what King Arthur called "might for right." The good are too often overwhelmed by the bad. Some well-intentioned soul picks up a half dozen cigarette butts only to find two dozen more the next day. The natural inclination is to shake your head, shrug your shoulders and stop fighting.

But we can't. Nice people, good people have to be tougher - more warrior-like. Nice people (because they're nice) don't usually call out mean people. The result? Mean people get away with being mean. It takes a warrior mentality to stand up to them. It may not help. But it may. Letting mean people know they're being mean may educate them. (There are jerks who don't know they're jerks.) It will also send the message that they can't get away with being a menace without being challenged.

But as much as the world needs warriors of virtue to fight society's riff-raff, the primary reason for developing a warrior mentality is not so much because of *whom* we're fighting. It's *what* we're fighting. Our most ruthless enemies aren't usually people. What keeps us from living extraordinary, happy, impactful, meaningful and satisfying lives are what JFK called in his 1960 inaugural speech - "the common enemies of man."

Kennedy's examples were "tyranny, poverty, disease and war itself." Yet the list can be expanded to include intrinsic battles. Battles we fight with *ourselves* against the seven deadly sins and against:

- addiction

- apathy
- bigotry
- bitterness
- boredom
- cynicism
- dishonesty
- fatigue
- fear
- frustration
- ignorance
- impatience
- laziness
- lust
- mediocrity
- pessimism
- procrastination
- rage
- resignation

Sometimes the enemy is disguised. Comfort, for example, doesn't seem like a threat. But comfortable people relax, which is OK – for a while. But comfort shouldn't be the goal. Is that why we're here? To live as comfortably as we can for as long as we can – then die? I don't want the theme of my eulogy to be "While Richards was here, he was comfortable." Besides, too much comfort for too long a time whittles away at motivation, destroys ambition and stunts growth. Comfort can be lethal.

Which begs the question, *Can we make things too comfortable for our kids?* The answer is a resounding YES! We don't want children to suffer, and we needn't throw artificial obstacles in their path. Life will naturally provide plenty of challenges, pain and heartache. Yet, we need to be careful about how much we shield our children from the storm that is reality. The hard, often brutal world is a ruthless teacher – but an effective one.

To fight our most formidable foes and flaws, kids need an arsenal of weapons. For example, armed with diligence, they can better battle slothfulness. Hall of Fame football coach Vince Lombardi, taught his teams that, "Fatigue makes cowards of us all." Fortified with fitness, kids can overpower fatigue.

But can virtues be instilled? Or are they simply inherent? Is it nature or nurture that determines who we are?

No educated person can ignore the obvious influence DNA has on a person's character. Genes are powerful, no doubt. University of Minnesota psychologist Dr. Thomas Bouchard conducted a fascinating case study of identical twins separated at birth and raised apart.[65] [66] He discovered that, although where and how each twin was reared varied, their adult habits, tastes and lifestyles were remarkably similar. They liked the same toothpaste, cut their hair the same way, had the same gestures and mannerisms and even had comparable speech patterns. Personality traits including leadership skills, levels of optimism, affinity toward risk taking, aggression and creativity were also alike.

For example, Daphne Goodship and Barbara Herbert were raised separately - Daphne as a Catholic and Barbara as a Jew. Reunited at 40, they were surprised to learn that each had suffered a miscarriage the same year. Eventually, both women gave birth to two boys and a girl - in that order. They recognized that they laughed and folded their arms the same way and learned that, for years, they had been cooking the same recipe from the same cookbook.

Even more implausible is the story of Oskar Stohr and Jack Yufe. Born in Trinidad, the twins were separated immediately. Oskar ended up in Germany, where he was raised a Catholic and became part of Hitler's youth. Jack stayed in Trinidad raised a Jew. As middle-age adults, they were reunited. And guess what? Despite growing up in different worlds, they found that they talked and thought alike, had comparable tastes (a hankering for spicy foods), walked with the same gait and even shared the odd habit of always flushing the toilet before they used it.

**Side Thought:** *Isn't it crazy that Bouchard could even find multiple sets of identical twins separated at birth and raised apart?*

Yet, despite discovering this powerful evidence that babies are born with environmentally unaffected traits and characteristics, Bouchard concluded that nature and nurture are *equally* important in the development of personality. Therefore, even if you strongly believe that children are "born that way," what they're taught and how they're raised is (at least) equally important.

Some things – preferences, interests, mannerisms - can't be changed. But virtues can be instilled and should be taught. In addition to the "seven heavenly virtues," here are other learnable weapons kids will need to defeat their external and internal adversaries:

- **Strong Moral Compass**
  Honesty, integrity, trustworthiness - doing what's right when nobody is watching

- **Tenacity, Perseverance and Resilience**
  *Fall seven times. Stand up eight.* -Japanese Proverb

- **Optimism**
  Martin Seligman, the University of Pennsylvania positive psychologist, insists it can be learned.

- **Confidence** (not cockiness)
  Real, *earned* confidence

- **Willingness to Face Fear**
  For students, small steps. Courage here isn't about scary, physical risks. It's about speaking up in (and out) of class, attempting something unfamiliar and uncomfortable or by going for it when

failure is a possibility.

- **Self-Discipline**
  The capacity to make that tough (and right) choice

- **Innovation**
  The inclination to *act* on creative thoughts and ideas, moving beyond dreaming. Finding ways to not just do things differently, but to do them *better.*

- **Fitness**
  A mindset, best if it's worked at *every* day

- **Communication Skills**
  The ability to listen, speak and write well are priceless.

- **Tolerance**
  (To a point, that is) Some things – the "common enemies of man" - should not be tolerated.

- **Manners and Respect**
  So rare, so attractive (especially in young people) - but not to the point of acquiescence

- **Compassion**
  The ability (and willingness) to empathize, especially with those who are hurting, oppressed, neglected, disadvantaged, and/or underprivileged

- **Initiative**
  Being *proactive* - one of the late Stephen Covey's *Seven Habits of Highly Effective People* - runs contrary to the "wait to be told what to do" school culture. But it creates progress.

- **Resourcefulness**
  Problems aren't overwhelming when we're armed with a "Find a way!" approach to obstacles (Lesson 13).

- **Forgiveness**
  Mother Teresa said, "People are often unreasonable and self-centered. Forgive them anyway."

- **Sense of Humor**
  Without it, the world is too cruel and too sad to endure.

- **Drive**
  Ambition, goals and an answer to this question: *What are you working toward?*

- **Fire!**
  Energy and enthusiasm are magnets. People want to be around people who are full of life.

- **Leadership**
  Leaders are less likely to succumb than followers.

Ideally, the inculcation of the warrior traits, characteristics and virtues will be done when kids are young, before they reach puberty. Instilling them in an amoral teenage boy who drinks, smokes, doesn't have a passion and spends the bulk of his time pursuing selfish pleasure is possible but unlikely. Once that initial teaching opportunity is lost, don't expect any sort of metamorphosis until after he turns 25 when his brain is fully formed and more capable of thinking rationally.

When I was writing my master's thesis on successful students, one of my professors encouraged me to take a serious look at the other side – unsuccessful students. So I took a job teaching an adult school English class. It was called "adult school," but only two students were genuine adults. The rest were high school students who had failed English and were trying to make up lost units.

It was a challenge. I spent a lot of class time trying to get them to listen, focus and learn. Genuine instruction had to share time with classroom management. It was annoying. But not just to me. Near the end of the course, the legitimate adult students (two women in their late twenties) had had enough.

"Please! Will you guys shut up?" one of them shouted, "I'm trying to learn!"

"I know," added the other one, "Can't you see that you're going to end up like us? We were just like you! Now, here we are trying to get our diplomas ten years later!"

Not surprisingly, their warning went unheeded. The kids just looked at each other and giggled. They didn't get it. They were stuck in that 12–25-year-old black hole where, barring some extraordinary occurrence, they aren't going to develop warrior traits until later – if ever.

Each day, the battle begins at dawn. The alarm clock rings. Laziness and productivity go at it. Not only does the value of our day depend upon who wins that battle, so does the meaning, purpose and significance of our lives.

## Assignment

Spend a week charting your battles. What (not who) are your worst enemies? Is it sloth? If so, what weapons do you need to overcome your laziness? Is it peer pressure? What can you do to develop the confidence you'll need to resist it? Is it apathy? What cause moves you so much that it forces you to care? Choose your weapons; prepare for war.

## The Five Kinds of Lives

Some lives are better than others. All men may be "created equal," but we sure don't live equally. There are different levels of effectiveness. There is no one way to live but there are definitely *better* ways to live. It's better to live honestly than dishonestly. It's better to be generous than to be selfish. It's better to be kind and compassionate than to be mean and malicious. It's better to find ways to contribute to the world than to look for ways to take from it. It's better to be a faithful husband or wife than an unfaithful one. It's better to take care of your body than to neglect it. It's better to work hard than to be lazy. The Nobel Peace Prize winner's life is better than the serial criminal's.

Obviously.

There are five kinds of lives, and the goal is to live a #2. That's realistic. If one of my students ends up living a #1, it would be beyond astonishing. But that's more fantasy than expectation.

It's all about scale. The difference between a #1 and a #2 or a #4 and a #5 is scale. In fact, the idea for this lesson came to me when I stumbled across a website called "The Scales of Good and Evil" put together by a Yale-educated biochemist and writer named Dr. Cliff Pickover.[67]

Dr. Pickover explored the question *Which human beings have lived the best and worst lives of all time?* It's fascinating. Check it out.

Some of the names on the list, especially the evil list, are the names you'd expect to see – Genghis Khan, Stalin, Pol Pot, Hitler… But some were not. For example, Dr. Pickover's number one on the evil side is Tomas de Torquemada, a name I wasn't familiar with

("...his name is synonymous with the Christian Inquisition's religious bigotry, and cruel fanaticism").

In other words, the guy pretty much started the hard-to-fathom concept of one religion (in his case, Christianity) hating another religion and those practicing it (in his case, Judaism) to the point where one religion's "faithful" kills the believers of another. De Torquemada took it to the extreme, torturing Jews – using that oh-so-Christlike 'burn them at the stake' method of execution.

De Torquemada's life is an example of a **#5 life** - the worst life a human being can live. Number 5's are born into the world and make life horrific for thousands, perhaps millions. Their evil reaches such a grand scale that when they die, the world celebrates. On the other end of the spectrum is a **#1 life** – the best life a human being can live. Names on Pickover's best-lived lives list include Jesus, Gandhi, Martin Luther King Jr. and Buddha. (Buddha is Pickover's choice for having lived the greatest life ever.) The list is open to debate – Pickover even encourages it. But one thing is clear: to live a horrendous life or a magnificent life, you have to affect the world permanently and colossally.

A **#4 life** is terrible, too. You're born, you're evil, you ruin people's lives, then you die. The difference between a #4 and a #5 is you didn't ruin as *many* lives, and your malevolent influence isn't as enduring or infamous. It's a matter of scale.

A **#3 life** is a typical life. You live, you die, but you're nondescript. Outside your family and tight circle of friends, your impact on the world – positive or negative – is minimal. Population scientists estimate that, currently, the ratio of living to dead people is 1/15. This means that their educated guess is that somewhere around 105 billion people have been born, lived their lives and died (starting 50,000 years ago when Homo sapiens first walked the earth). And how many of those 105 billion people do we know anything about (pre-Google and Facebook)?

Not many. Less than one percent.

Depressing, right? That's why a **#2 life** should be the goal. As remarkable as living a #1 life would be, how many Abraham Lincolns (ranked 7th on Pickover's list) can exist? Aspiring to live a #1 kind of life is like saying you want to be a supermodel, A-list movie star or the president of the United States. It takes incredible timing – a once-in-a-generation human being born into a time and place that desperately needs her (or him). It's within the realm of possibility, but just barely. However, a #2 life, a Rell Sunn kind of life, is within reach for all of us.

Rell Sunn lived a beautiful life. Born and raised in Makaha, Hawaii, her impact on her local community was enormous. Initially, it was her surfing prowess – she was one of the first women to surf professionally – that gained her fame. But she'll be remembered for way more than her surfing.

Diagnosed at 23 with breast cancer, she was given a year to live. She ended up living 16 more fulfilling years, positively affecting the lives of thousands. In addition to surfing, Rell was the first female lifeguard on Oahu. She was an accomplished free diver. She became a radio disc jockey. She worked as a counselor at a cancer research center and taught classes to local women on the causes, prevention and treatment of breast cancer. She founded the Menehune Surf Contest for underprivileged kids and found a way to take many of those kids to surfing competitions as far away as France.

Yet, outside Makaha and Oahu, certainly outside Hawaii, few know the name *Rell Sunn*. And if not for an award-winning documentary of her life (*Heart of the Sea: Kapolioka'ehukai*)[68], I would have never heard of her, either. And that's the point. You don't have to live a world-renowned, epic life to have an impactful, even legendary life. Rell even said we can all be like her. We can all aspire to make a significant local impact through passionate living and selfless caring.

Rell Sunn's life was about as good a life as it could have been. Over 3,000 people attended her funeral. Still, hers was not a world-famous #1 life. It was, however, the epitome of a #2 life.

One of the four parts of "The Prayer of Jabez" is about "enlarging our coast" (our sphere of influence) so we can lead/affect/teach/impact/inspire more people. That's why my mom referred me to it. She knew that, like Jabez (in the Bible, Chronicles 4:10), I wanted to reach more people.

I still do. I know I'm not living a #4 or #5 life. I hope I'm not living a #3 life. As of now, though, I'm not a #2. Maybe a 2.5. Maybe. But a 2 is still the goal. I pray that I have enough time left to get there.

**Note:** The whole numbers are an obvious simplification. A #3 represents the totally neutral (meaningless) life. No harm to the world but no contribution to it, either. Do these people actually exist? If they do, they may be those living with a *Have as much fun as I can for as long as I can* mission statement.

In reality, there are gradations. Most people are probably living somewhere between a 2.8 and a 3.2, which is a shame. It confirms what Michelangelo wrote - that, "The greater danger for most of us is not that our aim is too high and we miss it, but that it is too low and we reach it." It also confirms what Thomas Merton wrote – that "The biggest human temptation is to settle for too little."

I bet that Michelangelo and Merton would agree that aspiring to live a life with any score above a 2 – even a 2.1 - is unacceptable.

## Assignment

See the blue and take note of those living a #2 (or better) life. They're around you. They may not be famous on a grand scale, but they're probably well-known within their circles. Learn from these people. Aspire to "enlarge your coast" by living well, in your own way, using your own interests and strengths to improve the world.

Draw/Paint/Tattoo an eye-catching **#2** in a place where you'll be reminded that the goal is a #2.

(Maybe I believe in the vision board stuff more than I admit.)

## Money Making, Sales and Entrepreneurship

Although this is definitely one of the most vital lesson kids should learn, it's the one I'm least qualified to teach. As a kid, I wasn't taught it. I learned about it later in life. But when I tried to put it into practice… well, I'm far from wealthy.

Not long after having hip surgery, I was vacationing in Hawaii. Laid up, unable to run, surf or even hike, I spent a lot of time reading, studying and thinking about Robert Kiyosaki's *Rich Dad Poor Dad.* The point that most hit home was Kiyosaki's assertion that schools don't teach students moneymaking principles.[69] I identified too much with his "poor" dad – his well-schooled biological dad who, despite his PhD and high-paying job (in education), struggled financially.

So I decided to get rich. I took a chunk of equity from our house and used it as a down payment to buy two investment properties in Florida. This was in 2005, shortly before real estate (especially Florida real estate) crumbled. I cost my family thousands and thousands of dollars. It was a huge risk that didn't pay off.

I made a series of mistakes. If real estate had continued to soar as it had in the past (especially in Florida), I would have been rolling in dough. But I had no control over that. I relied too heavily on fate. Beyond that, I was hoodwinked into thinking that financial prosperity would come easily. That by investing and hoping money would come my way, I ignored one of life's basic truths – that under ordinary circumstances, pretty much everything will be way harder and take way longer than you originally thought (Lesson 44). This certainly includes making money!

I'm not wealthy or financially independent, but I do know this: Just about all of us need to learn…

- moneymaking 101
- how to sell
- how to be an entrepreneur

**Making Money**

Because I don't have good enough answers to the three questions (i.e. I don't have enough money), I don't feel comfortable teaching this - which is why I'm so sold on it being taught! (The way I deal with my insecurity is by inviting millionaires to speak to my students. I let *them* do the teaching.)

Economics shouldn't be a single-semester class taught to high school seniors absorbed by senioritis. When it's so condensed, students are typically only exposed to broad, basic economic theories. Understandably, they consider them irrelevant and impractical. Few have an interest in learning them. Instead, econ, business and moneymaking principles should be taught early and often. They should be taught all four years of high school. Right now, only 14 states require that a course in personal finance be *offered* (not necessarily taken), and only 22 demand that high school students enroll in economics.[70]

> *Just as it was not possible to live in an industrialized society without print literacy – the ability to read and write – so it is not possible to live in today's world without being financially literate. To fully participate in society today, financial literacy is critical.*
>
> - Annamaria Lusardi
> Denit Trust Professor of Economics and Accountancy
> George Washington University School of Business

When Zappos CEO Tony Hsieh was at Harvard, he learned that "Pizzas were very high-margin. A large pizza cost $2 to make but could be sold for $10 (or more with additional toppings)."[71] He didn't learn that in one of his Harvard classes. (Hsieh was a computer science major.) He learned it while running the campus's Quincy House Grille. That he learned it while working a part-time job was great for Hsieh, but the concept of "very high margin" needs to be taught in school, to everyone. Not just so that students can memorize its definition (a *margin* is the amount a product's price exceeds its cost), but so they can start thinking about what *they* can create and sell that has a very high margin.

In one semester, I can't come close to covering all the terms kids need to learn to become financially literate. But they need to learn concepts such as the *rule of 72* - the formula that gives a close approximation of how long it takes invested money to double. (Divide 72 by the interest rate. For example, $1,000 invested at 2% will become $2,000 in 36 years. But if it's invested at 12%, it will only take six years to double.) And I suspect that the younger kids are when they understand how *compound interest* works, the greater the likelihood that they'll use the daffodil principle - invest early and consistently - and become millionaires.

Learning the specialized vocabulary of an interest or passion is critical to mastering it. It's hard to be a great chef without knowing cooking vocabulary. You can't write code until you know computer science vocabulary. Athletes need to know their sport's vocabulary.

Still, most people don't *need* to know cooking, computer science, swimming or basketball vocabulary. But wouldn't you agree that just about every student needs to know financial vocabulary? Wouldn't you agree that every student ought to be taught how to make money?

## Sales

It's included on *The New Report Card* because if we can't sell, we can't succeed. When you think of the iconic writer, Robert Louis

Stevenson, you don't think business acumen. You think *Treasure Island.* Yet he wrote, "Everyone lives by selling something." Whether we work for ourselves or for someone else, if we can't sell what our business sells, we're in trouble. If we can't sell our ideas, what good is having them? And if we can't sell ourselves, we're going to be lonely, heartbroken, unemployed, poor and depressed.

Yet, how many sales lessons are included in the school curriculum? Should kids be taught specific "how to" sales skills? Yes! Sooner or later they're going to need them. When, how and what should be taught will vary, depending on the age of the students, the subject being taught and the expertise of the teacher. But making sure that students know how to sell is essential.

Start by ensuring that they know two of the most basic sales fundamentals:

1. Know your product.
2. Believe in your product.

Not every kid should be required to peddle something – although that isn't a bad idea. But all kids need to learn that the best sales professionals know their products inside and out and wholeheartedly believe in them. This extends to knowing and believing in *themselves* – musts for selling their ideas and themselves. Remember what my daughters and so many other women find most attractive in guys – confidence. And women who know and believe in themselves are attractive, too!

Elementary school students learn that design is everything. Beautiful coloring and neat handwriting are valued and admired. Kids who color and print well earn kindergarten and first grade respect. Unfortunately, somewhere along the education progression, the respect for design declines. How things look becomes less important. Beyond middle school, design is rarely evaluated. And, even when it is, it's not given much weight.

Yet, Tom Peters believes "everything is design." The author of

*In Search of Excellence* and *The Little Big Things* (bibles for majoring in business success) writes about the Tuf-E-Nuf mini striker claw hammer and how beautifully it combines function with form.[72] (Yes, a pretty hammer.) His point? If you can make a hammer look good, you can make anything look good.

Especially if you want to sell it. When customers compare products, when all else is equal – or even close to it, they'll choose the one with the more appealing design. As a teacher, I can tell you that design applies to homework, papers and projects. It takes a teacher about a half a second to determine if a student's work shows effort. The best students know that many grades are subjective – as are so many aspects of life – so they get good at selling their work to their teachers.

Examples of subjectivity and design's influence on opinions outside the classroom include Olympic events. There are the purely objective sports – running, swimming, jumping, lifting, ski and skate racing - that can be measured precisely. Then there are the subjectively judged events – diving, gymnastics, figure skating, the snowboarding half pipe, trampoline - that are won or lost on design.

Subjectivity is a huge factor in determining who gets hired, gets the investors, gets the business, gets the friends and who gets the girl or the boyfriend. How we present ourselves, our own personal design and style, are critical to our success and happiness. How we act, how we treat others, how we speak, how we look and how we carry ourselves matter!

## Entrepreneurship

In other words, "start your own." In school, kids get used to teachers telling them what to do. Which is fine if they get a job where their bosses are forever telling them what to do. But who wants that? Remember, autonomy motivates.

In the late 1950's, a promising young songwriter named Berry Gordy sold some of his best work to a company called Decca Records.

Most people would celebrate that success. Not Gordy. When he compared what Decca paid him to what Decca made from his hits, he realized that writing songs was not nearly as lucrative as *owning* songs. So he started a company that eventually became Motown in which he, along with Marvin Gaye, Stevie Wonder, Smokey Robinson and the Miracles, Diana Ross and the Supremes, The Four Tops, The Temptations and other R&B legends, made music history.[73] We need kids thinking like Gordy. Rather than relying on someone else, we need them to think, *Maybe for a while I may work for someone else, but it will just be temporary - a paid internship. It's only a matter of time until I start and own my own company.*

In the 1960's, as part of Lyndon B. Johnson's well-intended Great Society, the American government built huge housing "projects" in its inner cities. The typically high-rise, multiple-dwelling buildings were envisioned as a way to make housing affordable for all. The rent was low and often adjusted according to how much a tenant could afford to pay.

The key word is *rent*. Much to their dismay, government officials learned what real estate professionals had known for years: when you rent, there's no pride of ownership. You don't take your rented car to the carwash. Not usually, anyway.

It wasn't long before the projects became places infested with crime, infamous for their disrepair. Walls were covered with graffiti, windows were smashed, trash was strewn about and rats bred in the cellars and hallways. *Projects* became a synonym for cheap, undesirable, unwanted housing.[74] Even now, drive through any neighborhood and compare the upkeep of owner-occupied and rental properties. You'll find the difference startling.

In today's world, in which working for a single employer until retirement is practically unheard of, everyone needs to think like an entrepreneur. We all need to "start our own." And we can.

In the words of 2006 Nobel Peace Prize Winner Muhammad Yunus:

*All human beings are entrepreneurs. When we were in the*

> *caves, we were all self-employed. We were finding our food, feeding ourselves. That's where the human history began. As civilization came, we suppressed it and made it into labor. We are all labor. And a labor market. We became labor, because (they) stamped us, 'You are labor.' We forgot that we are entrepreneurs.*

How does this relate to students, teachers and school administrators? Peters writes:

> *Organizations should be no less than cathedrals in which the full and awesome power of the imagination and spirit and native entrepreneurial flair of diverse individuals is unleashed in passionate pursuit of excellence... a classroom in a primary school should obviously be such a cathedral.*[75]

So should classrooms in every other school. Principals should hire teachers who have the talent and motivation to become *intrapreneurs* – "employees who are given the freedom to create new products, services, systems, etc. and do not have to follow the corporation's (school's?) usual protocols and procedures."[76] Clearly, principals should support their teachers and staff, encouraging them to become intrapreneurs. Memorable learning happens when teachers are given the freedom to innovate.

And when principals, teachers and staff are thinking like intrapreneurs, the students immersed in that culture will begin to think like entrepreneurs. But only if they're taught to think like owners. They own their homework assignments. They own their projects. They own their education. Everything they do should show a pride of ownership.

The world desperately needs all types of entrepreneurs. Business entrepreneurs start companies that provide jobs, fill government coffers and deliver necessary or coveted goods and services. Social entrepreneurs contribute to the world by originating better ways to feed the hungry, heal the sick, educate children, deliver water and electricity and make athletic and other recreational opportunities available to those who wouldn't otherwise have them. Microfinance organizations including Yunus's Grameen Bank and Kiva make small business loans to entrepreneurs living in third-world countries and in difficult environments.

In the late 1990's, Apple Inc. ran an ad campaign that encouraged us to *think different.* Masterminded by the American advertising agency, Chiat/Day (now TBWA/Chiat/Day), the text of the *Think Different* campaign was a free-verse poem written by a Chiat/Day copywriter named Craig Tanimoto:[77]

> *Here's to the crazy ones. The misfits. The rebels. The troublemakers.*
>
> *The round pegs in the square holes.*
>
> *The ones who see things differently.*
>
> *They're not fond of rules. And they have no respect for the status quo.*
>
> *You can quote them, disagree with them, glorify or vilify them.*
>
> *About the only thing you can't do is ignore them. Because they change things.*
>
> *They invent. They imagine. They heal. They explore. They create. They inspire. They push the human race forward.*
>
> *Maybe they have to be crazy. How else can you stare at an empty canvas and see a work of art? Or sit in silence and hear a song that's never been written? Or gaze at a red planet and see a laboratory on wheels?*
>
> *We make tools for these kinds of people.*
>
> *While some see them as the crazy ones, we see genius. Because the people who are crazy enough to think they can change the world, are the ones who do.*

If we're going to make kids memorize anything, *Here's to the Crazy Ones* should be on the list. Because entrepreneurs change things. They invent. They imagine. They heal. They explore. They create. They inspire. They push the human race forward.

And don't we desperately need a push forward?

In the early 19th century, the Luddites tried to hold the human race back. They fought against technology and the Industrial Revolution. They resisted the mechanized looms that were replacing textile artisans. Their resistance was futile. Progress is inexorable.

The world is far, far, far from perfect. It desperately needs people with the will and energy to make it better. We must motivate students to want to find a better way to do things. So why aren't we teaching them to think differently? Why aren't we teaching students to think like entrepreneurs?

## Assignment

Most likely, you're not going to be taught money making, sales and entrepreneurship at school. So, become a self-taught business expert. Develop a specialized business vocabulary. Meet and talk to entrepreneurs and business professionals about their craft. Get into the habit of consistently checking out business and money websites such as Yahoo! Finance, CNN Money and Investopedia. Install their apps on your phone. When it comes to your education, think like an entrepreneur.

## Finish Strong (Like Bannister)

On May 6th, 1954 Roger Bannister of England ran a mile in 3 minutes 59.4 seconds. Before that day, no one had ever run a mile in under four minutes. Much has been written about that moment in history (including a memoir by Bannister himself). In 2000, *Sports Illustrated* named it (along with Sir Edmond Hillary's Mt. Everest ascent) the greatest athletic feat of the 20th century.

Kids don't know who Bannister is, though. Out of a class of 30-35 students, maybe two or three have ever heard of him. So, I share his story. About how he failed to medal in the 1952 Olympics in Helsinki, Finland. Before his feat, he wasn't well-known. Determined, but not well-known.

"Experts" said a sub-four-minute mile was a physical impossibility. That anyone who attempted it would pass out before finishing. Bannister didn't agree. He believed that if he combined his physical gifts – extraordinary lung capacity, for example – with hard work, he could do what most everyone said couldn't be done.

He trained relentlessly. Each day, with short rests in-between, he would attempt to run ten consecutive quarter-miles, each in 59 seconds or less. Perhaps because he was a medical student, Bannister believed the "experts" were wrong. He knew the barrier wasn't physical. It was psychological.

On the day of the race, two of his competitors, Chris Brasher and Chris Chataway, agreed to be his "rabbits." That is, they would sacrifice any chance they had of winning in order to set a blistering pace. If Bannister could stay with them for three and a half laps, then sprint to the finish, he'd have his chance to leave a legacy.

Four laps around the track make a mile. Bannister ran the first lap in 57.7 seconds and followed that with a 60.6 second lap. He was halfway there in less than two minutes. Then he struggled. A 62.4 third lap put him at 3:00.7. He'd have to battle winds and exhaustion and run the final lap in less than 60 seconds. Running away from Brasher and Chataway, Bannister willed himself around the track one more time. He ran the final lap in 58.7 for a 3:59.4 total. He did it! The world celebrated.[78]

But why teach it? Why should every kid know the Roger Bannister story? What are the lessons?

- The obvious one is to push past our mental limits that keep us from achieving our dreams. Less than two months after he broke the four-minute barrier, former mile record-holder John Landy broke Bannister's record. (Bannister later bested Landy in the "miracle mile" when they both ran sub-four-minute miles.) Since then, thousands of runners have broken four minutes. Some barrier.

- The "experts" aren't always "experts." We should respect them and listen to them, but what they preach shouldn't necessarily be accepted as gospel. The world isn't flat. The sun doesn't revolve around the earth. Heavier objects don't fall faster.

- Bannister's confidence development - his belief that he could do it came only after determined, tenacious training. Real confidence is earned with a ruthless work ethic.

- Failure motivates. If Bannister had been successful in his quest to win an Olympic medal, he may have retired afterward. Because he "failed," he set his sights on a goal that ended up being grander than a gold medal and gave him something few Olympians ever achieve – legendary status.

- Bannister didn't do it alone. He had help. If we want to achieve something special, something great, we need others working with us. Bannister had great coaches. He had Brasher and Chataway helping him on that historic day. And...

- He had a role model/mentor from whom he majored in success - he patterned his running style after 1936 Olympic champion John Lovelock.

- Eventually, it's up to us. Despite all the help, by the end of the race, Bannister was running by himself. Help is wonderful, but we can't totally depend on others. We have to take personal responsibility for our own success.

- Talent matters. The vast majority of humans, no matter how hard they train, could never run a four-minute mile. To reach our ultimate potential, we need to combine a solid work ethic with our natural gifts. Bannister could have worked just as hard or harder at throwing the shot put, but with his body-type, he still wouldn't have been any good at it.

- Learn to cook without a recipe. The best cooks start out following recipes. But once they've mastered cooking fundamentals, they don't need no stinking cookbook! They create new, unique concoctions. In his own way, that's what Bannister did. First, he mastered running fundamentals and training methods. Then, he went against accepted practices (running only long distances) and set up his innovative, quarter-mile split training method. Interval training is now widely practiced - but it wasn't then.

- Don't be afraid to be the first. Someone has to start the trend, change the belief or do something in a totally different way. Moreover, we remember the first person who does something innovative and important. Nobody remembers who won the gold in the 1,500 meter race at the 1952 Olympics. But we remember Bannister.

- Finish strong! Because of the way he finished the race, I teach my students about Roger Bannister on the first day of class after spring break. Even though he was fatigued as he entered the final lap, he wouldn't allow himself to relax. Instead, he pushed harder. He knew that he could rest after the fourth lap was complete. He didn't start resting 200 yards from the finish line as kids so often (metaphorically) do. The great gospel singer, Reverend James Cleveland, sang, "I don't feel no ways tired!" (in his fight against injustice). So often, fatigue is a state of mind. We can push through it.

If we begin to rest before the race is over, it's no thrill when we cross the finish line. So work hard right through the last day of school, the last part of practice, the last moment of the game, the last hour of work, the last seconds of studying, right down to the last moment of your life. Don't rest when there's still work to be done. There will be plenty of time for rest later. Be like Roger Bannister.

Finish strong.

## Assignment

First, to gain an appreciation for what Bannister did, as fast as you can, run one lap around a quarter-mile track. Make sure you time it. Not many people can run even one lap in less than a minute. Then, imagine averaging a minute per lap for *four consecutive laps*! Even though the current world-record in the mile is an inconceivable 3:43:13, what Bannister did in 1954 seems even more remarkable when one of us mere mortals tries it.

Second, teach "Finish Strong (Like Bannister)" to others. One of the best ways to learn and remember is to teach. With so many vital lessons attached to it, the Roger Bannister lesson should be universally taught. Help make it common knowledge.

# Afterward

## Knowing, ***Doing*** and Connecting

Education shouldn't be just about knowing. Knowing, although an important part of success, is only a small portion of the puzzle. What matters much more is *doing*. How often do kids say, "I know!" but then they don't do? Formal schooling is too much about knowing and not enough about doing. Knowing what Roger Bannister did is of little value if we don't use the lessons embedded in his story to improve our lives.

This book is about doing. It's not about what you *know* after you read it. It's about what you *do* as a result of having read it. Shouldn't this be the purpose of all schooling? What good is knowing something if you don't put it into practice? Consider Lesson 8: The Daffodil Principle (working at something consistently over a prolonged period of time). As vital as it is, it's simple to grasp. But it takes tremendous discipline to practice it. Or Lesson 19: How to Build Social Capital (learning what it takes to become the kind of person others want to be around). Being able to identify and explain attractive "Do-Bee" behaviors and repelling "Don't-Bee" behaviors might get you an A on a test, but so what? It's not just about knowing those behaviors, it's about applying them.

Finally, connect! If you study them carefully, you'll see how the missing pieces connect to solve the puzzle of life. The American writer, Elbert Hubbard, believed that, "It does not make much difference what a person studies – all knowledge is related, and the man who studies anything, if he keeps at it, will be learned."

Unfortunately, because of the way most schools are run - especially high schools, colleges and universities - there's little, if any, attempt to connect what's being taught in one course with what's being taught in another. Math, science, reading, writing, social science and the arts are linked, but they're typically taught in isolation. So students need to learn to look for and make connections on their own.

While locked in an Alabama jail cell, Martin Luther King Jr. had time to reflect on the deeper meanings of life. On whatever he could find - the margins of the *New York Times*, scraps of paper (sometimes even toilet paper) - he wrote his legendary "Letter from the Birmingham City Jail." It included some of the most meaningful, important and affecting thoughts in history. Among them were "We are caught in an inescapable network of mutuality, tied in a single garment of destiny. Whatever affects one directly, affects all indirectly."

May my words affect you. May you extend their ripple, affect others and improve the world. That's the purpose of education. It's not just for you. It's about using what you learn to boost, brighten and enlighten others' lives.

# References

[1] Muskal, Michael, 2012, March 19 "When high school is too much: 1 in 4 don't graduate, report finds" Los Angeles Times, Retrieved from http://articles.latimes.com/2012/mar/19/nation/la-na-nn-high-school-graduation-20120319

[2] Layton, L. (2014, April 28). National high school graduation rates at historic high, but disparities still exist. *The Washington Post*

[3] List of OECD Countries with the Highest High School Graduation Rates. (n.d.). . Retrieved from http://www.aneki.com/oecd_countries_high_school_graduation_rates.html

[4] Rubin, Gretchen, 2009, The Happiness Project, p.215-218, New York, NY, Harper Collins

[5] Kremer, J. (2013). *The college dropouts hall of fame*. Retrieved from http://collegedropoutshalloffame.com/n.htm

[6] Seligman, M. (2002). *Authentic happiness*. New York: The Free Press.

[7] Wagner, T. (2012). *Creating innovators - the making of young people who will change the world*. (p. 30). New York: Scribner.

[8] Leonard, G. (1991). *Mastery- the keys to success and long-term fulfillment*. New York: Plume.

[9] Gladwell, M. (2008). *The outliers - the story of success*. New York: Little, Brown and Company Hachette Book Group.

[10] See Csikszentmihalyi, M. (1990). *Flow*. New York: Harper & Row.

[11] Cherry, K. (n.d.). What is flow - understanding the psychology of flow. *About.com Psychology*, Retrieved from http://psychology.about.com/od/PositivePsychology/a/flow.htm

[12] Lipsky, D. (n.d.). Everything is Rent | Jonathan Larson & Rent. Retrieved January 4, 2015, from http://www.angelfire.com/in2/everythingisrent/jon.html

[13] Edwards, J. A. (1995). *Celebration- ten principles of more joyous living*. (pp. 39-49). Salt Lake City: Deseret Book Company. (Also, Search "The Daffodil Principle.")

[14] As quoted in: Saperston, E. (Producer) (2001). THE JOURNEY [CD].

[15] Delaney, B. I. (2007, October 21). *What did people use before toilet paper?*. Retrieved from http://voices.yahoo.com/what-did-people-toilet-paper-606096.html

[16] Goodgame, D. (2000, August 14). How the best got better - the game of

risk. *Time Magazine*, Retrieved from http://www.time.com/time/magazine/article/0,9171,997709,00.html

[17] Canfield, J. (2005). *The success principles - how to get from where you are to where you want to be*. (pp. 157-158). New York: HarperCollins.

[18] Godin, Seth (2009, February 1). The Tribes We Lead. *Technology, Education, Design (TED) Conference*. Lecture conducted from TED.

[19] Gabriel, P. (2011, January 11). *The influence of mahatma gandhi on martin luther king and the civil rights movement*. Retrieved from http://voices.yahoo.com/the-influence-mahatma-gandhi-martin-luther-king-7478078.html?cat=37

[20] Constitutional Rights Foundation. (n.d.). *Cesar chavez*. Retrieved from http://www.crf-usa.org/black-history-month/cesar-chavez

[21] Gruden , J. (2003). *Do you love football?*. (p.53) New York: HarperCollins.

[22] Weingarten, G. (2007, April 8). Pearls before breakfast.*The Washington Post*. Retrieved from http://www.washingtonpost.com/wp-dyn/content/article/2007/04/04/AR2007040401721.html

[23] Pausch, R. (Performer). (2008, May 26). Randy Pausch - The Last Lecture reprised [Web Video]. Retrieved http://www.youtube.com/watch?v=BODHsU3hDo4

[24] Collins, J. (2001). *Good to great*. (p. 75) New York: HarperCollins.

[25] Come clean. In (2004). WIKIPEDIA. Retrieved from http://en.wikipedia.org/wiki/Come_Clean_(Hilary_Duff_song)

[26] Saperston, E. (Producer) (2001). THE JOURNEY [CD and DVD].

[27] Vidmar, P. (2002). *Risk, originality & virtuosity*. (pp. 137-138). Sterling, VA: International Publisher's Marketing.

[28] Friedman, T. (2010, October 23). The election that wasn't. *New York Times*. Retrieved from http://www.nytimes.com/2010/10/24/opinion/24friedman.html?_r=2&partner=rssnyt&emc=rss&

[29] *"the hurt locker" screenplay (screenplay explorer)l*. (2010, February 10). Retrieved from http://screenplayexplorer.com/?tag=the-hurt-locker-script

[30] Coelho, P. (1988). *The alchemist*. New York: HarperCollins.

[31] *Holstee*. (n.d.). Retrieved from http://shop.holstee.com/pages/manifesto

[32] DEBAISE, C. (2009, September 22). Starting chipotle from scratch. *The Wall*

*Street Journal*. Retrieved from http://online.wsj.com/article/SB125319598236119629.html

[33] "2012 Form 10-K, Chipotle Mexican Grill, Inc.". United States Securities and Exchange Commission. Retrieved 2013-08-07.

[34] *Biography.com - bob geldof*. (2013). Retrieved from http://www.biography.com/people/bob-geldof-9308389

[35] Mycoskie, B. (2011). *Start something that matters*. (p. 6,19). New York: Spiegel & Grau

[36]Heather C. West, Ph.D. and William J. Sabol, Ph.D. BJS Statisticians, and Sarah J. Greenman, BJS Program Assistant. U.S. Department of Justice, Office of Justice Programs Bureau of Justice Statistics. (Dec. 2010 (Revised October, 2011)). *Bureau of justice statistics -prisoners* (NCJ 231675). Retrieved from website:http://www.bjs.gov/content/pub/pdf/p09.pdf

[37] Fisher, A. (2013, March 27). *Boys vs. girls: What's behind the college grad gender gap?*. Retrieved from http://management.fortune.cnn.com/2013/03/27/college-graduation-gender-salaries/

[38] Futures Without Violence. (2013). *Get the facts: The facts on domestic, dating and sexual violence*. Retrieved from http://www.futureswithoutviolence.org/content/action_center/detail/754

[39] Rosenthal, E. (2006, October 06). Domestic violence plagues women worldwide, study says. *New York Times/SF Gate*. Retrieved from http://www.sfgate.com/news/article/Domestic-violence-plagues-women-worldwide-study-2468667.php

[40] MedIndia. (2005, November 25). *Domestic violence: The silent killer of women worldwide*. Retrieved from http://www.medindia.net/news/healthwatch/Domestic-Violence-The-Silent-Killer-of-Women-Worldwide-5914-1.htm

[41] Hauslohner, A. (2010, July 07). Afghanistan: When women set themselves on fire. *Time*

[42] Russell, H. (2012, August 07). *NPR books, special series - 100 best books, "your favorites - 100 best-ever teen novels"*. Retrieved from http://www.npr.org/2012/08/07/157795366/your-favorites-100-best-ever-teen-novels

[43] *Single-parent families - demographic trends*. (n.d.). Retrieved from http://family.jrank.org/pages/1574/Single-Parent-Families-Demographic-Trends.html

[44] See articles/misson: *Menteach*. (n.d.). Retrieved from http://www.menteach.org/

[45] PLESHETTE-MURPHY, A. (2008, October 20). *Number of male teachers shrinking fast*. Retrieved from http://abcnews.go.com/GMA/Parenting/story?id=6070282&page=1

[46] Adams, J. (2010). *Gandhi: Naked ambition*. London: Quercus.

[47] Mandel, S. (2011, February 17). Alabama-auburn rivalry a double- edged sword for college football read more: http://sportsillustrated.cnn.com/2011/writers/stewart_mandel/02/17/alabama.auburn/index.html

[48] Pink, D. (Performer). (2010, April 01). RSA Animate - Drive: The surprising truth about what motivates us[Web Video]. Retrieved from http://www.thersa.org/events/rsaanimate/animate/rsa-animate-drive

[49] Quinn, L. (2010). *Life's too short to fold fitted sheets*. San Francisco: Chronicle Books.

[50] Buckingham, M., & Coffman, C. (1999). *First break all the rules - what the world's greatest managers do differently*. (p. 12). New York: Simon & Schuster.

[51] Johnson, S. (2010). *Where good ideas come from - the natural history of innovation*. New York: Riverhead Books.

[52] Gelb, M. J. (1998) *How to think like leonardo da vinci - seven steps to genius every day*. (p. 57). New York: Dell Publishing

[53] Johnson, S. (2010). *Where good ideas come from - the natural history of innovation*. (pp. 81-84). New York: Riverhead Books.

[54] Bliss, M. (1982, 2007). *The discovery of insulin: Twenty-fifth anniversary edition*. (p.50) Chicago: The University of Chicago Press.

[55] Rubin, G. (2009). *The happiness project*. (p. 288). New York: HarperCollins.

[56] Canfield, J. (2005). *The success principles - how to get from where you are to where you want to be*. (p. 88). New York: HarperCollins.

[57] Wong, D. (2010, May 01). How 'the karate kid' ruined the modern world. *Cracked*, Retrieved from http://www.cracked.com/article_18544_how-the-karate-kid-ruined-modern-world.html

[58] National Institute of Mental Health (NIMH). (n.d.). *Social phobia among adults*. Retrieved from http://www.nimh.nih.gov/statistics/1SOC_ADULT.shtml

[59] National Institute of Mental Health (NIMH). (n.d.). *Social phobia among children*. Retrieved from http://www.nimh.nih.gov/statistics/1SOC_CHILD.shtml

[60] Social Anxiety Support (SAS). (n.d.). *Social anxiety disorder: Did you know?*. Retrieved from http://www.socialanxietysupport.com/forum/f171/social-anxiety-disorder-some-statistics-177090/

[61] Koofi, F. (2012). *The favored daughter - one woman's fight to lead afghanistan into the future.* New York: Palgrave Macmillan.

[62] Ghosh, P. (2012, March 07). *Gorilla genome could hold key to the human condition.* Retrieved from http://www.bbc.co.uk/news/science-environment-17239059

[63] From Associated Press (Obituary). (2003, February 14). Kemmons wilson, 90; holiday inn chain's founder. *Los Angeles Times.* Retrieved from http://articles.latimes.com/2003/feb/14/local/me-wilson14

[64] on-line biographies. (n.d.). *Biography of gebhard jaeger.* Retrieved from http://www.onlinebiographies.info/oh/frank/jeager-g.htm

[65] Reiko, L. (2009, October 08). *Identical twins who were separated at birth: Amazing similarities.* Retrieved from http://lornareiko.wordpress.com/2009/10/08/identical-twins-who-were-separated-at-birth-what-are-they-like/

[66] Blair-Broeker, C., Ernst, R., & Myers, D. (2003).*Thinking about psychology - the science of mind and behavior.* (Fourth ed., pp. 42-44). New York: Worth Publishers.

[67] Pickover, C. (2001, 2002,2003). *The scales of good and evil.* Retrieved from http://sprott.physics.wisc.edu/pickover/good.html

[68] Lagarde, C. (Independent Lens). (2002). HEART OF THE SEA *kapolioka'ehukai* [DVD]

[69] Kiyosaki, R.T. (1997). *Rich dad poor dad.* New York: Warner Books.

[70] Council on Economic Education. (n.d.). *Survey of the states (2011).* Retrieved from http://www.councilforeconed.org/news-information/survey-of-the-states/

[71] Hsieh, T. (2010). *Delivering happiness - a path to profits, passion, and purpose.* (pp.27,28) New York: Business Plus - Hachette Book Group.

[72] Peters, T. (2010). *The big little things.* (pp. 377-378). New York: HarperStudio.
[73] Berry gordy jr. biography. In ENCYCLOPEDIA OF WORLD BIOGRAPHY. Retrieved from http://www.notablebiographies.com/Gi-He/Gordy-Jr-Berry.html

[74] Husock, H. (2009, June). *Public housing and rental subsidies.* Retrieved from http://www.downsizinggovernment.org/hud/public-housing-rental-subsidies

[75] Peters, T. (2010). *The big little things.* (p.431) New York: HarperStudio.

[76] dictionary.com. (n.d.). *intrapreneur.* Retrieved from http://dictionary.reference.com/browse/intrapreneur

[77] Hormby, T. (2013, August 10). *Think different: The ad campaign that restored apple's reputation.* Retrieved from http://lowendmac.com/2013/think-different-ad-campaign-restored-apples-reputation/

[78] Bannister, R. (2004). *The four-minute mile.* Guilford, CT. (50th Anniversary Edition ed.). The Lyons Press.

# Index

Made in the USA
Charleston, SC
07 February 2017